Just Shelter

Just Shelter

*Gentrification, Integration, Race,
and Reconstruction*

RONALD R. SUNDSTROM

OXFORD
UNIVERSITY PRESS

OXFORD
UNIVERSITY PRESS

Oxford University Press is a department of the University of Oxford. It furthers the University's objective of excellence in research, scholarship, and education by publishing worldwide. Oxford is a registered trade mark of Oxford University Press in the UK and certain other countries.

Published in the United States of America by Oxford University Press 198 Madison Avenue, New York, NY 10016, United States of America.

CIP data is on file at the Library of Congress

ISBN 978-0-19-094814-6

DOI: 10.1093/oso/9780190948146.001.0001

Printed by Integrated Books International, United States of America

MIX
Paper
FSC   FSC® C183721

To Nathan

"But they shall sit every man under his vine and under his fig tree; and none shall make them afraid . . ."

—Micah 4:4 (KJV)

Contents

Acknowledgments

I am grateful to everyone who supported me through my lengthy process of writing this book. Your encouragement, constructive criticism, and, most of all, your endless patience were invaluable and deeply appreciated. Naturally, all the mistakes in this book are my own, and many of its best bits result from the excellent feedback I received. It should go without saying—but in our era of sectarian political division, it must be said anyway—that all those who I am grateful to for supporting me in this endeavor may not agree with many of or all the conclusions I arrive at or positions I defend in this work. Indeed, I should expect not, since some of the most valuable comments I received were in the form of fierce criticism. I am grateful for that criticism because in its severity was also generosity and goodwill firmly grounded in a shared commitment to justice.

Thank you, especially to my husband, Nathan, who heartened and urged me on through the very beginning of this project. Further, although I had been grappling for many years with some of the issues in this book, such as the topic of integration, the idea of the book was born on a bicycle ride from the city of San Francisco and up the Marin Headlands with my friend and colleague, Evelyn Ho, who in addition to encouraging me to write the book, convinced me to get IRB approval to interview local housing policy experts and advocates—thank you for that inspiring discussion and, of course, the bike rides.

The interviews that I conducted with housing policy experts and advocates (whose identities I promised to keep anonymous) directed me to studies and data that shaped and helped me to repeatedly revise my analysis and arguments. I decided not to include quotations from those interviews; nonetheless, their views and interpretations and the conversations we had were formative. I thank them for generously sharing with me their time, expertise, and insights.

Additionally, throughout the years of writing this book, I received a wealth of support and criticism from many friends, colleagues, students, and audiences at academic and community events. Three groups were significant to that process: first, the Philosophy of the City Research Group and its organizers, Shane Epting, Michael Nagenboord, and Jules Simon, and the participants at its conferences in New York, San Francisco, Porto, and Bogota; second, the San Francisco Urban Film Festival (for which I am honored to serve as its Humanities Advisor) and its curatorial and production team: Fay Darmawi, Kristel Çelik, Robin Abad Ocubillo, Omeed Manocheri, Abigail Pañares, and Susannah Smith; and third, the participants of the 2021 Manuscript Conference hosted by the Jean Beer Blumenfeld Center for Ethics at Georgia State University, including Andrew I. Cohen (organizer and moderator), Andrew Valls (who nominated me for it), Casey Dawkins, Quill R. Kukla, Paul C. Taylor, Sharon Stanley, and others.

A few early chapters were shared and benefited from the criticism of several conferences and colloquiums, including at the American Philosophy Association, the Public Philosophy Network, the Hobby School of Public Policy at the University of Houston, the conference on Racial Equality at the CUNY Graduate School, the philosophy department at Vanderbilt University, the Political Science and Political Theory department at Radboud University in Nijmegen, Netherlands, the Politicogenetmaal conference at Leiden University, Netherlands, the Salzburg Conference in Interdisciplinary Poverty Research at the University of Salzburg, Austria, and the philosophy department at Occidental College. I am grateful for the comments of all the participants at those conferences and presentations, particularly Derrick Darby, Bart van Leeuwen, Johanna C. Luttrell, Sharon M. Meagher, Michael Merry,

Ian Olasov, Erica Preston-Roedder, and Tyler Zimmer. I also want to thank the anonymous manuscript reviewers and my editor at Oxford University Press, Lucy Randall, whose patience with me went above and beyond the call of duty.

At the University of San Francisco (USF), my research for this book was supported by my home department and the College of Arts and Sciences, and I am grateful for the responses to the project I received from friends and colleagues, including Rachel Brahinsky, Carol Brown, Glen Brown, Corey Cook, Tenoch Flores, Eileen Fung, Mark Goold, Rebecca Gordon, Evelyn Ho, Michael T. Iglesias, David H. Kim, Gerard Kuperus, Teresa Moore, Marjolein Oele, Kurt Organista, Pamela Balls Organista, Jeff Paris, Charles Petersen, Evelyn Rodriguez, Michael Root, Stephanie Sears, William Sullivan, DeAnna Tibs, and Brian Weiner.

I am also grateful for the work and efforts of several students at USF who read and responded to the chapters' early versions or served as my research assistants, including Kevin Clark, Amy Dundon, Akana Jayewardene, Shaya Kara, Neema Jyothiprakash, Jacqline Murrillo, and Eric Schroer. Lastly, the research for this book received the generous support of USF's National Endowment for Humanities Fellowship and USF's faculty writing retreats.

Introduction

The lack of a long-term, stable, and secure home and shelter, not in the temporary sense, but under the broadest understanding, is more than a simple material lack. It is a lack that undercuts, to the point of making nearly impossible, the healthy functioning of individuals and families. Those suffering from housing precarity cannot fully benefit from social goods nor fully participate as equal citizens in society (Waldron 1993). Due to these effects, housing crises involve more than a shortage of available housing, shortfalls in new construction, and so on; they are moral and political crises indicative of social injustice.

The United States is experiencing a housing and housing justice crisis, which, by some estimates, started in the early 2000s and was made worse by the financial crisis of the 2007–2008 recession; it involves both housing affordability and availability and continues unabated.[1] The situation indicates not just shortfalls in the construction of new homes or increased labor and material costs but also significant social, political, and economic inequalities in U.S. society.

The housing crisis is glaringly visible in many cities and towns throughout the United States, such as the San Francisco Bay Area, where I live and work.[2] The problem is evidenced by the increasingly visible tent encampments, stowed in the niches of neighborhoods, side streets, under overpasses, and the off- and on-ramps of freeways. And it can be seen in spikes of eviction, overdevelopment or underdevelopment, and growing justified concerns about the sustainability of the nation's towns and cities in the face of global climate change. These are instances of serious problems, and for those experiencing them, they cut to the bone. The harm, however, goes deeper than the mere lack of material resources and the lack of decent, affordable, and sustainable housing. It extends beyond housing to touch nearly every aspect of social and spatial organization, political power, economic opportunity, and the life chances of individuals and their families.

The sources of the housing crisis do not lie with the particular circumstances of the housing market of the early 2000s. The troubles reflect America's enduring class, racial, and ethnic divisions, a salient component of concretizing and conserving those divisions. It is the result of a history of state-sponsored discrimination in housing and land-use policy and the actions of neighborhoods and cities to enforce racial and class-based discrimination that has had long-lasting effects on access to housing and educational and economic opportunity (Rothstein 2017). Indeed, disparities in housing are generally a strong indicator of injustice in social-spatial arrangements, which warp what social scientists call the geography of opportunity (Chetty, Hendren, and Katz 2016). The warping of opportunity through social-spatial divisions has gone on for generations and has enabled the hoarding of wealth and opportunity and excluded Americans from benefiting from one of the primary ways American families have grown prosperous across generations: through property investment and inheritance. Whether called separation or segregation, processes of sorting have generated and preserved place-based class and racial stigmas that operate as tags of caste hierarchies. Segregated American neighborhoods, cities, towns, and regions have worsened our social and political divisions. We have segregated ourselves from each other due to a social and political sorting that feeds political sectarianism (Bishop and Cushing 2009). America has also made some progress on these challenges; for example, cities are more diverse and racially integrated now than ever (Glaeser and Vigdor 2021).

Nonetheless, as cities have become more ethnically and racially diverse, housing, income, and wealth inequalities have increased within them, spurring feelings of crisis about gentrification. Discrimination in housing persists nationally and affects the access of potential renters and homeowners to affordable and desirable residences and exacerbates already deep disparities in housing and a related wealth gap due to generations of state-sponsored discrimination in housing, real-estate lending, and land-use policies.[3] Homelessness has hit crisis proportions in major American cities, a notorious problem in California. According to the U.S. Department of Housing and Urban Development (HUD), 161,548 people were experiencing homelessness in California by January 2020, which increased from its previously high levels.[4] Additionally, rents and the cost of buying a home have increased with periodic respites brought on by economic dips or global crises such as the novel coronavirus pandemic that went global in the spring of 2020. Not enough affordable housing units for the working classes and the poor are available or built to satisfy demand. One study finds that in the San Francisco Bay Area, "over a third of Bay Area workers earn less than $18 per hour," making living and working in the area challenging enough. Still, worse off are minimum-wage workers (i.e., $12.50 per hour in Oakland and $13.00 in San Francisco) who "would need to work 4.7 full-time jobs to afford a two-bedroom unit" (Zuk and Chapple 2015).

In the Bay Area, over 25% of its 7.75 million inhabitants devote more than 50% of their income to housing. In Oakland, renters in households earning half or less of the city's median income (in 2015, the median income for renters was $34,195) are spending around 68% to 73% of their income on rent.[5] Renters in households earning the median income or more devote at least 30% of their income to housing. Plus, high eviction rates are adding to the housing insecurity of all but especially the poor. On top of that, increased financial precarity brought on by economic downturns connected to the COVID-19 pandemic threatened many Americans, from the very poor to the middle class, with increased housing instability. The brief respite for some on the cost of rent and the paying of it, brought on by the pandemic and the Centers for Disease Control and Prevention (CDC) moratorium on evictions, has run out, with millions of Americans facing eviction as those temporary protections have ended.

Cities and urban regions have not built enough housing to meet present challenges and rising demand for housing due to population and economic growth. The same metropolitan areas benefiting from economic development resist building housing for the middle-class workers who drive that growth, not the working class, poor, and homeless. Neighborhoods function as local plutocracies, motivated by social and economic incentives to create and maintain their exclusivity. They mean to keep others out, conserve their community character and lifestyle, and bolster their home values.

This work of political philosophy examines the core injustices of this crisis and its relation to enduring racial injustices. It posits that what is required to achieve justice in social-spatial arrangements, what some call "spatial justice," is to prioritize, in the crafting and enforcement of housing policy, individual moral equality and liberty, distributive justice, equal citizenship, and due to history and continuing practice and effects of racial discrimination in housing policy, corrective justice in the form of rectification programs that address the history of racism. To arrive at and illustrate this conclusion, I investigate aspects of the housing crisis closely related to the history of U.S. racial injustice, such as gentrification, segregation, desegregation, integration, and, to a lesser extent, homelessness, and offer liberal egalitarian reforms that gesture toward a broad view of justice that is reconstructive.[6]

The ideas that *reconstruction* points toward are the topic of Chapter 1, "Justice and Social Spatial Arrangements"; with its foundation in formal moral equality, liberty, distributive justice, and democratic equality, reconstruction begins with a liberal egalitarian framework of spatial justice as applied in nonideal, real-world conditions. What makes this a work of nonideal political philosophy is that it addresses real-world conditions of injustice in social-spatial arrangements and ultimately calls for the social and political reconstruction of those arrangements. Theories of justice dedicated to the determination of accounts of justice in ideal conditions, what is termed "ideal theory," do not typically address concepts such as spatial, racial, or gender justice because they focus on ideal conditions, which assumes that, among the parties involved, there will be universal understanding and full compliance with the derived (or otherwise determined) principles. Therefore, in ideal theory, categories of justice that address specific injustices tied to a social marker, such as gender or race, are technically irrelevant. For those not familiar with this strategy (and for plenty who are), ideal theory seems, on its face, absurd and, at best, an out-of-touch academic exercise, irrelevant to real-world concerns. A relevant component of this objection to ideal theory emphasizes that its intentional lack of an analysis of oppressive social dynamics— which it does to achieve universal and impartial application in ideal conditions—incapacitates its ability to address real-world situations. What is worse, according to such objections, is that ideal theory provides ideological cover for oppressive interpersonal relations and social structures through, for example, the employment of ideals such as race neutrality or "colorblindness" to preserve unjust conditions and the privileges of groups that profit from them. Despite such dismissals, ideal theories of justice are valuable for setting normative guidelines for correcting injustice in nonideal conditions. The neglect of nonideal conditions in the construction of ideal approaches too often leads to neglecting those conditions when theories of justice are applied to the real world.[7] This work addresses nonideal conditions directly. And considering the relevant nonideal conditions of housing insecurity and its harms, accounts of justice in social-spatial arrangements should begin with the ideas of fundamental moral equality and liberty. That is the ethical basis of social equality and distributive justice; it justifies the demand that social-spatial arrangements reflect and enable moral and social equality and individual liberty. Furthermore, it is the ethical foundation of a basic right to housing, just as it is the foundation for other basic rights, such as freedom of conscience, or more complex rights, such as the right to education.

This history of U.S. housing, land-use policy, and the U.S. housing market has been a long-running demonstration of how the moral and social equality of Americans, subjected to class, racial, ethnic, and religious discrimination, has precisely not been respected, and how the federal government, in league with local governments, housing industry groups, and neighborhood associations, purposely thwarted distributive justice and positively pursued the opposite. It is a history in which Americans, judged to be of the wrong sort, were told to know their place and get back into it. The exemplar of this injustice in social-spatial arrangements is the history of U.S. residential segregation, which primarily targeted African Americans, which is the subject of Chapter 2, "Open Cities and Reconstructive Justice." The chapter concentrates on state-sponsored housing segregation and discrimination in post–World War II housing policy, partly because of its direct link with the United States' postwar economic boom and its immediate connection with the enduring wealth gap between black and white Americans. For example, in 2013, the median net wealth of white families was $142,000, while for African American families it was $11,000, and $13,700 for Hispanic families (Shapiro 2017, 16).[8] This is a dramatic gap sparked by the history of housing discrimination and has long-lasting negative effects. Because of the history and enduring effects of class and racial discrimination in U.S. housing and land-use policy, corrective justice to mitigate, reverse, and repair the resulting injuries is necessary and justified. However, the account of spatial justice based on the ideas of formal moral and democratic equality and distributive justice, as mapped out in Chapter 1, is based on ideal theory. Ideal theories prepare the way for correction; they define the "ought" and mark the gap between it and its failure, but, as outlined earlier, they provide a scant guide to, and insufficient tools for, the work of correction. Thus, frustrated critics altogether turn away from liberalism toward *illiberal* views in the hopes of radical social, political, and economic transformation.

Chapter 2 answers these concerns and completes my account of spatial justice by arguing that rectification policies should be implemented to address the history of racism in housing and land-use policy. Such a commitment to corrective justice to directly address enduring injustices is precisely the correction that liberalism *itself* needs, which is a lesson from Charles Mills's "radical black liberalism" (Mills 2017, 11). It is on this basis that this chapter argues for three things: the full enforcement of the U.S. Fair Housing Act of 1968; a reasonable right to housing; and pragmatic rectification policies that directly address the effects of class and racial residential segregation. These policies should be consistent with U.S. constitutional law and aid all citizens burdened by intergenerational poverty and concentrated disadvantage; those who are stuck in place and prefer to exit to access opportunities elsewhere; and those who want to stay put and build opportunities where they are. These reasonable and pragmatic reforms would transform the geography of opportunity, touching every town and city, and that is what spatial justice and the reconstruction of American communities would look like.

The analysis of gentrification in Chapters 3 and 4 demonstrates the implications of this approach. Even more than the topics of segregation and integration, gentrification is an issue that has caught America's attention, and it is associated with a host of other urban political problems. Chapter 3, "The Trouble with Gentrification," reviews the main conceptual and empirical concerns about gentrification, which, as it turns out, trouble popular conclusions about its causal relation to displacement. It argues for two things: First, gentrification-based displacement may not be the problem that critics charge it is. Second, the focus on gentrification in "superstar cities" (the global urban centers of finance, entertainment, and technology [Glaeser 2011]) obscures other more widespread injustices in social-spatial arrangements and the consequences of the history of housing discrimination against non-whites, exemplified by the African American experience of state-sponsored residential segregation, discrimination in housing, and land-use policy and neighborhood disinvestment. The excessive focus on the experiences of superstar cities, with the recent shocks of reinvestment they experienced, obscures older and continuing patterns of disinvestment that have affected people and places distant from the fashionable centers that grab our collective attention.

That analysis leads, in Chapter 4, "The Harms of Gentrification," to an analysis of the ethical and political objections to gentrification. The harms of gentrification are typically associated with displacement, and I categorize these objections as involving (1) distributive inequalities, (2) loss of community character, and (3) social inequalities. The first and third categories of harm are grave injustices and the source of enduring inequality. The second category of injury, the loss of community character, is essentially a stand-in for the disadvantages of social inequality. In response to standard views of these harms, I maintain that groups do not have legitimate claims to any territory based on social identity alone; individual rights and access to opportunity, especially concerning vulnerable minorities, are typically undermined by such territorial claims. Furthermore, I explain that these harms are deeply related to the history of racial segregation and discrimination in housing; indeed, the most visible complaint about gentrification is its effects on traditionally black and Latino neighborhoods and its pressures on poor residents. To address this enduring injustice, and to get at the nub of the injustices that shadow contemporary objections to gentrification, I advocate for the pragmatic reforms introduced in Chapter 2.

Gentrification indicates deeper injustices in social-spatial arrangements, as much as it is an instance of such inequities. In the United States, what lies beneath it is a history of the continuing effects of class and racial segregation and, to paraphrase the sociologist Orlando Patterson, an ordeal of (half-successful, half-failed) integration (Patterson 1998). Chapter 5 examines this long-standing nub of spatial injustice in the United States. The discussion about segregation and integration in contemporary political philosophy is primarily about what segregation is, its harms and potential benefits, and whether individuals and groups should integrate. The chapter reviews those issues and then asks whether any anti-segregation strategy is morally and politically legitimate. On the one hand, there is formal desegregation where all are allowed access to public places and institutions (e.g., parks, neighborhoods, schools), and individuals pass through, participate in, or use them as they see fit. Desegregation takes no stance on interracial or cross-class community formation, nor does it build in an expectation of, encourage, or especially value cross-group interaction or communication. On the other hand, integration is understood as the official promotion or orchestration of interracial interaction, communication, and cooperation, with the larger social goal of encouraging friendship, community, and civic sorority and fraternity.

However, in the political-philosophical debate, the ideas of integration most focused on are demographic "evenness" and mobility. "Evenness" comes from a specific measure of segregation, the dissimilarity index, a statistical representation of the distribution of groups in a specified geographic area, such as a neighborhood, zip code, or city. Likewise, the idea of mobility, as applied to an individual or family, has been the focus of the integration debate because of several federal and state housing policies that have attempted to increase levels of integration by offering support to families to move out of areas of disadvantage to ones that have comparatively more resources and potentially greater access to advantages.

I am sympathetic with contemporary arguments against integration—insofar as it has been envisioned through measures of neighborhood demographic evenness or its administration through government mobility programs that have affected the "ghetto poor," mainly poor black and brown families stuck in neighborhoods marked by concentrated disadvantage (Shelby 2016, 82–83). However, I cannot quit the ideal of integration, and I do not think Western democratic societies should do so either. It is so related to the ideas of openness of opportunities and communities, democratic communication, and national belonging that it is nearly axiomatic that the latter requires the former. Therefore, I argue that societies have a moral and political duty to desegregate and that integration viewed primarily through the lens of evenness is inadequate. There is no moral imperative to engineer demographically even neighborhoods and cities. Likewise, the expectation that poor residents of underresourced communities must "integrate" (i.e., be relocated) is illegitimate. All the same, as I argue in Chapter 6, "Reconstructing Integration," every neighborhood, city, and region should be open; individuals and families should have fair and equal opportunities to access housing in those communities, towns, and cities. From the vantage of liberalism committed to reconstructive justice, integration is nearly synonymous with open communities and opportunities. This is a legitimate and just version of integration and a vision of integration as national reconstruction.

The broad implication of this book is that the requirements of justice supersede the neighborhood amenities that many Americans put above the provision of decent housing for other human beings, such as the conservation of community character or the expectation that homeless shelters or affordable housing developments be placed anywhere else other than their neighborhoods. In short, my argument hammers home that NIMBY-ism (an acronym for Not In My Back Yard) is morally and politically illegitimate and, more often than not, racist. Spatial justice is inconsistent with reactionary attitudes toward housing policy, whether expressed by the political Right, who want to conserve racial and class exclusions, or by members of the progressive Left, who want housing for all but simultaneously oppose housing development in their communities.[9] It is also inconsistent with dominant neoliberal views about the distribution of social-spatial arrangements, which leave those arrangements up to market vagaries. This makes a *reconstructive* theory of spatial justice discomfiting; it holds that the needs of the poor and the housing insecure have greater moral and political weight than the upper-middle- to upper-class comforts that so many Americans expect in their neighborhoods and the defense of which are used to thwart the equality, liberty, and access to opportunities of other citizens. Justice in social-spatial arrangements is the *price of the ticket* of American reconstruction.

1

Justice and Social-Spatial Arrangements

The U.S. Housing Crisis

In his remarkable book on eviction and housing insecurity, *Evicted: Poverty and Profit in the American City*, Matthew Desmond wrote:

> Whatever our way out of this mess, one thing is certain. This degree of inequality, this withdrawal of opportunity, this cold denial of basic needs, this endorsement of pointless suffering—by no American value is this situation justified. No moral code or ethical principle, no piece of scripture or holy teaching, can be summoned to defend what we have allowed our country to become. (Desmond 2016, 303)

Desmond is right. The American housing crisis is severe. It must be addressed through policy and public political discourse, including journalism, and especially through storytelling, as Desmond has done, from those suffering the heaviest burdens, for the sake of informing the public and expanding social support for the reforms that are needed to meet the challenge.

Political philosophy has a role in addressing this crisis. It provides a framework for understanding the ethical and political theoretical stakes of the challenge, how the crises involving housing affordability, exclusionary land-use policies, and the distinct conflicts around gentrification, displacement, segregation, and integration are injustices. They are instances of injustice that undermine moral equality and equal citizenship and are flagrant demonstrations of not only unfairness—or inequity as many would state it today—but also material manifestations of life-crushing and society-rotting oppression. By considering different theoretical frameworks and based on the core principles and ideals it operates with, political philosophy justifies and advocates for guiding principles directed at ideal ends. Although those ends are ideal, they should consider nonideal conditions so that the principles, demands, and policies they support are pragmatic and feasible. Pragmatic deference is especially appropriate when political philosophy is applied to the world of actual practices within associations and institutions, or what philosopher John Rawls called "local justice" (Rawls and Kelly 2001, 11).

This book is a work about local justice having to do with social-spatial arrangements, or what others also call "spatial justice." Desmond's encapsulation of the damage done, and thus the stark moral wrongs and social injustice of the American housing crisis, points to an instance of spatial injustice: the unjust arrangements of this nation's built environment within its cities and towns, and, specifically, the building, provision, administration, and location of housing. In this chapter and the following chapter, I (1) outline a liberal egalitarian theory of justice in social-spatial arrangements. This theory is applied to the ongoing challenge of housing segregation in Chapter 2 and later chapters to the conflicts over gentrification, displacement, desegregation, and integration. As I move through this analysis, I argue for (2) the full enforcement of anti-discrimination law in housing, (3) the provision of a reasonable right to housing, and (4) pragmatic corrective justice to address the enduring consequences of the United States' history of state-sponsored housing discrimination. What results is a view of justice in social-spatial arrangements that is broadly reconstructive.

An account of what justice requires in social-spatial arrangements begins with examining its components. First, I discuss the phrase "spatial justice" and my use of it and the alternative phrase "justice in social-spatial arrangements." I then review the chief demands that come from various ethical, political, and theological sources for justice in urban planning, housing, and community development; this leads to an initial position that accounts of justice in social-spatial arrangements should begin with the idea of moral equality. This fundamental value is the ethical basis for further claims of democratic equality and distributive justice. It provides a starting point for discussing how social-spatial arrangements reflect and enable both ideas. It is also the starting point for a right to housing as it is for other basic rights such as freedom of conscience, or other complex rights, such as the right to education.

Appeals, however, to basic moral equality are not sufficient to deal fully with the complicated injustices and inequalities related to the urban crisis, such as segregation and gentrification-based displacement. Therefore, this account depends on the idea of democratic equality, with its focus on equal concern, civic equality, and nondomination. While social inequalities are behind the material inequalities that characterize the urban crisis, the prominent features of that crisis are material in nature. Hence, injustices in social-spatial arrangements are distributive injustices. They are largely due to unjust conditions; they undermine individual rights and liberties, impede interpersonal, specifically familial, duties to care, and curtail opportunities, thus eroding moral equality, diminishing human flourishing, and making democratic equality impossible. This chapter concludes that those suffering from these injustices deserve corrective justice so that they and the local communities they are part of can thrive.

Correcting the enormous "degree of inequality" and "withdrawal of opportunity" that Desmond condemns requires more than ending the lack of shelter. Addressing the shortage of affordable housing, the instability that comes with it, and the economic inequality and precarity that form its background would be a reform just as enormous as the injustice itself. It would require the

reconstruction of American communities. Despite the monumental effort and expense entailed, this chapter concludes that it
is imperative to do so if we are to end the "pointless suffering" we
see, or intentionally do not see, in our streets and neighborhoods
throughout this country.

However, the provision of shelter and reforms to housing,
land-use, and community development policies in the American
nonideal context does not sufficiently respond to the enduring
effects of the segregation of our neighborhoods, towns, and cities,
of our social-spatial arrangements generally. Liberal ideal theories,
including those that lean egalitarian, tend to ignore or underesti-
mate the deep effects of group-based inequality, as is evident in the
history of segregation in the United States. The subsequent chapter
takes up this issue to examine what corrective justice regarding
social-spatial arrangements requires.

Spatial Justice

Before analyzing justice and social-spatial relations, a brief clarification of terms is in order. Urban theorists commonly use the
phrase "spatial justice" when referring to theories of social-spatial
arrangements. Spatial justice, territorial justice, or references to the
idea of the just city are phrases used to signify the concept of just
and equal social-spatial arrangements. Those phrases parallel other
subcategories of justice, including procedural, distributive, civil,
criminal, and corrective justice. The usage of "spatial justice" raises
the question, as Justin Williams insightfully points out, whether
spatial justice is distinct from the other subcategories of justice.
Does it usefully point to types of equality? Is it useful as an independent category of analytic analysis?[1] There is a spatial expression
of distributive injustice, but as Williams argues, spatial distributive injustice is not conceptually independent of distributive justice. Other subcategories of justice could be similarly accused; for

example, is there a meaningful distinction between liberty and spatial liberty, or equality and spatial equality? Adding the adjective "spatial" adds little explanatory or conceptual value because the idea of spatial justice is dependent on, or reduces to, other higher-order conceptions of justice and equality. It denotes nothing distinct, and its usage risks reifying a general idea to the extent that it obscures its conceptual dependency.

The term "spatial justice" could be compared to other terms that denote justice or equality from a particular perspective, set of interests, or methodology, as with gender justice, racial justice, transitional justice, or reparative justice.[2] However, they are more useful categories of analysis because they capture more than just different perspectives. Each term points to significant sociological patterns of differing treatment or sociological or economic outcomes of categorizing people or groups. "Spatial justice" does not do so. What is worse, spatial justice is an amorphous category that takes no account of the distinctions among local, national, and international or global justice and is used to support indeterminate demands of questionable legitimacy, such as vague calls for the appropriation of private property to fulfill the undefined needs of city inhabitants (Harvey and Potter 2009; Harvey 2013). All the same, at its best, the term signals a spatial or geographic perspective on moral and democratic equality, liberty, and distributive justice (Soja 2010; Fainstein 2010). Insofar as that is the case, the term is not fully redundant and serves as a useful shorthand.

There are alternatives, but they also fall short. For example, one could scale down and speak of the "just city" or "urban justice," which also refers to justice in their areas of concern. But scaling down is unsatisfactory because the scope of justice and social-spatial arrangements is more significant than the city level—the same problem afflicts calls for the "right to the city." Nonetheless, I defer to the shorthand and contemporary academic usage, although I use it interchangeably with the longer phrase "justice in social-spatial arrangements."

Therefore, for this discussion, "spatial justice" is shorthand for "justice in social-spatial arrangements," which refers to the arrangements' procedural and distributive fairness (the planning, design, building, and placement) of the elements of the built environment. It includes procedural and democratic concerns about the planning of the built environment and distributive and democratic concerns about who has access to, benefits from, is burdened by, and is responsible for those resources.

Additionally, in the sections that follow, the concepts "geography of opportunity" and "spatial foundations of equality" are used when referring to aspects of justice in social-spatial arrangements (Galster and Killen 1995; Briggs 2005a, 1–16). Their virtue is that they prompt the visualization of the basic structures of society and how the goods, services, and opportunities associated with them map onto society, thus revealing points and patterns of inclusion or exclusion and relations of reciprocity or isolation. These are not reducible to other categories of social justice. There is no redundancy in references to justice and the geography of opportunity and the spatial foundations of equality. All the same, these terms do not fully substitute for the idea of spatial justice (understood as justice in social-spatial arrangements). They refer to conditions that mark, by their presence or absence, the social and material conditions for civic belonging in communities, towns, and cities, so they directly relate to the concepts of equality, liberty, and distributive justice.

Equality and Social-Spatial Arrangements

Liberal egalitarians are concerned with the fair distribution of rights, liberties, resources, and opportunities; they should, therefore, be equally concerned with the geography of opportunity and the spatial foundations of equality and inequality because social-spatial arrangements affect the lives of individuals, the value of liberty, and the health of communities. Social-spatial arrangements tell a moral and political story about who and what society values: This is for us, not them; you are allowed here, but not there. This type of story, written in concrete, steel, and asphalt, through walls, fences, and freeways, broadcasts a tale about whose lives matter. Peter Marcuse (2002) succinctly describes this injustice with his distinction between the "ghetto" and the "citadel," and Richard Florida's (2017) references to "winner-take-all urbanism" and the "city of the elite" make the same point.[3] In its concern about distributive justice, liberal egalitarianism focuses on the justice of the basic structure of society, which, in John Rawls's formulation, includes "the political constitution and the principal economic and social arrangements."[4]

The basic structure of society is an abstract concept that consists of society's principal political, economic, and social institutions and the laws, policies, and norms that guide them. These arrangements are not, however, just abstract ideas. They are embedded in physical structures and are arranged spatially—they are the background of individual and family life (Rawls 2001, §4.1, 10). How they are arranged and who thereby has access to them has a profound effect on the life chances of individuals. Justice in social-spatial arrangements, therefore, is concerned with the spatial aspects of background justice. What is more, the profound impact of social-spatial arrangements goes beyond access to resources; those arrangements directly influence the effectiveness of individual liberties and the social standing of individuals and groups as citizens. Social geography also impacts how we relate to others and ourselves as citizens, legitimate residents of communities, and even as moral persons.

Basic Equality

Therefore, thinking about justice and social-spatial arrangements begins with recognizing basic moral equality, which applies universally across all humans and arises from, and is based on, the idea of human dignity (Waldron and Dan-Cohen 2012; Waldron 2017).[5] Basic moral equality is a cornerstone of, of course, *personal morality*, but it equally applies to matters of *political morality*.[6] It sets a baseline for how, as a society, we treat moral others and our fellow citizens, and as such it has implicit social, political, legal, and economic implications. Thus, in regard to social-spatial arrangements in most societies and certainly in ours, to be treated as a moral equal, and to have dignity, or at least effective dignity, requires the right to be in a home: to nurture ourselves and our families, to be alone with our thoughts, or to be with those we welcome in a place we call our own. A home is a place for privacy, rest, a base for families, a uniquely valuable asset, and a place to keep one's possessions; it is one of the fundamental bases of private life, personal autonomy, and social belonging. A home requires more than minimally sufficient and temporary shelter; it is not just basic shelter—a momentary lean-to to catch some sleep in and get out of the rain—it must be decent housing, shelter that is fit for human beings.[7] It is an index of, as W. E. B. Du Bois recognized early in his studies of black life in the United States during the first years of the twentieth century, the social and economic condition of individuals, families, and groups ([1903] 1999, 91; [1899] 2014). Therefore, *if* it is not a condition of dignity, having a home is, at minimum, its intimate attendant. As such, moral equality, and ultimately, dignity, is the normative foundation of housing as a human and civil right.[8] This is why social-spatial arrangements matter both morally and politically. Although U.S. federal law has not codified the importance of decent housing—or at least minimally sufficient basic shelter—its relationship to equal dignity, access to opportunity, and equal citizenship has long been recognized. For example, the U.S. National Housing Task Force in 1988 stated:

> [A] decent place for a family to live becomes a platform for dignity and self-respect and a base for hope and improvement.

. A decent home allows people to take advantage of opportunities in education, health and employment—the means to get ahead in our society. A decent home is the important beginning point for growth into the mainstream of American life.[9]

As a platform of dignity and "hope and improvement," a home is an entry to another aspect of dignity directly connected to social-spatial arrangements: the right to be in, use, and traverse social spaces. The right to access social spaces is concomitant with the right to life, the right to exist, and the right to inclusion in common social life and activity. Home and access to social spaces outside one's front door is not just a material condition; it is access to opportunity and status as equal persons and citizens in the American republic.

Democratic Equality

More is at stake with justice and social-spatial arrangements than distributive justice. Social-spatial arrangements are also a signal and instantiation of equality in social and civic relations—precisely what is not communicated in America's race and class residential and educational segregation patterns and its geography of inequality. According to Elizabeth Anderson, the point of equality is to establish a "social order in which persons stand in relations of equality" (1999, 312; 2010a, 18). And relational equality is, in turn, motivated by the acceptance of moral equality and the denial of hierarchies that rank humans according to their assumed intrinsic worth, or rather, hierarchies that assert major differences in kind between groups, such as is found in racial and other caste-based hierarchies (Mills 1998, 16–17; Anderson 1999, 313; Waldron 2017, 19–28). As Anderson puts it, standing in relations of equality means that no citizen must "bow and scrape" to others (1999, 313).[10] Anderson calls this sort of equality *democratic equality*, and it is also commonly referred to as a type of *relational* or *social equality* (Anderson 1999). To be clear, I am using the idea of democratic equality, following Christian Schemmel's (2015) distinction, to refer to "justice-based relational equality" rather than "relational equality." The latter sort of equality, namely the relation sort, focuses on equal affective and psychological relations, and is too dependent on interpersonal subjective feelings rather than the objective administration of justice.[11]

Democratic equality is clearly motivated and justified by basic equality, but it is also intrinsically related to ideals of distributive justice. Conceptions of social egalitarianism need some corresponding conception of distributive justice, but they may support competing schemes of distributive justice, as long as those accounts of distributive justice support more rather than less equal relations.[12] Although one conception of distributive justice does not immediately follow the idea of democratic equality or Anderson's requirements of equal relations (2010a, 106–108), it leads to prioritizing the goal of democratic equality as a constituting element in principles of justice.

The goals of democratic equality, for example, are evident in Ronald Dworkin's view of a liberal community marked by reciprocity. It is tempting to dismiss the idea of reciprocity because it seems to reduce to merely fair political or economic contractual exchanges. Still, Dworkin's view includes an idea of moral integration that goes beyond a narrow conception of reciprocity. According to Dworkin, integration occurs when "citizens identify with their political community" and "they recognize that the community has a communal life and that the success or failure of their own lives is ethically dependent on the success or failure of the communal life" (Dworkin 2000, 231).[13] Moral integration requires that citizens recognize that their life has equal value as the lives of their co-citizens, or as Dworkin stated, "an integrated citizen accepts that the value of his own life depends on the success of his community in treating everyone with equal concern" (Dworkin 2000, 233).

Likewise, a thick sense of reciprocity is central to Rawls's theory of justice. It begins with the idea that citizens are fundamentally free and equal and includes the disposition of citizens to relate to other citizens as such (2001, 18–24 and 196).[14] It is expressed by Rawls's second principle of justice, especially in its affirmation of democratic equality. It involves the recognition that in a well-ordered society, the relevant parties are involved in a system of social cooperation characterized by fair terms of cooperation that include each participant's rational advantage or good.[15]

Indeed, the ideas associated with the value of relational equality, such as equal concern and the rejection of inequality based on caste or arbitrary status, justify procedural fairness and distributive justice. Apart from the patent injustice of unfairness in procedures or the effects of distributive injustice, the reason we care about residential or educational segregation, the lack of housing for the homeless, or the displacement of those facing economic precarity is because of what those arrangements say about the concern a society has for its members and the different levels of status, as persons and citizens, that a society unjustifiably assigns to those members. Most if not all primary goods are irreducibly social. Their possession indicates status, and the lack of their possession or access indicates stigma; this is especially true of goods such as education and housing (Taylor 1995). Lorraine Hansberry's *A Raisin in the Sun* (1954) unforgettably communicated this social dynamic and has served as a monumental condemnation of the racial segregation of communities.[16] The scenes that it depicted were not restricted to America in the 1950s and 1960s; residential segregation through de facto and barely hidden de jure means continued and continues to be carried out. Consider this example, contained in Sam Fulwood III's analysis of the effects of the Fair Housing Act:

Anthony Foxx recalls looking out from the backyard of his grandparents' Charlotte, North Carolina, home during the late

1970s and early 1980s to see a concrete fence two blocks away
that bordered Interstate 85 and walled off his neighborhood. If he
ventured out the front door and turned right at the corner, he saw
Interstate 77. His childhood home was quarantined by asphalt
highways, isolated from the rise of the city by the comings and
goings of unknown people passing through, but never stopping
in, his neighborhood. This delimited his view of the world and
shaped his childhood. "Had I been born 10 years before, where
those fences were would have been through-streets with houses
and people," said Foxx. "My neighborhood has one way in and
one way out, and that was a choice." (Fulwood 2018, 43–44)

The concrete quarantine of Anthony Foxx's childhood has
parallels across America. A quick view of the map of the city of
Oakland, for example, reveals a system of freeways that box in
the black neighborhood of West Oakland. Those concrete walls
do more than signify distribution injustice and the fencing-off
of opportunity. Social spaces are arranged to make concrete social inequalities and to make visible and physical a lack of equal
concern and disparities in status. This, along with distributive
inequalities, is what Loïc Wacquant calls the process of "relegation" that is part of creating conditions of "advanced marginality." It is seen in different forms: from American ghettos to
French *banlieues* (Wacquant 2008, 2016). There is a geography to
equal access to opportunity, social stigmatization, and relational
equality. Besides deprivations of resources and opportunities, this
was one of the principal objections to forced racial segregation in
residence, education, and public accommodations, and it remains
a concern for the current advocates of integration who seek to not
only mitigate status inequalities but also promote a sense of collective civic equality. It is also related to the housing insecurity
and unaffordability that characterize the current urban crisis, and
it is linked to gentrification and the tense interpersonal relations

among class and racial groups within gentrifying neighborhoods. Considerations of justice and social-spatial arrangements shine a spotlight on the value of democratic equality as a category of equality that is not just a feature of abstract formal relations; it is embodied in social relations and embedded in the physical structures of urban environments.

Despite the importance of democratic equality, or even basic equality, it is not the focus of critical approaches to the right to housing or those movements that organize under the banner of "the right to the city." Instead, those critical approaches adopt a Marxist wariness toward what they imagine are ' "bourgeois rights" and focus instead on critiquing the commodification of housing and cities as part of their criticisms of modern capitalism or ne-oliberalism (Harvey 2013; Harvey and Potter 2009).[17] In contrast, Thad Williamson's and Susan Fainstein's respective accounts of jus-tice and social-spatial arrangements rely on ideas that point to the value of democratic equality, as does Casey J. Dawkins's account of housing justice (Dawkins 2021). Williamson applies Rawls's ideas of reciprocity and Ronald Dworkin's view of civic virtues (2010, 123–128 and 154–155). In addition to his standard that social-spatial arrangements should neither function as a "driver" nor "vehicle" of distributive injustice, he adds the further criteria that those arrangements should indicate and facilitate reciprocity (Williamson 2010, 123–128, 154–155). Concrete walls that cordon off residents blatantly do not. Fainstein argues that three values, equity,[18] diversity, and democracy, characterize a just city (2010, 2011). Democratic equality is in the background of these values because they all communicate that all residents and their interests should receive equal concern. Dawkins's account of housing justice draws on liberal egalitarianism, as well as historical accounts of the natural right to homestead and civic republican views of housing and the common good that are directly tied to social and especially democratic equality (2021, 35–88).

Distributive Justice

Given the good of democratic equality, distributive justice is a natural place to start examining social-spatial arrangements. We need
a vision of distributive justice that leads to a radical reformation of
housing, land-use, and community development policies as a part
of a larger vision of social policy guided by the ideals of basic and
democratic equality. This is needed to counter the mechanisms,
like NIMBY-ism and racial stigmatization, that cause and reinforce
social closure and the group inequalities used to justify those social
closures. Policies that open communities and, with it, opportunities
would instantiate a reconstruction of the basic structures of society
for the common good.

The fairness of arrangements will be achieved through tan-
gible infrastructure, the layout of towns and cities, access to those
spaces, and the right to reside in them. But distributive justice on
its own is not enough. The value of equal democratic relations that
motivates distributive justice in the first place must be kept in sight
to form national expectations of what distributive justice looks like
in urban planning. What could result are distributive outcomes
for communities beyond the idea that a home, be it apartment or
house, is simply a unit of housing—a piece of private property,
storage for personal property, and a base for accessing opportunity.
A unit of housing is more than human storage. To invoke Charles
Taylor's view of primary goods, a stable and decent place to live is
an irreducible social good connecting individuals to society and its
basic structures. As one U.S. government report put it, a home is "a
platform for dignity and self-respect and a base for hope."[19]

Distributive justice concerns the fairness and legitimacy of the
distribution of rights, liberties, primary goods, and services. It
applies to the people within and under the jurisdiction of a state;
thus, it is a matter of domestic justice rather than international or
global justice and administered through systems of local justice.
Included within its domain are issues of "predistribution," such

as pretax pay rates, minimum wage laws, redistribution through taxes, and the provision of resources and services (Hacker and Pierson 2010). The goals of distributive justice include providing resources required to make equal rights and liberties effective and administering fair equality of opportunity. Typically, schemes of distributive justice help fair access to opportunity by laying out broad standards to guide procedural fairness and outlawing unjustified discrimination in public affairs and other domains the public has decided to regulate, such as commerce, medicine, or education. Achieving the goal of equal opportunity converges with its other primary goal of a just redistribution of resources (e.g., material goods and services). Most theories of distributive justice focus on starting points, sometimes called "starting gate" theories. Such theories do two things. First, they justify the provision of a decent or fair start for individuals so that they may pursue their life plans under fair conditions, and, secondly, they argue that distributive schemes, as carried out by policies, should make up for or mitigate the effects of unchosen social or natural disadvantages (Kymlicka 2002).

In application to the question of how social-spatial arrangements can be just or unjust, we can inquire, following Thad Williamson, whether they are intrinsically unjust or undermine justice (Williamson 2010, 110–114). Williamson argues that social-spatial arrangements are intrinsically unjust when they unjustifiably or inequitably deny individual moral and political equality, restrict individual liberty, or thwart distributive justice. In this scenario, social-spatial arrangements are a "driver" of injustice (115–117). The classic example of an intrinsically unjust social-spatial arrangement is state-sanctioned or de jure segregation, including de facto segregation, as experienced in the United States from the era of Jim Crow segregation through the passage of the Civil Rights Act of 1964 and its slow and inconsistent implementation through the 1970s. Although individuals are granted formal liberties, as codified in civil rights, unjust, discriminatory exclusions null the effective worth of that liberty. Likewise, if individuals are subjected to those exclusions, they are denied the goods and services due to them as citizens, are subjected to explicit distributive injustice, are denied or have no fair path to access opportunity, and suffer immiseration and the diminishment of their life chances (115–120).

On the other hand, social-spatial arrangements may not be intrinsically unjust, but they undermine justice because of many independent factors. Social-spatial arrangements serve, in this case, as a "vehicle" of injustice. In Williamson's account, policies that are not intentionally discriminatory but have a disparate impact on protected classes of people fall into this category.[20] Thus, Williamson concentrated on suburban and exurban sprawl because of its adverse effects on residential and educational racial segregation, disparities in infrastructure spending, urban poverty, and the experience and practice of citizenship (Williamson 2010). The current state of high housing costs, the lack of development and availability of affordable housing, and other features of the urban crisis are also in this category.

Justice as Fairness in Urban Theory

Rawls's theory of justice is one of the principal accounts of distributive justice in the spatial, city, and housing justice literature. It, along with Marxism, is a touchstone in discussions about justice and social-spatial arrangements. Thad Williamson's analysis is explicitly Rawlsian, and Rawls's influence is apparent in Susan Fainstein's account, although she adopts the language of equity and capabilities to frame her discussion of resources, and it is part of the mix in Dawkins's egalitarian and civic republican account of housing justice (Fainstein 2010, 2011; Williamson 2010, 110–114; Dawkins 202, 13–32).[21] Even David Harvey's (1973) early account of spatial justice, one of urban theories most prominent neo-Marxist theorists, was based on Rawls's theory of justice. Moreover, a liberal egalitarian framework is embedded in much of the spatial justice and just city literature, especially in discussions of desegregation, integration, and gentrification. In the book *Gentrifier*, for example, John Joe Schlichtman, Marc Lamont Hill, and Jason Patch address the titular issue in an explicitly egalitarian manner in their argument that the benefits of reinvestment, such as improvements in public safety and infrastructure, should be shared by all the neighborhoods in a city, and not be dependent on gentrification. They make a case that housing agencies should work to protect the most vulnerable from displacement when community reinvestment occurs (2017, 125–126). As we will see later, this position reflects the aim of the difference principle and the principle of fair equal opportunity, and the example demonstrates why geographers and urban affairs scholars continue to be attracted to Rawls's theory.

Rawls's account of justice as fairness starts with the recognition that a person's starting point in life affects their life chances because the basic structure of society favors some starting points rather than others. These starting points are determined by what is essentially a lottery of birth and are unearned; therefore, society ought to ameliorate these undeserved disadvantages. Rawls famously proposes the thought experiment of the "original position" where individuals are denied knowledge of their particular social identities and conditions through the mechanism of the "veil of ignorance"; although the individuals in this thought experiment do not know their position in society, they do know that it is marked by social divisions and inequality (Rawls 1999a, 3–18; 2001, 1–32).

Epistemologically cocooned by the original position and the veil of ignorance, and thus theoretically isolated from potential biases, the participants derive two principles of justice for an ideal society: the *basic liberty principle*, which determines equal basic liberties and rights, and the *difference principle*, which guides the distribution of *primary goods* to individuals through the basic structure of society (Rawls 1999a, 52–56; 2001, 42–50).[22] Primary goods are divided between social and natural goods. Social ones are the supporting elements of life made possible by the basic structure of society, including individual rights, housing, education, health care, social and economic opportunities, and so on. Natural goods start with the basic capabilities humans are born with, made possible or not by their circumstances, health, intelligence, and other capabilities (Rawls 1999a, 78–81; 2001, 57–58). The key innovation of the difference principle is that it holds that all inequalities must be attached to "offices and positions open to all" and that insofar as inequalities obtain, "they are to be to the greatest benefit of the least-advantaged members of society."

Justice as fairness is an ideal theory and was not meant to be applied directly to nonideal conditions.[23] It aims to determine what justice as an abstract idea requires for constitutional, or what Rawls termed "domestic," justice. The result, Charles Mills and others have argued, is that Rawls's view of justice as fairness abstracts away the conditions of nonideal contexts to achieve its goal, so it famously does not explicitly deal with, for example, sexual and racial domination and oppression as well other group-based or caste inequalities.[24]

Applied, however, to a contemporary accounting, it offers a framing of why such group-based injustices are wrong and unjust. Its components and principles are unsuited for direct application to nonideal conditions involving group-based inequalities. One reason is that not accounting for nonideal conditions in the first place can be interpreted as ignoring those conditions. Ideal theory could be taken as a framework that assumes that the social mechanisms that perpetuate those injustices, such as status inequalities and opportunity hoarding, are, in fact, just or even natural.

Although its principles and components should not be directly applied to questions over the provision of housing or the formation of communities, it applies as a normative guide to domestic laws by being embedded in constitutional principles (Freeman 2007, 200–209). Constitutional principles, in turn, serve as a mandate and a reference point in the formation and implementation of domestic law, such as the Civil Rights Act of 1964 or the Fair Housing Rights Act of 1968, that seek to outlaw injustices and establish justice, and to themselves guide what Rawls called "local justice," which concerns state, regional, and municipal policy (Rawls 2001, 11–12).

Geography and the Fair Equality of Opportunity

A key feature of Rawls's theory that is crucial for thinking about justice, and especially local justice, in social-spatial arrangements is the idea of fair equal opportunity. The principle of fair equal opportunity is embedded in the "difference principle," the second principle of justice in his theory of justice, and according to Rawls, the principle of fair equality of opportunity is the best interpretation of the difference principle.[25] Opportunities should not just be formally open to all without consideration to individual starting points or the conditions from which they develop the requisite talents, abilities, and willingness to pursue opportunities; instead, fair equality of opportunity strives for *substantive opportunity* in which individuals have the necessary conditions and a fair chance to develop the requisite talents, abilities, and willingness to pursue opportunities in the first place.[26] The normative ideal of fair equality of opportunity is in stark contrast to societies marked by social closure and the mechanisms, such as opportunity hoarding, that result in and embody durable inequalities.[27]

Whether the standard of fair equal opportunity on its own can achieve substantive opportunity is a source of profound worry and the subject of Chapter 3 (Scanlon 2018, 53–56). Those concerns put aside, for now, fair equality of opportunity necessitates providing resources to individuals and households so that society may achieve fair equality of opportunity. Works of political philosophy, even those dedicated to ideal theory, stress the necessity of sufficient education, but other resources are equally important, such as health care, a healthy environment, and, significantly, a decent home and community.

Those resources are spread out across the built environment and that affects who has direct and indirect access to them, so there is a geography to opportunity (Dawkins 2017). Cities and communities characterized by substantive opportunity are open, in opposition to places marked by social closure with few opportunities. Accordingly, the idea of the geography of opportunity is a concept that is closely associated with the idea of equal opportunity and fair access to it. It is a geography revealed by opportunity mapping, which is a sociological and economic method that investigates where opportunities or resources are located in any given locale from an area that corresponds to a zip code through the whole nation.[28] For example, researchers pick some social index (e.g., poverty, rental rates, childhood mortality, economic mobility, transportation infrastructure) and map its incidence, and then overlap that with maps of specific populations (e.g., racial groups, income levels) or another index to get a visible representation of where opportunity exists and its proximity or distance from any given group. This practice enables researchers and the public to see where opportunity clusters and the separation between sites of opportunity and marginalized groups. It uncovers social-geographical impacts, or, as Xavier De Souza Briggs put it, that "Location matters—for economic returns, quality of life, and many other reasons" (2005a, 17). In the United States, race correlates with the geography of opportunity, with predictable results showing that where blacks and some Latinos are located, there are relative disparities in access to resources and opportunities. Robert Sampson has shown through his empirical research how this racialized lack of opportunity shows up as "spatial logics" and in "neighborhood effects" of locales.[29] These and other findings linking race, place, opportunity, and outcomes have been verified and extended by research showing that individuals' life chances are profoundly affected by their race and where they develop from children into adults.[30] This research demonstrates that spatial foundations of inequality are linked to a lack of resources, infrastructure, access to opportunity, and the concentration of disadvantages.

The idea of the geography of opportunity echoes Rawls's theoretical insights about the effects of the basic structure of society and how it favors some starting points over others. Two implications of this research have a bearing on the theoretical political debate about justice and social-spatial arrangements: First, social-spatial arrangements are a nontrivial feature of justice and equality for nonideal and ideal theory. Second, race and racism are also nontrivial features of nonideal and ideal theories of justice for societies with a significant history of race and racism, so much so that principles dealing with racial justice are required, which most liberal egalitarian theories of justice fail to deal with squarely except those, like black radical liberalism, that confront the problem directly (Shelby 2016; Mills 2017; Valls 2018). Distributive justice and democratic equality are central facets of the liberal egalitarian analysis of social-spatial arrangements, but they are inadequate on their own to deal with the legacy of racial injustice and inequality.

The caveats about substantive opportunity and racial equality aside, using justice as fairness as a touchstone, we can inquire whether and to what extent social-spatial arrangements meet equal liberty and distributive justice standards. Concurrently, we can be heedful of whether those arrangements also indicate democratic equality. The primary American examples of arrangements that did not meet these standards were the underresourcing and political domination of Native American communities and reservations (Wilkins and Stark 2018) and the history of housing discrimination and segregation, especially against African Americans. Take, for instance, the difference principle, which holds that "Social and economic inequalities are to satisfy two conditions: first, they are to be attached to offices and positions open to all under conditions of fair equality of opportunity; and second, they are to be to the greatest benefit of the least-advantaged members of society" (Rawls

2001, 41–42). The social inequalities manifest in neighborhoods characterized by segregation and concentrated disadvantage strikingly fail both conditions. That these arrangements are not "to the greatest benefit of the least-advantaged members of society" is apparent in the high levels of poverty and low levels of employment in those neighborhoods but also its enduring effects on the wealth gap. In 2013, for example, "the median net wealth of white families was $142,000, compared to $11,000 for African American families and $13,700 for Hispanic families" (Shapiro 2017, 16). Through its convergence with educational segregation, this wealth gap contributed to an income gap; the median white family income in 2017 was around $60,000, but the median black family income was around $37,000 (Rothstein 2017, 184). This disparity is largely the result of America's history of housing discrimination. As Richard Rothstein points out:

> By the time the federal government decided finally to allow African Americans into the suburbs, the window of opportunity for an integrated nation had mostly closed. In 1948, for example, Levittown [New York] homes sold for about $8,000, or about $75,000 in today's dollars. Now, properties in Levittown without major remodeling (i.e., one-bath houses) sell for $350,000 and up. White, working-class families who bought those homes in 1948 have gained, over three generations, more than $200,000 in wealth. (Rothstein 2017, 182)

What is at stake here is not just income and wealth but education and other goods and services—access to a healthy environment, health care, nutritious food, transportation, and political power—that make anything like substantive opportunity possible.

If the principles of justice in Rawls's justice as fairness were to be applied through local policy to social policy, even with the caveats registered herein, the results would dramatically alter the geography of social-spatial arrangements in the service of justice. For example, the U.S. Department of Housing and Urban Development (HUD), other federal agencies, and corresponding state agencies would have to take positive steps to close the wealth gap. Cities and communities could no longer wash their hands of their collective responsibility to provide decent homes for poor and working-class families. NIMBY-ism may survive, but it would have to be offset by redistribution policies that afforded resources to communities across class and racial boundaries. Take, for example, the practice of exclusive neighborhoods, such as Orinda, California, that police enrollment in their school districts to ensure that students from nearby and poorer cities, such as Oakland, do not enroll in their public schools. Orinda is 82% white, the median home price is $1,609,500, and the median rent is $5,101.[31] A case featuring Orinda from 2014 is illustrative of the NIMBY-ism and resource-hoarding behavior made possible by current housing, tax, and education policies:

> In 2014, Vivian, a seven-year-old Latina, was thrown out of Orinda's public schools because a private detective hired by the school system determined that her family did not officially reside there. Vivian stayed with her mother, a live-in nanny for an Orinda family. Her case highlighted school officials' limited sense of the "public" they served—although she stayed with her mother in the community where her mother lived and worked, because Vivian and her mother could never live in Orinda on their own, Vivian was seen as a trespasser, poaching a community resource to which she was not entitled. Vivian had crossed an invisible border, gaining richer educational resources without proper documentation. Her citizenship was not questioned; her address was. (Shapiro 2017, 81)

Under the guidance of the principles of justice, such exclusions would either be illegal because they infringe on Vivian's and her mother's equal liberties and if it were deemed that the exclusion per se did not infringe on their liberties—to access resources where they lived—then Orinda would have to pay because the exclusion would have to meet the requirement that it be to the "greatest benefit of the least-advantaged members of society" (Rawls 2001, 41–42).

In addition to providing positive support to achieve fair equal opportunity, distributive justice also supports citizens' access to political power. On the most basic level, the provision of resources enables and motivates participation in political systems by aiding the supply of time and resources for citizens to access polls and communicate with their representatives. It also provides an education that informs and motivates citizens to participate in mutual governance. It is part of the dynamic of equal concern and reciprocity that underwrites democratic equality. Indeed, deliberative democratic approaches are prominent in debates within urban theory about spatial justice and how communities determine what good and right urban policies are. For example, Feinstein's (2010) account of the just city reflects the importance of democratic participation in accounts of justice and social-spatial arrangements, as does philosopher Iris Marion Young's advocacy of democratic regional governance in urban justice (Young 1990, 2000). Citizens should have a say in urban policy, and their voices should be heard in discussions about social-spatial arrangements if equal citizenship means anything. However, if the requirements of equal liberty and distributive justice are to be satisfied, citizens' demands, even when framed by the idea of "localism," must be limited by constitutional restraints. There is a danger in the boundaries that communities assert to make sense of themselves and divide the included "we" from the excluded "them." These assertions of limitations are written into the idea of community and expressed in democracy; those boundaries define collective life, but they also demarcate belonging and distribution (Walzer 1983, 31–35).

Civic republicans and liberals that see an ideal in the expression of community identification across civil society hold that the function within a democracy that divides insiders from outsiders, friends from enemies, needs to be universalized across civil society for the sake of the realization of some common good. Yet this same function is one of the undergirding features supporting durable inequality and the exclusion, marginalization, and exploitation that come with communal demarcation. Skepticism, therefore, about the results of direct or participatory democratic methods in dealing with questions of social-spatial arrangements is justified. Democratic governance has primarily served to underwrite and preserve status inequality, particularly regarding race and class, through the hoarding of public resources and opportunities— this is essentially the core problem with NIMBY-ism, and related attitudes and acts of exclusion, including exclusionary and restrictive zoning policies, and the resulting racial and class segregation and stratification. This problem, and the need to contain the excess of the tyranny of politically manufactured majorities over the form of communities and who gets to live in them, is at the core of racial residential segregation and class-based exclusions that drive residential displacement (Rothstein 2017; Doughty 2020). This problem is displayed prominently in the troubled history of desegregation and integration programs for education and housing after the *Brown v. Board of Education* (1954) decision and the passage of the U.S. Fair Housing Act (1968). It is a feature of controversies over gentrification, and it continues to operate in the attitudes and activities of homeowners acting like monopoly-seeking cartels in blocking fair and affordable housing (Macedo 2011; Monkkonen 2016; Scheutz 2022). Justice in social-spatial arrangements entails supporting citizens' access to political power and giving them a voice in urban policy, but not the ability to restrict who can be their neighbors. In areas with severe housing shortages, this includes constraining community members from limiting how many neighbors they should have.

If we, as a society, take basic and democratic equality seriously, distributive justice is categorically required. Theories of justice, such as those offered by classic liberalism (what some would rather label as "neoliberalism"[32]) or libertarianism, which support laissez-faire market-based distributions, and that include varying degrees of protection for even basic equal opportunity (e.g., such as a conception of opportunity as careers open to talents), fall short in this regard. Their purported respect for persons *qua* persons and liberty, restrained only by a fundamental principle of "no harm," which itself is limited to a basic set of rights, and rejection of state-imposed distributive patterns, is purely formal and fails to deal with socially imposed patterns that cause and embody durable inequality.

In the political imagination of classic liberalism and libertarianism, individuals are maximally free in their private and social spheres; in their purview, this includes most, if not all, economic life, and that freedom includes the freedom to be excluded, discriminated against, segregated, and socially abandoned. Such a narrow and atomistic conception of freedom is unfreedom because it identifies as the core of freedom the right of choice exercised primarily through private and market exchanges. This limited conception of freedom is entirely negative and includes no guarantee against arbitrary and unjustified stigmatization, exclusion, and marginalization in those exchanges. Indeed, it provides only thin theoretical moral and legal equality guarantees. This is not just the freedom to choose but to be subject to the right of others *not* to choose others, all to devastating effect. Laissez-faire liberty is a negative and nakedly discriminatory liberty that fuels segregation and NIMBY-ism. It connects Anthony Foxx's experience in Charlotte, the segregation of Levittown, and Vivian's experiences in Orinda. American racism, abetted by classic liberal conceptions of liberty and property, endorsed the arrogance and entitlements that the character Karl Lindner, from Hansberry's *Raisin in the Sun*, epitomizes, and libertarianism in the 1970s arose to justify such views under cover of the freedom of choice (Bagenstos 2014). Thus, consider the implications of Robert Nozick's libertarian maxim, "from each as they choose, to each as they are chosen," application to the private and social sphere (even when no public resources are involved). It is both an invitation to and cover for segregation and other forms of social closure (Nozick 1974, 66).[33] This view sanctions preexisting conditions of de facto discrimination, exclusion, and segregation, concretized through generations of de jure policy and practice, which neither theory fully addresses. Nozick's version of libertarianism includes a rectification principle that holds that property obtained violates just original acquisition and transfer must be rectified. However, there is little recognition in Nozick's account of the rectification due to black Americans and other victims of extensive and state-sponsored discrimination in the protection of rights, liberties, and provision of public goods—such as, famously, access to federally guaranteed home mortgages that powered the postwar middle class, which under even his stringent view, would have been unjust. Taking libertarianism seriously, perhaps even more seriously than libertarians, means taking the prospect of correcting for these substantial harms seriously. Rectification for these injustices in social-spatial arrangements is due, but not based on the narrow grounds given by property rights assertions; rectification is justified based on the demands of distributive justice and democratic equality, based on equal citizenship. It is to that topic, and segregation as an exemplar of American injustice in social-spatial arrangements, that we now turn.

2
Open Cities and Reconstructive Justice

Corrective Reform

Frustration abounds with standard liberal egalitarian accounts of justice. The complaint is that its focus on distributive justice is too narrow. It is missing an analysis of the social dynamics that lead to oppression or even intentionally passing over domineering interpersonal and structural relations for the sake of class and racial domination. In short, liberal egalitarian concepts of justice are accused of not only being insensitive to neoliberal and racist hegemony but also being in their service by providing ideological cover. Thus, the applications of liberal egalitarian theory to the basic structures of society, such as education, employment, criminal justice, and social-spatial arrangements, are accused of promoting "reform"—a word that in the worlds of social and political theory can be reasonably interpreted as near slanderous—which merely affirms present structures. If reformers authentically cared about justice, this criticism goes, they would strike a radical posture toward the hegemony of dominant late-capitalist and neoliberal ideology and urge structural or systemic transformation. Or, in a word, revolution.[1]

Despite such scathing criticisms, liberal conceptions of distributive justice continue to appeal to urban theorists. Equality, fairness, and liberty have staying power when we focus on housing people and opening communities and opportunities instead of guillotine dreams of radical systemic transformation.[2] Liberal egalitarianism has the resources that serve as the basis for necessary reforms to correct the deep and enduring injustices in unjust social-spatial arrangements. So the instinct to return to the political values and virtues of liberalism and egalitarianism when thinking through the ethical and political theoretical challenges of social-spatial arrangements is correct and pragmatic.

Therefore, this chapter defends the application of liberal egalitarianism to urban policy. It reviews objections, common to the Left, that liberal egalitarian approaches merely justify piecemeal reforms to ameliorate some injustices, but they do not support radical or so-called transformative reforms that would fundamentally alter or abolish underlying oppressive and dominative systems. This chapter responds to these objections by defending a nonideal liberal egalitarian account of justice in social-spatial arrangements. It argues that applying laws based on political and legal equality and fair equal opportunity would be reconstructive from the neighborhood to the national level. As a primary example of a potentially radical reconstructive law, I consider the U.S. Fair Housing Act of 1968. The full enforcement of the Fair Housing Act and other related policies to ensure fair equal opportunity would make substantial changes to the demography of American towns and communities and the geography of opportunity. But those changes, as massive as they might be, would not be enough to make communities and cities truly open: opportunity hoarding makes substantive opportunity elusive and drives enduring inequality. A reasonable right to housing is required to address this problem, but as reconstructive to American communities and cities as a federal right to housing might be, it still falls short. The full enforcement of the Fair Housing Act and the formation of a right to housing would be a prime example of distributive justice actually carried out, but they are entirely forward-looking. Achieving distributive justice and democratic equality requires addressing the deep and enduring consequences of structural racism; it requires a vision of justice that is backward-looking enough to make forward-looking administrations of justice substantive. Doing so requires addressing the effects of residential segregation, racial discrimination in housing, housing policy, and finance regarding social-spatial arrangements. That is the price, heavy as it may be, to reconstruct our social-spatial arrangements so that they meet the demands of justice. Thus, nonideal liberal egalitarian accounts— or for that matter, normative ideal accounts—of social justice, motivated by basic and democratic equality and committed to distributive justice, must also affirm a principle of corrective justice.

Reaching for Transformation

Despite the applicability of liberal egalitarianism to urban policy, it has faced a range of criticisms in urban theory that parallel those from political philosophers. The major complaint about liberal theories of justice, including John Rawls's conception of justice as fairness, is that they do not address nonideal conditions as an ideal theory.[3] The world that we confront, where the problems of segregation and economic and housing precarity exist, is nonideal and requires additional or entirely alternative principles that address those actual nonideal conditions.[4] Additionally, justice as fairness and its two principles of justice pertain only at the constitutional level and directly affect the institutions that comprise the basic structure of society (Rawls 2001, 10–11). After being adjusted to deal with nonideal conditions, they apply to—but do not wholly determine—what Jon Elster called "local justice," which concerns state, regional, and municipal policy (Elster 1992; Young 1994; Rawls 2001, 11–12). This objection to ideal theory is paired with the complaint that it is also forward-looking, in that the participants in the original position formulate principles of justice to guide the basic structure of society going forward from some theoretical point, which may hamper its application to backward-looking issues, such as past injustices (Mills 2017, 139–159).

These are fair concerns, but as pointed out repeatedly by other political philosophers, addressing nonideal conditions and backward-looking issues is not the role of *justice as fairness*. Instead, it is to formulate a guiding reasonable utopian ideal (Pogge 2007). This does not negate the development of adaptations and applications of ideal theory to nonideal conditions or the addition of backward-looking policies to deal with enduring injustices. The development of theories of justice for nonideal conditions is expected, as seen in Williamson and Fainstein's work, this application, and especially Charles Mills's criticisms of Rawls's liberalism and his development of black radical liberalism. A nonideal liberal egalitarian analysis provides a reasonable and politically legitimate normative foundation for reforming unjust and unequal social-spatial arrangements. They are rooted in recognition of universal moral equality, set democratic equality as their ideal standard, and in doing so, affirm the need for both equal rights and liberties and distributive justice in theory, yes, but more vitally in practice.

But, for all of that, there is a deeper problem with forward-looking theories of justice. Approaches that concentrate on justice in abstraction, in some imagined counterfactual—Rawls's (1999) original position is the paradigmatic example—depend on the imposition of blind spots to illuminate some idea, distinction, or principle.[5] The problem is that they may encourage applying those very same blind spots to nonideal conditions. Setting aside thorny complications and social identities is theoretically helpful in negating bias in idealized decision procedures. However, at the same time, it encourages being imperceptive to how race, gender, and class matter (Young 1990; Pateman and Mills 2007; Mills 2017). The race insensitivity affected by Rawls's mechanism of the veil of ignorance portrays an idealized ideal that is patently untrue and unreasonable (Mills 2017, 73–80). Worse, it encourages a willful ignorance about nonideal conditions—Mills called this an epistemology of ignorance—and dresses it up as a normative ideal (Mills 1998, 21–40; 2007). That normative ideal too easily translates into a race blindness in nonideal conditions, which provides an excuse to ignore enduring injustices. This blind spot can hamper any hope of the realization of fair equal opportunity and the larger goals of distributive justice and democratic equality. Likewise, there is concern about the normative support that liberal egalitarian theories seemingly impart to neoliberal free-market policies. The accusation is that liberal egalitarianism ends up supporting welfarist policies that ameliorate the disparities created by the free market but do not challenge underlying marginalizing and exploitative conditions.[6] Worse, as this criticism has it, liberal theories, egalitarian or not, provide ideological cover for hegemonic structures by giving the rulers superficial universalist ideals that justify their continuing power and reasons to the ruled for why they do, in fact, consent to their own domination. The frustration toward free-market, libertarian, and ameliorative liberal-welfarist policies demonstrates a desire for a more radical egalitarian framework.

Peter Marcuse laid out a distinction, influential among scholars of urban affairs and planning, between the first two approaches, which he labeled as "market principles" and "welfare-oriented principles," and a more transformative alternative, which he called "over-riding social justice principles." He describes them in the following passage, which addresses gentrification, but his categorization is general:

1. Market principles—neo-liberal policies. Gentrification can be allowed to proceed according to strict market principles with public policy facilitation, the justification to be found in various ways: ideological commitment to the free private market, concern for physical condition, "sustainability," increasing the tax base, "freedom of choice," etc., with no explicit attention to the social justice of the result;

2. Welfare-oriented principles—liberal policies. An analysis of the distributional impact of policies planned according to other principles and for other purposes can add considerations

of social justice to the mix, including a variety of measures to control the displacement aspects of gentrification, such as eviction controls, relocation aids, mixed income requirements for new construction, etc.

3. Over-riding social justice principles—transformative policies. Such an approach would begin with a consideration of the needs of the residents and users of the neighborhood subject to the economic pressures of gentrification, and would prevent displacement through a variety of techniques including limiting new investment, regulating occupancy prices, appropriate land use and zoning controls, and, where necessary, targeted public investment. (Marcuse 2013, 3–4)

Marcuse equates liberalism with the first (neoliberal) and second (liberal) policies and distances them from the transformative third category. His typology parallels Nancy Fraser's distinction between *affirmative* and *transformative* redistribution. Affirmative redistribution reforms, according to Fraser, "such as means-tested welfare and affirmative action, seek to redress maldistribution by altering end-state patterns of allocation, without disturbing the underlying mechanisms that generate them" (Fraser 1996, 45–46; 1997, 23–27). The affirmative approach contrasts with what she calls *transformative redistribution*. The transformative approach seeks to redress end-state injustices precisely by radically altering the underlying framework that generates them. By restructuring the relations of production, transformative redistribution would change the social division of labor, reducing social inequality without creating stigmatized classes of vulnerable people perceived as beneficiaries of special largesse. Fraser also identified a middle way between the two types of redistribution, which she called "non-reformist reforms." Such reforms do not strive to alter the "underlying framework" of society.

Nonetheless, they would "set in motion a trajectory of change in which more radical reforms become practicable over time" (Fraser

2003, 79). Fraser's and Marcuse's distinctions are evocative. Yet, insofar as Fraser or Marcuse's critiques associate "affirmative distribution" with Rawls's view of justice and liberal egalitarian conceptions of distributive equality, they are wrong. They are incorrect about how justice as fairness conceives of distributive justice and miss its foundational ties to moral and democratic equality.[7] The goals laid out in justice as fairness, as Rawls argued, are inconsistent with laissez-faire and welfare-state capitalism because both do not respect the fair value of equal liberties and impede fair equality of opportunity. In contrast, according to Rawls, the principles of his account of justice as fairness are more likely realized by either a "property-owning democracy" or a liberal socialist regime (Rawls 2001, 135–140).[8]

Furthermore, their call for "overriding social justice principles" and transformation raises questions about what precisely may rightfully be overridden or transformed. The distinction between welfare-oriented (or nonreformist reforms) is indeterminate; for example, take rent control, targeted location-based investments, or zoning reforms. They attempt to "transform" communities, and all have been supported by liberal reformers. In Rawls's theory of justice, the first or equal liberty principle overrides schemes of distribution or social and political ordering that deny individuals effective equal liberties. Correspondingly, the second principle of justice, which contains the principles of fair equality of opportunity and the difference principle, overrides schemes of distribution that would undermine fair equality of opportunity and do not benefit the least-advantaged members of society. However, methods of radical redistribution that called for equality of holdings or outcomes would not override the protections of the equal liberty principle. Thus, liberal egalitarian schedules of justice, including those committed to transforming society away from structural injustices, would be less open-ended than Fraser's and Marcuse's calls for transformation. All the same, it is not equivalent to the "affirming" underlying unjust structures and systems.

These limitations aside, aspects of Marcuse's transformative alternative echo the form, if not content, of the aims of liberal egalitarianism. The same applies to Fraser's category of "non-reformist reforms," which Susan Fainstein adopts to characterize the pragmatic urban policies she supports (Fainstein 2010, 18). Liberal egalitarianism begins with recognizing equal citizenship and affirms all citizens' equal liberties and rights. However, those rights and liberties (e.g., property and the ability to collect rents from one's holdings) are not absolute. Inequalities must be justified and consistent with the maintenance of fair background justice. As Thomas Scanlon explained in *Why Does Inequality Matter?*, any inequalities must be justified as institutionally necessary, as the result of fair procedures, and with substantive opportunity as a background condition (Scanlon 2018, 41). Thus, Marcuse cites some of the proposals consistent with a liberal egalitarian approach. For example, Marcuse supports "regulating occupancy prices" in the form of rent stabilization or rent control (leaving aside, for now, the issue of whether such policies are effective), ending restrictive zoning, and "targeted public investment" such as in the form of community reinvestment programs or the provisioning of publicly subsidized housing. However, what policies and practices social justice principles would override may not lead to all the techniques that Marcuse endorses. He, for example, supports limiting new investments. However, suppose he means banning them or rejecting all market-based solutions, as some not-in-my-backyard (NIMBY) or anti-development activists insist. That case may contradict the ends (the provision or subsidizing of housing) that so-called transformative policies seek to accomplish.

What is more, concerning social policy generally and housing, community, and land-use policies specifically, changing the "underlying structure" is a tall order. One truly radical transformative idea would be to decommodify all housing. For that to be democratically legitimate, it would require garnering the support of the majority in the nation and fundamentally altering U.S. political structures. Consider the necessary changes imagined by this sort of radical structural transformation. It would involve radically altering U.S. property, housing, and land-use law, changing decades of constitutional interpretation, and likely the U.S. Constitution. It is not even clear with this formulation what could count as transformation short of scraping the entirety of the nation's social, political, legal, and economic structure. This question leads to the more substantial objection that Marcuse's view supports undermining or negating individual equal basic liberties. His view implies eliminating the right to engage in regulated market exchanges of privately held homes and buildings. Even in a limited manner to address the cluster of problems associated with the urban crisis, doing so is inconsistent with reasonable conceptions of justice. Indeed, as morally bold as the call for radical transformative redistribution pretends, they are equally morally misbegotten; they are disconnected from the normative ideals of basic and democratic equality, equal liberty, and fair equal opportunity (Rawls 1999c, 96–116; 1999a, 434–441; 2001, 184–188).

Open Communities and Substantive Opportunity

In the Longfellow neighborhood in North Oakland near where I live, there is a mural of a multicolored polygon that used to be accompanied by Henry Wadsworth Longfellow's often-quoted paean to cities, "I have an affection for a great city. I feel safe in the neighborhood of man and enjoy the sweet security of the streets."[9] The passage is worth reading in its original form because the security that Longfellow praised was not about the feelings of personal safety—an idea that is common enough in the thoughts that Americans have about cities and which is often inflected with race and class prejudices—instead, he praised the comfort and uplift that he received from being witness to the plentitude

of human experiences and strivings. It is a celebration of imma-
nence, the openness of the city, and being open to its varied to-
tality. Longfellow's perspective was romantic when he wrote that
passage in 1837, and he apparently floated above the hard realities
he enjoyed witnessing as a flaneur. All the same, his sentiments express the view that the openness of cities is a good that contributes
to the democratic health of society, and while his appreciation is
mainly aesthetic and spiritual, we can join in his praise from the
perspective of the ideals of justice and democratic equality. Cities,
towns, and neighborhoods are public spaces, and insofar as they
are supported by and made possible by the public, they ought to be
open. Openness is a condition for democratic equality, the effective
freedom of residents and citizens, substantive opportunity, and the
sustainability of society.

The openness of cities, towns, and neighborhoods means
that those locales' residences, goods, and services ought to meet
basic and democratic equality and distributive justice demands.
Specifically, as openness relates to distributive justice, the first
clause of Rawls's difference principle is relevant; that "social and economic inequalities" are "are to be attached to offices and positions
open to all under conditions of fair equality of opportunity" (Rawls
2001, 41–42).

Individuals should have a substantive opportunity to reside in the
cities, towns, and neighborhoods of their choice. Inclusion should
not be based on social identities and be subject to the mechanisms
of group-based inequality, such as discrimination based on caste
or racial stigmas. This opportunity is dependent on and supports
more general substantive opportunities in which individuals have
the necessary conditions and a fair chance to develop the requisite talents, abilities, and willingness to pursue opportunities in
other parts of their lives. The absence of substantive opportunity,
as is evident through the history of segregation in America and
racial and class-based disparities in housing, and the closely related disparities in education, wealth, and so on, reinforces adverse

social-geographic effects and racial stigmas. Closed cities and communities are a vehicle and a driver of enduring injustice. To achieve substantive opportunity and address enduring injustice in housing, procedural fairness in the housing market and policies must be mandated and effectively enforced to outlaw and mitigate racial and other forms of group-based discrimination. Doing so would be reconstructive.[10]

The U.S. Fair Housing Act

In the context of the United States, achieving substantive opportunity in housing would mean finally and fully enforcing the dual mandates of Title 8 of the 1968 Civil Rights Act, better known as the Fair Housing Act. That act is the United States' primary law addressing the history of urban and housing policy discrimination, exemplified by its history of housing segregation, which will be further discussed in Chapter 5. Sections 804 and 805 of the act make up its first mandate, which prohibits discrimination against protected classes in renting and selling housing by individuals and businesses. Section 808 (e)(5) contains its second mandate, which directs the Department of Housing and Urban Development (HUD) to *affirmatively* further fair housing.[11] The first mandate has had limited success, evidenced by ongoing discrimination in housing, and the second has largely been neglected (Squires 2018a; Fulwood 2018). The first mandate is forward-looking in that it forbids and seeks to mitigate ongoing discrimination. The second mandate is an administrative demand to execute the first mandate. It instructs HUD to institute and support local policies addressing past and enduring racial discrimination patterns in housing. That requirement may mean ending segregation patterns, concentrated poverty and disadvantage, and altering policies that negatively impact affected groups. Doing so requires being attentive to the history of American racial residential discrimination and some level of backward-looking concern to make forward-looking reforms effective. In short, addressing past harms is a precondition for improving the outcomes of future-oriented reforms. For example, establishing fair equal opportunity in housing policy should include proposals that address past inequities, such as a right of return policies for those displaced by the destruction of public housing, increases in housing subsidies, the building of affordable housing in neighborhoods that previously excluded them through zoning, outlawing discrimination against holders of housing vouchers, and providing more community development resources to areas affected by concentrated poverty and disadvantage.

With Julián Castro as the director of HUD, the Obama administration announced in 2015 the Affirmatively Further Fair Housing (AFFH) Rule that emphasized the original intent of the 1968 act to address the history of racial residential segregation. It ordered states, local governments, public housing agencies, and any institution or agency that receives subsidies or participates in any HUD program to assess their fair housing issues and develop plans to achieve the goals of both parts of the Fair Housing Act.[12] The full enforcement of the Fair Housing Act would go a long way in protecting the equal liberties of citizens. It would be a program guided by the ideals of distributive justice and consistent with the aims of substantive opportunity. Outlawing discrimination and mandating that states and municipalities take affirmative steps to address their history of residential segregation is a necessary feature of procedural fairness in the housing market. Its support by federal, state, and local governments is an indicator of political fairness. Its enforcement, or lack thereof, indicates whether society expresses equal concern for its residents and is indeed open to all citizens.[13]

From its inception, the milquetoast enforcement of the Fair Housing Act can undoubtedly be labeled as ameliorative and deserves ridicule. It was subverted by enduring patterns of racist

exclusion in American communities and cities and by applying neoliberal housing market principles that made an end run around
the Fair Housing Act's goals.[14] The insincere enforcement of the
act's goals could not withstand the force of mortgage lending
practices that favored the upper-middle classes and the wealthy.
The evasion of the Fair Housing Act by affluent communities
includes zoning practices that excluded affordable housing, made
fair housing goals impossible to achieve, and entrenched the desire
of communities to exclude the ghetto poor. When the federal, state,
and local municipalities enforce the Fair Housing Act, it is at best
an example of the sort of welfare-oriented liberal policies criticized
by Marcuse, Fraser, and Fainstein that end up engaging in reforms
affirming the underlying enduring injustices.

Imagine the result of forcing the compliance of both its parts
on all American cities and communities. The aggressive enforcement of the act would be reconstructive. It would not only be so in
some general qualitative sense, but it would also be a step toward
reconstructing the American communities, where too many have
assumed that it is their democratic right to exclude the poor and to
conserve their communities' racial or ethnic character.

The Lack of Substantive Opportunity

As laudable as enforcing both parts of the Fair Housing Act would
be, critics who accept the higher bar for transformative redistribution rightly criticize laws such as the Fair Housing Act for being
limited to forward-looking reforms. Furthermore, this limitation is compounded by the additional limit of being guided by
the U.S. Supreme Court's standard of postracial jurisprudence,
which holds that the only legitimate role for considering race in
legal proceedings is to prevent direct discrimination. Laws and
policies that use racial or ethnic categories to ameliorate or rectify past race-based discrimination in housing, education, health

care, and the distribution of primary goods are currently unconstitutional (Darby and Levy 2016). Thus, the full enforcement of the Fair Housing Act would ultimately be yet another instance of an ameliorative reform that reaffirmed underlying unjust systems. It would not achieve substantive opportunity—fair and equal opportunity not undermined by historic and enduring state-sponsored injustices, in a word, segregation—in the provision of state and federal housing benefits or the housing market.

This grave problem provides a window into why applying abstract and race-blind principles of justice, even in a political and economic system closer to a property-owning democracy than current neoliberal systems, may not transform American housing and urban policy to good effect for those formerly excluded. Fully enforcing the Fair Housing Act and the AFFH rule is an imperative of public morality. Its full enforcement would be significant and, in concert with policies that promote and protect a right to housing, housing affordability, and stability, their full implementation would alter every American community subject to fair housing laws. However, it is not a panacea, nor do its proponents think it is (Squires 2018b).

All the same, it is important and instructive to pay attention to how, even with its full enforcement, the Fair Housing Act would not override the accumulated disadvantages incurred by enduring racial injustice. Since it is not a backward-looking law, its enforcement does not address past exclusions and displacements; it does not rectify the substantial damages done by America's history of residential discrimination. Thus, it is ineffective in dealing with the resulting black-white wealth gap. These limitations mean that even with the full and aggressive enforcement of the Fair Housing Act, victims of state-sanctioned residential discrimination would not be compensated for the loss of wealth resulting from intergenerational transfers of real estate–generated wealth. Even after robust reforms of the Fair Housing Act, affected individuals would not have the capital to buy homes; they were denied and access to the neighborhoods—with the backing of the local, state, and federal governments—that excluded them.

Additionally, the aspects of the urban crisis that a fully enforced Fair Housing Act would address do not capture all the facets of that crisis and injustice in social-spatial arrangements. The Fair Housing Act would likely mitigate some of the visible signs of housing instability, but it would not directly address the problems of homelessness and the high rates of evictions, nor would it deal with the general lack of affordable housing for residents across economic classes. The Fair Housing Act outlaws discrimination against what U.S. law recognizes as protected classes, but being poor or working class is not one of those protected characteristics. The second mandate, which directs state and local agencies to affirmatively further fair housing, might lead to programs that address this problem; for example, policies could promote inclusive rather than exclusive zoning or encourage affordable housing development. The problem, though, is that these reforms would be a secondary effect, so it would not be necessary to expand them after meeting the general goals of the mandate. This scenario illustrates how substantive inequality can remain even under ideal conditions.

The functional impairment involved in substantive inequality converges with shortcomings in liberal egalitarian theories of justice that stand in the way of realizing their goals. For instance, Rawls's second principle of justice governing distributive justice is not likely to lead to substantive opportunity because even after adjustments due to predistribution and redistribution, the most well-off may still hoard opportunities. While the lower and middle classes benefit from increases in public resources, such as education and political power, the wealthy may provide more significant developmental, educational, and social resources to their progeny. The quality of public schools may exponentially increase, and a more substantial number of Americans may afford elite private schools, but the wealthy have the resources and options to escalate their investments in their children (Anderson

2010, 11–22; Scanlon 2018, 66–70). Those children would likely be better educated, connected, and have a wider breadth of experience, increasing their ability to communicate with, relate, and appeal to those making admission and employment decisions. The "fairness" of equal opportunity would still be subject to opportunity hoarding, and ceasing such behavior patterns would inevitably lead to dilemmas involving feasibility and clashes with individual rights (Scanlon 2018, 67). Perhaps to a lesser degree than America has now, the result would be class and racially segregated American housing patterns and disparities in the geography of opportunity and wealth.

Similar problems affecting the equal liberty principle would result, as Iris Marion Young argued, in restrictions of liberty of groups and segments of society vulnerable to marginalization or stigmatization, including groups or categories of persons, such as women, the disabled, or transgender persons (Young 1990, 48–63). Such marginalization and stigmatization can result simply from individual and group tastes and judgments enacted through ordinary social networks—all of which are justified by freedom of association or conscience. Suppose procedures are implemented to negate or diminish the effects of group inequality. In that case, the problem still appears in status inequalities due to income, wealth, and the differences in merit caused by the opportunity hoarding that results from the broad educational inequality still allowed by the second principle of justice. The economically well-off would esteem and associate with those in their class, justified in their mind by their standards of merit, which follow from their educational, professional, and wealth attainments. All of this just serves to undergird and preserve not only status inequality but also opportunity hoarding.

In response to the problem of the lack of substantive opportunity, Thomas Scanlon writes that "it is an objection to society if qualified individuals have no significant chance to qualify for desirable careers requiring higher education unless they are born into a wealthy family" (Scanlon 2018, 56). He calls this the "self-realization rationale" for substantive opportunity. Scanlon's analysis pinpoints a vital aspect of the normative objection to our society's deep and enduring inequalities and inequities. The self-realization rationale can and should be extended to housing and community policy. It is an objection to society if financially qualified individuals have no significant chance to rent or purchase a desirable home unless they are family members of the "right" race, ethnicity, nationality, or religion. It is also an objection to society if individuals who labor in, have lived in, or just prefer an urban or rural area have no significant chance to rent or purchase a desirable home or even stay put unless they are wealthy. Their opportunity to live in the area of their choice in which they need to live is not fair or equal, not to mention substantive; society is not open to them and thwarts their self-realization and life chances. Deeper than that, such inequality and injustice fail to treat them equally and respect their basic and democratic equality.

Rectifying Enduring Injustice

The lack of substantive opportunity as a feature of distributive injustice, in addition to the disrespect for basic and democratic equality, and society's dogged unresponsiveness and lack of will to accept what James Baldwin called the "price of the ticket" to achieve our nation, leads directly to the despair and anger rumbling through this nation's history of civil rights protests and civil unrest.[15] Baldwin's insight and the insight that runs through the history of black American political thought is that realizing justice requires dismantling the racial injustice that runs through American social life, institutions, and structures. What is not needed is to perceive substantive inequality as merely an incidental problem (e.g., the result of individual bad luck or bad decisions); such views are biased toward the preservation of the status quo and suffer from blind spots to unjust advantages (Shelby 2016, 2–4).[16]

An effective answer to the nested injustices that comprise racial injustice, and other forms of group inequality, requires a "systemic-injustice framework" that addresses the mechanisms of group inequality. The systemic-injustice framework identifies the problem not with a symptom that the dominant society finds antisocial or as a sign of individual or communal ill health; instead, it inquires whether disparities are the result of structural injustices, structural or institutional racism, or unjustified discrimination, and it leads to the implementation of principles of corrective justice (Shelby 2016, 12).

A systemic-injustice framework applied to social-spatial arrangements would focus on the systems—local statutes, policies, governance, and lack of enforcement of civil rights mandates—that preserve inequalities. It would lead to two overarching principles aiming to transform social-spatial arrangements to make them closer in line with the ideals of equality and justice while respecting the limits of individual equal liberties. The first is that housing is a civil as well as a human right. For this to be practical, it would need to be established through local, state, and federal mandates that communities should receive equitable levels of public resources and investment and that all communities should have fair and reasonable access to public services and institutions. But even that transformation may not adequately address the history of racial discrimination in housing. A systemic-injustice framework in social-spatial arrangements must confront and correct the difficult realities of how injustice is embedded in American social-spatial arrangements. This includes the well-documented history of public and private dispossession, discrimination, segregation in housing, and disinvestment in poor and segregated communities. For such a vision to be practical, consistent with equal liberties (including individual property rights), and constitutionally sound, it would have to be framed as *rectification* for present substantive inequality and be guided by a principle of priority for the most economically and housing insecure.[17]

A Reasonable Right to Housing

Basic equality is the deep motivation behind the expectation of justice in social-spatial arrangements, so it has distributive implications and implies at least a fundamental right to housing. This right means a simple place for individuals to rest, have some privacy, gather family, and keep their possessions, such as declared in Article 25 of the United Nations' 1948 Universal Declaration of Human Rights:

> Everyone has the right to a standard of living adequate for the health and well-being of himself and of his family, including food, clothing, housing and medical care and necessary social services, and the right to security in the event of unemployment, sickness, disability, widowhood, old age or other lack of liveli-hood in circumstances beyond his control.[18]

This rudimentary vision of an individual right to housing was reiterated in Article 11 of the 1966 International Covenant on Economic, Social and Cultural Rights, which recognizes that "the right of everyone to an adequate standard of living for himself and his family" includes "adequate food, clothing, and housing, and to the continuous improvement of living conditions."[19] States may fulfill this fundamental right by providing a minimal amount of shelter that initially may be temporary, with the condition that the means for "continuous improvement of living conditions" be somehow provided.

Domestically, a version of this basic right is seen in the New York Supreme Court case *Callahan v. Carey* (1979), which decided that Article XVII, section 1, of the State of New York's constitution included the right to shelter for the homeless. That article states, "The aid, care, and support of the needy are public concerns and shall be provided by the state and by such of its subdivisions, and in such manner and by such means, as the legislature may from time to time determine."[20] This is a right to a minimally sufficient level of shelter, and it has led to the creation of hundreds of shelters in New York City; in 2019, there were more than 63,000 homeless people, including families with children, sleeping in those shelters.[21] As is evident from the underwhelming practical legacy of the U.N. Declaration and the contentious repercussion of Covenant and the *Callahan v. Carey* decision, the basic right to housing can be satisfied through a subsistence level of provision. Optimally, participants would have access to other essential goods and services, such as food, education, health care, and at least a basic level of opportunity to acquire employment. Bare provisioning, such as this, would be consistent with a system of natural liberty or system where opportunities are open to talents, as favored by classic liberalism and sufficientarian versions of egalitarianism. The goal would be a type of sufficiency that states could achieve without further consideration of issues, such as the desirability of locales or proximity to goods, services, or opportunities beyond minimal requirements.[22]

However, most of a state's residents require not just intermittent shelter but a home. American politicians repeatedly voiced this need, such as in President Franklin Delano Roosevelt's State of the Union Address in 1944, which though frequently discussed, was not implemented. In his call for a "second Bill of Rights," he includes a decent home in addition to employment, food, clothing, recreation, and education:

> We have come to a clear realization of the fact that true individual freedom cannot exist without economic security and independence. "Necessitous men are not free men . . ." These economic truths have become accepted as self-evident. We have accepted,

so to speak, a second Bill of Rights under which a new basis of security and prosperity can be established for all—regardless of station, race or creed. Among these are: . . . the right of every family
to a decent home. All of these rights spell security. And after this
war is won, we must be prepared to move forward in the implementation of these rights, to new goals of human happiness and
well-being.[23]

A decent home is one of the requirements for a free life, a life free
from the conditions of domination and oppression. A decent home
for each is the basis for "security" and "prosperity" for all. FDR's
vision of a second bill of rights goes well beyond basic equality to
the heart of social and democratic equality demands. It underlines
how the ideal of democratic equality and principles of distributive
justice provide a normative foundation for the right to housing
and a guide to filling its components. Likewise, the value of relational equality comes roaring through the Black Panther Party's
1966 10-point program that included the fourth item, "We want
decent housing, fit for shelter of human beings."[24] This more profound sense of equality is also present in the U.N. Committee on
Economic, Social, and Cultural Rights' interpretation of the "adequacy" standard in the Declaration and the Covenant statements
on the right to housing.[25] In that committee's view, the right to adequate housing goes beyond temporary shelter; it is key to a life of
"security, peace, and dignity" and a mere commodity.

A liberal egalitarian scheme of distributive justice on its own
could be the basis of a right to housing, especially if connected to
a principle that prioritizes equal liberties. Applied to questions of
social-spatial arrangements, it would go beyond justifying the provision of minimally decent housing by requiring housing policies
attentive to the spatial factors that undergird fair equal opportunity.
These factors include but are not limited to proximity and access to
public and private resources and services, such services that materially enact reciprocity and serve to publicly recognize the equal

worth and status of all the community's residents. Guaranteeing fair opportunity to access housing in open communities and providing housing for the needful responds to the moral demand behind the call for "fit shelter for human beings."

Reforms based on a principle of distributive justice could, on their own, lead to a transformative housing policy that would be markedly better than our current geographical unjust patterns of opportunity. But distributive schemes that lack the guiding role of democratic equality do not address the demands of substantive opportunity because they do not effectively address the mechanisms of social closure, such as opportunity hoarding, nor do they meet the challenge of enduring group-based inequalities. Egalitarian planners, guided by the values of basic and democratic equality and distributive justice, should be wary of housing policy outcomes that subvert substantive opportunity and contribute to status inequality.[26]

The combined justification for a right to housing guides its potential content. The U.N. Committee on Economic, Social and Cultural Rights indicated the elements of a right to housing through its interpretation of the adequacy standard in Article 25 of the U.N. Universal Declaration of Human Rights. According to their interpretation, a right to housing should include "adequate privacy, adequate space, adequate security, adequate lighting and ventilation, adequate basic infrastructure and adequate location with regard to work and basic facilities—all at a reasonable cost" (U.N. Office of the High Commissioner for Human Rights 1991). Their position resonates with that of Chester Hartman, who includes "affordability, physical quality of the unit, the social and physical characteristics of the neighborhood environments, and secure tenure" (2006, 183); David Bryson, who includes, in addition to those qualities, stress on the importance of the quality of location and protections against exclusion and discrimination (Bryson 2006, 194); and Casey J. Dawkins, who advocates for a right to housing as a right to secure tenure (Dawkins 2021, 246). What stands out in these various outlines of a right to housing is proximity to social and political institutions and goods and services, such as access to private and public transportation and educational institutions, access that gives meaning to fair equal opportunity, legal and political equality, and equal citizenship.

The U.S. Constitution does not justify a federal right to individual housing, so critics may retort that a liberal egalitarian demand for a right to housing is just as practically unreasonable as the radical calls for a right to housing and the decommodification of the housing market (Burkhart 2003). This short-sighted objection views the call for a right to housing under zero-sum lenses. A constitutional amendment guaranteeing an individual right to housing, while normatively justified, is not the only path to establishing such a right. Another approach is to tie housing to state and locally mandated services, such as education, mental health, addiction treatment, and homelessness mitigation (Bryson 2006; Hartman 2006; Alexander 2015). The right to housing, guided by this model, could result from an accretion of policies across all levels of government.

Another option is to spread the New Jersey model of a "reasonable right to housing" across the country as established by that state's Mount Laurel 1 and 2 decisions. The first decision held that

> every . . . municipality must, by its land use regulations, presumptively make realistically possible an appropriate variety and choice of housing. More specifically, presumptively it cannot foreclose the opportunity of the classes of people mentioned for low and moderate income housing and in its regulations must affirmatively afford that opportunity, at least to the extent of the municipality's fair share of the present and prospective regional need therefor.[27]

These cases established a state's "constitutional obligation to provide a realistic opportunity for a fair share of its region's present and future needs for housing for low and moderate income families through its land-use regulations."[28] Although local municipalities continue to resist this obligation and the other aspects of the housing crisis afflicting New Jersey, these decisions, along with the state's Fair Housing Act, have established the responsibility of municipalities to take on their fair share of affordable housing. Critical in this approach is that the "reasonable right to housing" or "fair share" model does not assert a direct individual right to housing but puts the burden on municipalities to take a fair share in developing, providing, and maintaining affordable housing. This model does not support the absolute right of individuals to appeal to a particular town, city, or municipality to demand housing in a specific place or neighborhood, regardless of economic, environmental sustainability, or other feasibility constraints; instead, it supports individuals' and families' access to a substantive opportunity to live where they need to live. Additionally, this model avoids the constitutional soundness problem and is feasible; for example, the United States spends some $195 billion on the mortgage interest deduction on individual federal income taxes, which exclusively subsidizes the property of mainly middle- and upper-class Americans.

In contrast, it spends roughly $46 billion on public housing and subsidized housing programs (Collinson, Ellen, and Ludwig 2015).[29] These amounts reflect the nation's priorities and the vested interests of property owners and the real estate and banking industries. It is feasible to shift our federal spending to prioritize stable and decent housing for the poor, working, and the lower-middle classes. Doing so would likely bring down housing costs across the country.

Further, laws and policies that patch together something like a right to housing could be grouped with other reforms to slowly realize the right to housing and contribute to a national movement for its federal establishment.[30] These other reforms include aforementioned policies, such as inclusive or "upzoning" ordinances that eliminate single-family zoning and outlaw discrimination against subsidized housing vouchers. Additionally, many other proposed reforms put pressure on local municipalities that continue to resist taking on any share of affordable housing, much less their fair share. Notably, establishing the individual right to housing and the municipal obligation to provide a fair share of housing serves as political and legal leverage against municipalities that continue to shirk their responsibilities. The resistance of NIMBYs and of communities that refuse these obligations should not be underestimated, but their resistance and their local preferences do not negate the more significant societal responsibility to care for its residents and to support equal citizenship and social and political stability. Opponents to local mandates of housing reform policies cite quality of life, traffic and parking congestion, fear of crime, concerns about the environmental effect of housing development, and local control. None of those concerns supersede the normative demands of basic equality, democratic equality, and distributive justice. One's comfort in their neighborhood should not come at the cost of another individual's fundamental rights and status as equal citizens and residents. Individuals ought to have a right to housing, but they should not have a right to determine who does and does not get to live in their communities. Individuals have the right to be included, but beyond their front doors, they ought not to have the right to exclude.[31] This is the price and the imperative of open cities and communities.

Corrective Justice

The ignominious legacy of housing, community, and land-use discrimination in public policy, especially against African Americans, dates at least from the Compromise of 1877, with the end of Reconstruction and the rise of Black Codes and Jim Crow laws and practices. The date could be pushed backed to the Homestead Act of 1862, which resulted in the first significant wave of subsidies for white landowners and homeowners, mainly at the exclusion of blacks and Native American sovereignty interests (Painter 1976; Edwards et al. 2017). However, the modern era of urban and housing policy discrimination began with the Serviceman's Readjustment Act of 1944, which served as the basis for the Veterans Affairs (VA) loan program and the development of Federal Housing Administration loans. The state-sanctioned discrimination built into those programs, buttressed by nationwide nodes of discrimination by state and local governments and the real estate and banking industry, is behind the current urban crisis and the black-white wealth gap (Coates 2017, 163–208; Rothstein 2017).

The problem of enduring racial injustice illustrates why advocating for distributive justice or democratic equality is insufficient. Neither value fully addresses the past effects of racism and racial oppression in social-spatial arrangements, which are enduring and mark all aspects of the urban crisis in the United States and other nations with histories of racial and ethnic discrimination. Mainstream liberal egalitarian theories that do not squarely confront this history end up genuflecting to mealy ameliorative positions. Without addressing this legacy, the idea of fair equal opportunity, much less substantive opportunity, smacks of emptiness and is justifiably met with cynicism. Thus, corrective justice, in some form, is morally required (Kaplan and Valls 2007; Valls 2007, 2018).[32]

There are different forms that corrective justice can take, from direct reparations in the form of money transfers or group-specific policies meant to materially address past wrongs to symbolic acts of reparation in the form of public apologies or monuments that serve to recognize, condemn, and commemorate the injustice, educate the public, and function as a moral beacon. It also encompasses particular legal forms, such as tort law in the United States, criminal justice penalties requiring convicts to financially pay for damages done to their victims or to pay through community service for the harms done to the local community, or reparative justice programs that seek to repair communal and social bonds. Reparations can also apply to policies that do not correct, repair, rectify, or make right all the harms of past wrongs but are normatively motivated by those wrongs and seek, for practical reasons, to address some of their pressing instantiations (Kaplan and Valls 2007; Valls 2019). Direct material reparations and policies that seek to address the enduring effects of past injustice are focused on in the present work because they are the most pertinent to this analysis of corrective justice and social-spatial arrangements; all the same, even though I do not specifically address symbolic reparations, they are crucial because they justify the building of sites of commemoration that serve as moral beacons and contribute to the social imagination that supports such transformative acts of justice and democratic equality (McCarthy 2002, 2004; Weiner 2005; Spinner-Halev 2012, 85–119; Valls 2018, 44–75).

Direct Material Reparations

The first type, direct reparations, is most clearly justified by political theories emphasizing compensation for harms, especially unjustified property loss. Libertarian accounts of justice that focus on rectification, such as Robert Nozick's theory of entitlements, provide the most transparent and prominent defense of direct reparations. He argues that there are three principles needed to adjudicate the fairness of current entitlements: just acquisition, just transfer, and the rectification of injustice in holdings which is activated when property has been unjustly initially acquired (e.g., theft) or unjustly transferred (e.g., stealing or cheating) (Nozick 1974, 150–153). With these three principles, Nozick's libertarianism is backward-looking in that it judges the fairness of current distributions by the history of property acquisitions and transfers. The libertarian principle of rectification is morally compelling in its straightforwardness. Taking the principle of rectification seriously leads to the conclusion that what is due is nothing short of direct remuneration for the territorial losses and loss of life suffered by Native American indigenous groups from (at least) the flagrant breaking of treaties and illegal acts of war; the loss of property and life incurred by the descendants of Africans enslaved in America; the losses of property, life, and citizenship by the descendants of Mexicans who lived in the territories seized by American during the Mexican American War, and the victims of the public failure to enforce equal protection and due process; and state-sanctioned discrimination against individuals from participating in publicly funded or sponsored programs or private markets over which the government has extended its control. The principle applies, for example, to state-sponsored discrimination involving the VA loan program or even the private housing market or mortgage market after the 1968 Fair Housing Act. And this is a bare sketch of a list of rightful claimants to direct material reparations from the United States.

There are substantial philosophical, political, psychological, and legal objections against direct reparations. The philosophical objections raise questions about which wrongs are due reparations, which victims and to what extent they deserve reparations, and the causal relations between current inequalities and those past harms (Loury 2000, 2007; Spinner-Halev 2012, 22–49). Plus, given the stratospheric costs of direct reparations—including the potential substantial redistribution of property—there will be fundamental moral and political conflicts between reparation claims and individual property rights that will have no solution likely to be accepted as legitimate by the competing stakeholders. The psychological concerns about reparation are related to differences in attitudes about the importance of race and racism in American society, implicit biases against other groups, and the general tendency for individuals to refuse collective guilt for historical wrongs and to resent and blame the victims—these attitudes may significantly shift after the Black Lives Matter protests over the summer of 2020, although whether that shift is enduring is an open question (Wohl, Branscombe, and Klar 2006; Darby and Levy 2016,

135–139).[33] The legal objections to reparations relate to the infeasibility of race-specific remedies, given the dominance of postracial interpretations of the U.S. Constitution and civil rights law (Darby and Levy 2016). These objections combine to feed the political barriers to direct reparations.

I would include among the calls for direct material reparations proposals for remedies that focus on the legacy of housing discrimination and its effects on African Americans, among other groups. For example, Richard Rothstein suggests that the government identify suburban developments that followed the Federal Housing Administration's discriminatory practices, purchase several homes in those areas that correspond with the national African American population of around 15%, and then sell them to qualified African Americans at 1950s prices (Rothstein 2017, 202–203). Rothstein acknowledges that this proposal is not politically or likely constitutionally feasible. Still, he thinks it would directly address the history of the country's state-sanctioned racist and exclusionary housing practices.

In addition to the practical and political obstacles to specific proposals for reparations, there are problems with the libertarian conception of rectification. First, it is of a piece with the philosopher Robert Nozick's theory of justice in holdings and its singular focus on entitlement. In its purview, distribution patterns are irrelevant to questions of justice in holdings because liberty disrupts patterns. Second, it has a broad conception of consent that is not mindful of oppressive conditions and dominates choices beyond the most blatant forms of forced property seizures. Third, it ascribes a high degree of personal responsibility for consensual decisions, even in conditions that others reasonably identify as exploitative or domineering. Racial discrimination in housing by private individuals or homeowner associations is not, under the entitlement theory, a wrong to be rectified, and class-based discrimination by private and public entities is permitted. Finally, the significant limitation of the libertarian model is precisely its dependency on conceptions of justice based on entitlement to, distribution of, and rectification of just holdings—in other words, property. But what needs repair goes beyond essential property claims and reaches caste- or group-based inequalities, status inequalities, and enduring injustices. Libertarian accounts of rectification allow persons to have a *price*—thus, losing sight of the normative core of repair in a liberal society, which is acknowledging wrongs and establishing moral and democratic equality.

Pragmatic Rectification

What we mostly see in calls for reparations is a blending of policy reforms that are normatively motivated by reparations arguments that, on the one hand, intend to achieve symbolic repair through the national acknowledgment of enduring injustices and, on the other hand, to rectify, to some degree, the enduring effects that afflict the least well-off. Ta-Nehisi Coates, for example, sums up his case for reparations by directly channeling James Baldwin's terms and tone and casts it as a painful yet necessary act of remembrance required to achieve our country. He writes,

> And so we must imagine a new country. Reparations—by which
> I mean the full acceptance of our collective biography and its
> consequences—is the price we must pay to see ourselves squarely.
> The recovering alcoholic may well have to live with his illness
> for the rest of his life. But at least he is not living a drunken lie.
> Reparations beckon us to reject the intoxication of hubris and see
> America as it is—the work of fallible humans. (2017, 202)

Coates is open-ended about the actual policies that would result from his call (2017, 200–201).[34] His approach leaves room for policies that, while race-neutral, aim to have disparate positive effects of mitigating and reversing the patterns of disparate negative impacts that are both the drivers and vehicles of racial injustices. It imagines and demands a politically and legally feasible form of corrective justice that blends principles of reform and rectification. Doing so makes it pragmatic and broadly reconstructive for the nation.

To achieve, in Baldwin's phrasing, "our country" requires respecting democratic equality and actualizing the freedom of residents and citizens by realizing substantive opportunity. A pragmatic rectification is consistent with this broad vision, as well as with a liberal egalitarian vision of justice in social-spatial arrangements. Furthermore, it is compatible with liberal egalitarian theories of distributive justice, although those theories fail to address the problems with substantive opportunity and enduring group-based inequalities. Although liberal egalitarian theories do not build in a principle of rectification, with a systemic-injustice framework, they can guide a principle of rectification that applies to nonideal circumstances (Shelby 2004, 2016; Valls 2018).[35] This addition is not exogenous to liberal egalitarianism and arises from internal pressure within its core values and virtues. Those values and virtues are magnified by focusing on democratic equality coupled with an awareness of historical injustice and enduring inequality.

An objection to the pragmatic rectification supported by this approach is that it counts as a form of compensation but not reparation (Boxill 1972, 119). In this view, compensation aims to offset the effects of brute or bad luck; for example, government aid to victims of natural disasters, while reparation is due to those whose rights have been infringed by others (Boxill 1972, 116). The normative basis of each differs in crucial ways; in particular, reparation has at its moral core the idea of repair and of "making right," while compensation is an aid in achieving fair equal opportunity. The recipients of reparations are determined by their status as victims of past wrongs, while compensation is dispensed to those in general need. The upshot is that rectification might address racial injustices and specific group-based inequalities. However, because it attempts to be practical by aiming for political feasibility and constitutional soundness, it misses the moral mark and cannot adequately repair those harmed by historical injustices.

What pragmatic rectification for housing injustice calls for are programs that target households suffering from the effects of inter-generational poverty, concentrated disadvantage, and context im-mobility. A wide variety of programs could achieve this goal. Such relief would have currency for the victims of the American system of residential racial segregation and most of the households in the most disadvantaged neighborhoods. Reducing this goal to the cat-egory of compensation strips it of its normative intent and justi-fication; it is not merely concerned with leveling the playing field but instead motivated by the goals of democratic equality, effective freedom, and substantive opportunity. Viewing it as compensa-tion would reduce it to mere property relations when concerned with equal democratic relations. Yes, it responds to concerns about practical feasibility, but it is motivated by the normative demand of enduring injustices. Pragmatic rectification is not direct material reparations for past wrongs. Even so, it can be a form of and work with other versions of symbolic reparations. It advocates for relief for the least well-off in a form that not only is politically and legally feasible but also affirms equal civic belonging.

3

The Trouble with Gentrification

Bad Techies

Gentrification is both a symbol of injustice and a process that can contribute to further injustices. It serves as a symbol because of its material manifestations in changing streetscapes, storefronts, and residential demographics of status inequalities and distributive inequities. Some are confronted with this condition in daily saunters, trudges, or dashes through their neighborhoods. Although each instance of gentrification does not cause or lead to further injustices, it is commonly thought of as a process that does so. Moreover, what we call "gentrification" is the result of several factors that have led to demographic turnover and economic change. Public policies to redevelop and revitalize cities have driven this change, along with rapid job growth in some parts of the economy (e.g., famously, in technology industries), increased traffic congestion, lengthened commutes, and an expanded taste for urban amenities that have led many to seek residences closer to urban centers. This mezzo-level activity, on the regional or city level, is connected to macro-level forces, on the level of national and global industries and financial markets, and feeds micro-level activity, on the level of the neighborhood, such as an increased preference for urban amenities and changes in the feel or vibe of street life (Kennedy and Leonard 2001, 9–14). The standard view in left academic and activist circles is that gentrification is indicative of social and distributive inequalities, and because it causes displacement, it is unjust.

In this chapter, I consider the main conceptual and empirical concerns about gentrification that trouble popular conclusions about its causal relation to displacement. Those concerns affect the normative analysis of gentrification, a topic taken up in the next chapter. Identifying and defending competing conceptions of gentrification is an ongoing project in urban affairs and policy, sociology, and geography. This chapter does not settle that debate; instead, it analyzes the concepts of gentrification and displacement to identify their confusions and conflations. This investigation then prepares the way for a normative analysis of gentrification that avoids the problems with popular conceptions of gentrification. First, I argue that gentrification-based displacement may not be the problem that critics charge it is. Second, the focus on gentrification obscures other larger injustices in social-spatial arrangements and the consequences of the history of housing discrimination against non-whites as exemplified in the African American experience.

Citizens and residents of metropolitan areas are rightfully interested in and worried about gentrification's relation to injustice and its positive and negative effects on the quality and character of urban neighborhoods and the civic life of cities and, in turn, nations. Areas in the grip of gentrification can seem unbalanced or chaotic or, in the eyes of others, vibrant and exciting. In this context, one can understand why some refer to neighborhoods undergoing gentrification as "frontiers" and its new adventurous, risk-taking residents as "pioneers." Wealth is being "discovered," and formerly "wild" spaces are being "settled." Such settler and colonialist rhetoric associated with gentrification are now so well-known as to be banal. It should be no surprise that this rhetoric angers long-term residents because it insults their dignity by marking their lives and communities as invisible, inconsequential, or worse, as an instance of savagery that is needful of pacification. The heyday of this rhetoric in the United States was in the 1970s and 1980s and was associated with its major cities (Smith 1996).

The careless meanness of this rhetoric, with its racial and class inflections, has not been lost on gentrification's critics and is part of the context for the writer Rebecca Solnit's (2013) description of Google's "invasion" of San Francisco through the visible signal of gentrification, the Google Bus. In her essay, the Google Bus stands in for technology companies, such as Google, Yahoo, Apple, Facebook, and Genentech, that use luxury double-decker buses to transport employees of firms from San Francisco and other Bay Area cities to where those companies are based in Silicon Valley, south of San Francisco. She writes:

The buses roll up to San Francisco's bus stops in the morning and evening, but they are unmarked, or nearly so, and not for the public. They have no signs or have discreet acronyms on the front windshield, and because they also have no rear doors they ingest and disgorge their passengers slowly, while the brightly lit funky orange public buses wait behind them. The luxury coach passengers ride for free and many take out their laptops and begin their work day on board; there is of course wifi. Most of them are gleaming white, with dark-tinted windows, like limousines, and some days I think of them as the spaceships on which our alien overlords have landed to rule over us. . . . Silicon Valley has long been famous for its endless work hours, for sucking in the young for decades of sixty or seventy-hour weeks, and the much celebrated perks on many jobsites—nap rooms, chefs, gyms, laundry—are meant to make spending most of your life at work less hideous. The biotech industry is following the same game plan. There are hundreds of luxury buses serving mega-corporations down the peninsula, but we refer to them in the singular, as the Google Bus, and we—by which I mean people I know, people who've lived here a while, and mostly people who don't work in the industry—talk about them a lot. . . . My brother says that the first time he saw one unload its riders he thought they were German tourists—neatly dressed, uncool, a little out of place, blinking in the light as they emerged from their pod. The tech workers, many of them new to the region, are mostly white or Asian male nerds in their twenties and thirties. . . . All these youngish people are on the Google Bus because they want to live in San Francisco, city of promenading and mingling, but they seem as likely to rub these things out as to participate in them. (Solnit 2013, 1–2)

Solnit's depiction of the tech workers, the "techies" as Bay Area residents call them, follows the standard form of othering: they are not one of us, they are not from here, they do not follow our practices, and they are a little odd, like German tourists. Her depiction of them is meant to be humorous but is smug and exclusionary. It is a performance of a type of urbane xenophobia that includes hipsters yet ridicules them for their affectations but excludes techies from authentic communal belonging.[1] In Solnit's judgment of them, they are subject to a local form of civic ostracism (Kim and Sundstrom 2014). She sees them as a threat to the city as a refuge to "dissidents, queers, pacifists and experimentalists" (Kim and Sundstrom 2014, 4; Solnit and Schwartzenberg 2000). Solnit does not, however, pause to consider the dissidents, queers, pacifists, and experimentalists among the Google Bus riders, thereby rubbing out their individuality and the complex phenomenon of gentrification, just as she accuses these so-called pod-born techies of potentially erasing the local urban life.

Her animus against individual techies is misdirected. They serve as a surrogate for her real target, which are the technology companies of Silicon Valley whose mores are shaped by tech-utopian, left-libertarianism, whose business models celebrate and seek "disruption" and characterize positive or creative interpersonal exchanges as "collisions." Those industries have failed to provide adequate housing for their employees and contracted service workers. They have not effectively used their economic power to leverage in suburban cities, where they are based, to increase the number of housing units in their municipalities, leaving the larger cities, with their middle, working-class, and poor residents to suffer the consequences (Zuk and Chapple 2015).

The Concept of Gentrification

Several problems in the San Francisco Bay Area and nationally are bundled together under the label of gentrification that drives the anxieties that Solnit expressed. First, there is the larger and general state of economic and political inequality in the United States. This is related to the second problem that housing costs, either through the rental or purchasing of individual homes, are unaffordable for an increasing number of Americans. This problem is directly related to the particulars of regional housing markets where there is an imbalance between the number of low-wage or middle-class jobs in the area and the number of homes affordable to them, such as is apparent in the Bay Area and other regions experiencing technology or industrial booms. The third problem is a general lack of affordable or subsidized housing for low-income to extremely low-income families (Cervero 1989).[2] A fourth problem, obscured in the housing policy literature, is that this housing crisis is compounded for middle- and low-income groups that have concurrently suffered from residential and educational segregation, intergenerational and concentrated poverty, and profound disadvantages in what Patrick Sharkey calls contextual mobility.[3]

Instead of focusing on the effects of gentrification on low-income groups who have long suffered from concentrated poverty and housing discrimination, Solnit worries whether San Francisco and other cities that have attracted the creative class remain welcoming to them along with everyday people. This peculiar focus on artists in her polemic, and the story of wealthier creatives pushing out poorer ones, usefully reveals problems with the concept of gentrification that have been there since the term was coined. These problems include (1) conceptual confusion and inflation of the term "gentrification," a confusion that extends to the categories of "gentrifier" and "gentrified"; (2) the assumption of a unitary cause or exclusive set of causes of gentrification; and (3) the assertion that gentrification is morally wrong and politically unjust, a claim based on the observation that gentrification correlates with the displacement of long-term residents.

There is so much confusion about the idea of gentrification that urban studies scholars have called the concept "chaotic" because it collects different causes and processes. Furthermore, the confusion around gentrification has not faded even as the concept expands (Rose 1984).[4] Ruth Glass created the term in her study of London in 1964, and she identified it as the process by which working-class neighborhoods were being taken over and improved by the middle classes of the time, resulting in the displacement of the working classes and the change of the "social character" of the neighborhood. She understood that economic forces were behind gentrification, but she saw it primarily in terms of neighborhood rehabilitation (Glass 1964). However, the general idea of working-class displacement from their neighborhoods was first written about by Friedrich Engels in 1872, and he, of course, saw the process as evidence of class antagonism and the exploitation and marginalization of the proletariat.

Engels's analysis lies behind Neil Smith's influential neo-Marxist account of gentrification (1996). Smith defined gentrification as the process and result of capital investments in urban neighborhoods, including housing, business, and other amenities. He wrote:

> Gentrification is the process . . . by which poor and working-class neighborhoods in the inner city are refurbished via an influx of private and middle-class homebuyers and renters— neighborhoods that had previously experienced disinvestment and a middle-class exodus. The poorest working-class neighborhoods are getting a remake; capital and the gentry are

coming home, and for some in their wake it is not entirely a pretty sight. (Smith 1996, 32)

While current discourse identifies the gentry as "hipsters" and "techies," Smith saw them as the "yuppies" of the late 1970s through the 1990s. His is a supply-side definition that emphasizes production, and key to his view is the economic theory of the "rent gap" described in a summation of his structuralist economic view:

> Gentrification is a structural product of the land and housing markets. Capital flows where the rate of return is highest, and the movement of capital to the suburbs, along with the continual devalorization of inner-city capital, eventually produces the rent gap. When this gap grows sufficiently large, rehabilitation (or, for that matter, redevelopment) can begin to challenge the rates of return available elsewhere, and capital flows back in. Gentrification is a back-to-the-city movement all right, but a back-to-the-city movement by capital rather than people. (Smith 1996, 70)

The effect of gentrification on the poor and working classes, according to Smith, is displacement, which he claimed was related to the mean-spirited politics of the 1980s that were anti-urban, anti–civil rights, and pro-privatization. These policies were so vindictive toward urban areas and their current residents that Smith labeled cities gripped by those policies as revanchist cities (Smith 1996, 44–45).[5] "Neoliberal" is what contemporary critics call such policies, especially as they promote privatization and deregulation (Rodrick 2017; Chapple and Loukaitou-Sideris 2019).

In contrast to Smith's supply-side view, other definitions emphasize the role of demand-side consumption forces in gentrification, particularly the changes in taste for urban living of the young and affluent (Ley 1996). However, others define gentrification as transforming working-class and vacant neighborhoods for middle-class residences and commercial use or simply reinvesting capital in declining neighborhoods (Kennedy and Leonard 2001; Schlictman, Hill, and Patch 2017). Those definitions depart from Smith's economic analysis and his assertion of a revanchist intent, which remains influential despite the lack of direct empirical evidence for such a broad claim.

Housing organizations that advocate against gentrification, evictions, foreclosures, housing discrimination, and for renters' rights operate with concepts of gentrification that are customized to their political theories and idealized ends. For example, in the San Francisco Bay Area is Causa Justa :: Just Cause (CJJC), which has a definition of gentrification influenced by Neil Smith's claim that rent gaps are the underlying condition for gentrification:

> We define gentrification as a profit-driven racial and class reconfiguration of urban, working-class and communities of color that have suffered from a history of disinvestment and abandonment. The process is characterized by declines in the number of low-income, people of color in neighborhoods that begin to cater to higher-income workers willing to pay higher rents. Gentrification is driven by private developers, landlords, businesses, and corporations, and supported by the government through policies that facilitate the process of displacement, often in the form of public subsidies. Gentrification happens in areas where commercial and residential land is cheap, relative to other areas in the city and region, and where the potential to turn a profit either through repurposing existing structures or building new ones is. (CJJC 2011, 11–12)

There are serious problems with all these definitions. The trouble with Neil Smith's and other derivative supply-side definitions is that it does not explain all occurrences of gentrification or capture its varied effects. There are clear instances of gentrification that are not driven by the "movement of capital," for example, when so-called urban pioneers seeking to take advantage of low housing costs move into a blighted or economically depressed community. The real estate industry may take that as their cue to exploit the rent gap in a neighborhood, but early gentrifiers did not necessarily do so because of the machinations of the real estate industry. The same applies to demand-side explanations. This causes problems with who is classified as a "gentrifier" and what places are "gentrified," and these problems multiply when an organization employs an ideologically laden definition that potentially conflicts with its other interests; for example, Smith struggled with whether women, who gained greater access to professional jobs in the 1970s, counted as gentrifiers, or whether white gay entrants in formerly ethnic enclaves did so as well. This problem is visible in CJJC's definition, which emphasizes the effects of gentrification on non-white neighborhoods. If we were to take their definition seriously, it would not readily apply to instances of gentrification in white working-class urban communities such as the ones studied by Engels or later by Glass.

Because it is hazardous to hinge a normative analysis of gentrification on the veracity of any of these causal claims, it is prudent to separate the apparent harms and injustices and focus on them and their divergent and varied causes, rather than an amorphous villain called "gentrification" that bundles together widespread anxieties and complaints about change and status differences with significant material and economic disparities and inequities and social inequalities.[6] Despite the confusion around the definitions of gentrification, it is not a wholly chaotic or incoherent concept. However, there is no shortage of examples of the concept's inflation and its transformation into "gentrification as everything," such as the so-called gentrification of the mind or food (Schlichtman, Hill, and Patch 2017, 9–16). A normative analysis of the effects of the processes that parties call gentrification can go forward without depending on a particular conception or its questionable assumptions. This analysis, therefore, is not wedded to the causal factors that critics of gentrification ultimately seek to condemn; namely, capitalism. Additionally, just as a particular causal factor should not be attached to the concept of gentrification, neither should its potential harms be included in its definition. Doing so begs the question about its normative status. Another consideration is that displacement, the potential harm most associated with gentrification, suffers from its own conceptual confusion.

Growing caution about defining the concept of gentrification is evident in research about regional effects of gentrification; for example, the Center for Community Innovation's *Mapping Susceptibility to Gentrification: The Early Warning Toolkit*, which reports that displacement is sometimes but not necessarily linked with gentrification, defines it as:

> a process of neighborhood change that encompasses economic change in the form of increases in both real estate investment and household income, as well as demographic change in the form of increases in educational attainment. These changes may be highly correlated with racial/ethnic transition as well, though this is not measured directly. Although some change could be coming from within, as existing residents improve their economic circumstances, most is driven by exogenous forces, as evidenced by home price appreciation. Thus, we differentiate gentrification from revitalization more generally, which consists simply of improvements in neighborhood income (due either to newcomers or changes for existing residents). (Chapple 2009, 1–2)

A similar definition offered by Daniel J. Hammel and Elvin K. Wyly stresses the replacement, but not necessarily displacement, of poor and working-class residents with those from the middle and upper classes. According to them, gentrification is "the replacement of low-income, inner-city working-class residents by middle- or upper-class-households, either through the market for existing housing or demolition to make way for new upscale housing construction" (Hammel and Wyly 1996, 250). A more cautious, stripped-down version of this sort of definition is provided by the *Encyclopedia of Housing*, which defines it as "The process by which central urban neighborhoods that have undergone disinvestments and economic decline experience a reversal, reinvestment, and the in-migration of a relatively well-off, middle- and upper-middle-class population" (Van Vliet 1998, 198).[7] My analysis relies on this minimal definition.

It is important to emphasize that gentrification is a process, something each of those careful definitions notes. It has an "early" stage, denoting when changes or reinvestments initially occur, and "late" changes, where the changes have nearly or fully transformed a neighborhood. It can take the form of "upscaling" that increases a neighborhood's "socioeconomic context," including the value of its built structures and economic activity and its social status, or it can appear as the "upgrading" of its "built environment" (Chapple and Loukaitou-Sideris 2019, 46). There are positive and negative effects associated with each stage (Kennedy and Leonard 2001; Chapple 2009; Schlictman, Hill, and Patch 2017, 87–110). Each stage in this process involves events on the macro- or national and global level (e.g., speculative investment in luxury high-rise condos, otherwise called "vertical money"), the meso- or city and metropolitan level (e.g., changes in zoning policies or demographic shifts), and the micro- or neighborhood level (e.g., the establishment of services and businesses that cater to the taste of the young, hip, and affluent) (Schlictman, Hill, and Patch 2017, 87–110).[8]

Gentrification is also usually preceded by a previous process of disinvestment. Gentrification is sometimes thought to be just the reinvestment side of the process, as with the minimal definition, or it is taken to name the whole process, including the preceding cycles of disinvestment. Doing that, however, inflates the concept, turning all instances of abandonment, neglect, or ghettoization into gentrification, thus obscuring the specific conditions and causes of those events. This provides a convenient set of counterexamples to inflated definitions of gentrification that would include all instances of places that experience disinvestment: those places that experience disinvestment but not subsequent reinvestment.

John Joe Schlichtman, Marc Lamont Hill, and Jason Patch provide a helpful distinction that captures the dual processes associated with gentrification. In their book, *Gentrifier* (2017, 89), they identify a set of "de-'s" and "re-'s" associated with disinvestment and reinvestment, respectively. Their catalog for the de-'s includes demarcation (i.e., redlining), devaluation, deterioration, deindustrialization, departure, demolition, decoupling (i.e., razing of neglected affordable housing without building replacement units), decentralization (i.e., encouraging flight from the neighborhood of privileged groups), destabilization, defunding, and delinking (i.e., neighborhood isolation). For the "re-'s," they list revaluation, revitalization, reprioritization, refunding, retainment, restoration, rediscovery, redefinition, reconnection, reinvention, and renaming (Schlichtman, Hill, and Patch 2017, 89, 96–110).

Gentrification is also not just a narrow urban issue; it is a regional phenomenon that will require regional policies to ameliorate any of its potential harms. This highlights the mistake of declaring "a right to the city" when a right to the city may not be the critical issue. For example, in 2012, the City of Mountain View, a suburb of San Francisco, stopped Google from developing 1,100 housing units for its employees. Additionally, although the city sought to build office space accommodating over 42,000 workers, it capped the development of new homes at 7,000.[9] This is an example of NIMBY behavior that dogs all policy proposals to deal with any facet of the housing crisis and is an example of the failure to develop adequate housing for all classes to preserve or conserve the character of a suburban community.

Two or Three Cheers for Gentrification

There are few public defenders of the displacement of the working class or poor from urban neighborhoods undergoing economic redevelopment and the inward migration of the "gentry," but they exist. Those who cheer on gentrification—(two cheers from Peter Byrne [2003] and three from Duany [2001])—are concerned about displacement and call for increased support of affordable housing for those who are experiencing housing precarity and have moved or remained. However, they claim that gentrification is, on balance, healthy for neighborhoods. They point out the economic and social benefits to neighborhoods, increased tax revenue and property values, improved neighborhood amenities, the dilution of concentrated poverty, new opportunities for cross-race or class social mixing, and increased responsiveness from local politicians and institutions to community needs (Kennedy and Leonard 2001, 14–24; Duany 2001; Byrne 2003; Fiss 2003, 117–118). Residents in these communities, including the poor and working class who remain, reap the benefits of these improvements. For such residents, the improvements are sometimes appreciated (Freeman 2006, 4).

And then there are the defenders of gentrification who see it as yet another symptom of modern progress and view reactions against it as reactionary.[10] According to this view, the gentrification that results from the wealth that businesses in metropolitan areas generate is the outcome of the choices of individuals and households who select housing based on what they can afford and what they desire or need to flourish. These choices by private networks disrupt established patterns in housing and public infrastructure (e.g., Google Buses or ride-share companies supplanting public transportation). These changes are thought to be the inevitable byproducts of economic and technological development, bringing new conveniences, opportunities, and freedoms that many in the neighborhood love.

Here's the Thing about Displacement

The first defense of gentrification is correct that some of the "re-'s" are positive, but those benefits diminish in the face of the current housing crisis. The second defense of gentrification is engaged in willful ignorance of the dynamics of urban change that cast the changes in the urban landscape as simply "natural" and the evolution of the housing market. The history of urban change is not solely a story of the redevelopment, reinvestment, and so on; it is as much a story about the history of the "de-'s" that are often not factored in or accounted for in the cheering for gentrification. These "de-'s" are linked to legacies of injustice in the form of social and political inequalities and economic inequities, and the harms of these legacies are many and well-documented. In the area of housing, which is intrinsically connected to education, employment, community building, and wealth generation, among other social indicators, this legacy includes a history of dispossession, exploitation, segregation, and discrimination, including the legalized exclusion of blacks, Latinos, and Asian Americans from participation in federal programs that established and protected wealth in the form of housing subsidies and tax breaks, and disinvestment that gutted the equity that the excluded managed to establish in segregated neighborhoods (Massey and Denton 1993; Powell and Spencer 2003; Pietila 2010; Sharkey 2013, Rothstein 2017). Native Americans faced similar exclusions, though their history includes their attempted genocide by the U.S. government, forced removal from their ancestral lands, and concentration on reservations. Tribes and their members were denied access to a wide array of opportunities, including opportunities to build wealth, equality in education, and access to employment. Concerning housing justice, these more sizable national-level disparities led to housing disparities on tribal lands. Because of that, in the mid-twentieth century, many Native Americans were relocated to urban areas under the American Indian Relocation Act of 1956 and not provided with sufficient resources to thrive. This ugly legacy continues to affect Native American families in cities (Fixico 1986; Wilkins 2011; Keeler 2016).

Anti-gentrification academics and activists count displacement chief among the housing justice-related harms that resulted from these legacies. For example, the geographer Richard Walker wrote in the preface for Cause Justa :: Just Cause's displacement report that:

> To housing and social justice organizations across the United States, gentrification is a scourge. They have seen the damage done to hundreds of thousands, if not millions, of families, and the disruption of schooling, friendships, and habits accompanied by the costs of finding new housing, jobs, support networks, and more. They witness the cruel unfairness of the way the suffering falls so disproportionately on the heads of innocent children, poor parents, and people of color. (CJJC 2014, 3)

Walker's insight gives us the sense of a problem of great magnitude and harm, especially if we conjecture that similar numbers of displacements are occurring across each of the gentrifying neighborhoods of each major metropolitan area in the United States and across the globe. Nevertheless, here is the thing about displacement due to gentrification: the evidence about its magnitude and effects is ambiguous. Some critics even say there is little direct evidence for large-scale displacement (Vigdor 2002). To say that research has called into question claims about the magnitude and harm of gentrification is an understatement (Kennedy and Leonard 2001; Braconi and Freeman 2002, 2004, 2005; Vigdor 2002; Byrne 2003). Lance Freeman and Frank Braconi find in their study from 2005 that:

> the probability of being displaced ranges from 0.9% to 1.4%. The predictions suggest that the incremental increase in the

probability of displacement as a result of gentrification is small, perhaps in part because displacement is a relatively rare occurrence regardless of what type of neighborhood one resides in. The probability of being displaced in a gentrifying neighborhood is about 0.5% higher than in a nongentrifying neighborhood. It should also be recalled that this definition of displacement includes moves for health reasons, divorce, joining the armed services, or other involuntary reasons and thus probably overstates the amount of gentrification-induced displacement.... Overall, the models suggest at most a modest link between gentrification and displacement. The relationship between mobility and gentrification is not statistically significant. Although displacement was significantly related to gentrification, the substantive size of this relationship is very small, as indicated by the predicted probabilities. Finally, poor renters do not appear to be especially susceptible to displacement or elevated rates of mobility. Taken together, the results would not seem to imply that displacement is the primary mechanism through which gentrifying neighborhoods undergo socioeconomic change. Nevertheless, it is true that gentrification was related to displacement in this analysis. (Freeman and Braconi 2005, 480)

Additionally, researchers have found that poor residents are just as likely to remain in gentrifying neighborhoods (McKinnish, Walsh, and White 2010; Ellen and O'Regan 2011) and that most long-term residents approve of changes and improvements due to gentrification (Sullivan 2006). These are shocking claims to those familiar with discussions of gentrification through the press and on social media platforms. However, those claims are at the center of the discussion for urban policy scholars due to empirical research that questions the assumptions about the effects of gentrification.

Before analyzing the implications of these claims for normative analysis of gentrification, the idea of displacement needs clarification. The definition of displacement that Freeman, Braconi, and

Vigdor used is a careful one that only includes "those who are forced to move for reasons that are beyond the household's control and related to conditions in the dwelling or the surrounding neighborhood" (Freeman 2005, 465; Kennedy and Leonard, 2001, 5; Grier and Grier 1978, 8). It is also worth pointing out that these studies use a generous standard for displacement; for example, Freeman's 2005 study included in its standard for displacement such factors as divorce or enlisting in the military, yet they still uncovered a low incidence of displacement (Freeman 2005, 469).[11] A simple definition of "displacement" is to take over someone or something from their proper place; applied to residential displacement, it connotes the coercive forcing of an individual or household to leave their preferred or current residence.

The reaction to this research from geographers and urban policy scholars committed to anti-gentrification positions has been to voice concern about the "eviction" of "critical" methods from gentrification research and to call for an expanded conception of displacement (Lees, Slater, and Wyly 2008, 195–236; Slater 2009). A leading contender is Marcuse's three-faceted conception of displacement. For Marcuse, research must consider the following three types of displacement to understand the full effect of it: (1) direct last resident, which includes those who were compelled to leave due to eviction, an unaffordable rent increase, or some other tactic meant to pressure current residents to leave; (2) direct chain, which includes those who left the neighborhood during a previous period of disinvestment; and (3) exclusionary displacement, which includes those who cannot, but would like to, move into the neighborhood because of its higher housing costs (Marcuse 1986, 155–157).

This expansion has led to conceptual inflation, just as has occurred with gentrification; for example, Chapple and Loukaitou-Sideris begin to define displacement as "a situation in which incumbent residents have fewer options within, are forced out of, or cannot move into neighborhoods"—so far so good—but then they go on to say that it "may also be nonphysical, such as a sense of loss of place and belonging, erosion of cultural cohesion, loss of community supports, and/or diminution of political power" (2019, 48). This definition includes alienation from a place, which is a feeling most people experience for several reasons. To label every one of those experiences as displacement opens the door to a great deal of subjective judgment about what counts as displacement and who counts as displaced; it will involve significantly different political and aesthetic judgments about which experiences of spatial alienation, change of community character, cultural shifts, and diminution of political power tied to demographic-geographic changes is deserving of sympathy and attention.

Despite such excesses, Marcuse's expanded definition of displacement is constructive. His three types are reflected in Schlichtman, Hill, and Patch's distinction between disinvestment displacement and reinvestment displacement, and both types of displacement are important for thinking about the harms that critics package under the banner of gentrification (Schlichtman, Hill, and Patch 2017, 89, 96–110). However, it is only the latter type that is relevant for pinpointing the harms of gentrification; this does not excuse or dismiss the harms of disinvestment displacement; instead, it leaves it to be dealt with by different arguments.

Marcuse's distinction also reveals that gentrification studies have a time-slice problem. Following the minimal definition of gentrification and then selecting a time-slice that features "the replacement of low-income, inner-city working-class residents by middle- or upper-class households" (Hammel and Wyly 1996, 250) misses the masses displaced by direct-chain displacement. On the other hand, including direct-chain displacement risks making everything gentrification and obscuring its distinct harms, systems, and causes, such as the demolition of affordable housing and the forced removal and relocation of residents. Granted, sometimes the causes and systems involved with the "de-'s" are connected with the "re-'s," but that is not necessary, and the presence of such connections is not necessary for normative criticism of the "de-'s" or "re's" to proceed.

Additionally, including exclusionary displacement initially makes intuitive sense, but it is by its nature suppositional and can absurdly include large numbers of people who cannot afford, for a variety of reasons, to relocate to their preferred neighborhoods. Including exclusion as a form of displacement is an instance of conceptual inflation and is not needed to conceptualize exclusion as a potential sign of injustice; for example, drawing on the idea of the geography of opportunity, exclusion from cities or neighborhoods due to a lack of available or affordable housing could be viewed as "exclusion from (proximity to) opportunity."

Another problem with reports that make large-scale displacement claims is that they depend on statistics of turnover or succession that have not conclusively established displacement. Studies that use succession statistics to track racial and ethnic demographic shifts, increases in the cost of rents, median housing values, changes in household income, and the proportion of renters to homeowners in neighborhoods in various stages of gentrification have successfully documented early and late gentrification, but they too quickly label that change as displacement. They have not established whether those who left the neighborhoods in question did so because of gentrification, the demographic composition of "gentrifiers," and whether those residents who left because of either displacement or succession were harmed or benefited because of the change in their residence.[12]

In reaction to this challenge and the methodological problem of tracking displacement, some researchers dismiss the distinction between voluntary and involuntary residential turnover. Questioning the voluntariness of an individual's or household's decision to move is wise because most choices are conditioned and limited by their context (e.g., by the cost of living in their metropolitan area). This should lead to humility in claims about limited evidence of reinvestment displacement, but it is also not a reason to entirely dismiss the distinction between voluntary and involuntary moves and consider all succession as reinvestment displacement. However, that is exactly what happened in scholarship on the subject; for example, Miriam Zuk and Karen Chapple (2015) call the distinction a "dichotomy" and judge it false. They write:

> although the distinction between voluntary and involuntary moves is conceptually sound, it is nearly impossible to analyze quantitatively and at scale. Some scholars have therefore eliminated the dichotomization of voluntary and involuntary displacement from their studies, either due to data limitations . . . or ideological disagreement . . . and have characterized displacement as the loss of any vulnerable populations including low income households, renters, and people of color among others. (Zuk and Chapple 2015, 5)[13]

Based on anecdotes from their qualitative research and their assessment of statistical patterns of neighborhood composition, Zuk and Chapple adopt this view, but in doing so, they give just cause to advocates of gentrification who are skeptical of its harms to dismiss their study as biased and ideologically driven. They essentially admit in the quoted passage that there are grounds to accuse them of fallacious reasoning because they are begging the question or, in other words, engaging in a false inference. If the distinction between "voluntary and involuntary moves is conceptually sound," then why give in to the methodological limitations and count all moves in gentrifying areas as displacement if not for ideological commitments? Sounding the alarm about gentrification and making false inferences may be useful for community housing organizations committed to direct action against gentrification, but inflated alarms do not promote reasonable political discussion or lead to compromises with varied stakeholders who may not share the ideological commitments of the researchers. It is enough to refer to the features of the housing crisis, such as discrimination in housing or the lack of affordable housing, rather than inflate the crisis with politically popular umbrella terms overloaded with ideological baggage.

All the same, the empirical implications of the disputes about the concept of displacement do not significantly affect the normative analysis of the harms of gentrification.[14] They dampen the claims about the magnitude of gentrification-based displacement but do not negate all of its potential harms nor affect the categorization of the harms. Furthermore, examining competing conceptions of gentrification and displacement provide distinctions that are helpful for thinking about the specific harms related to segregation, housing discrimination, and disinvestment and investment displacement. Stepping back from the rhetoric around gentrification and displacement allows room for identifying and highlighting other injustices and their harms that are otherwise obscure. For example, the rhetoric about gentrification can miss displacement caused by eviction in poor and segregated nongentrifying areas or the eviction problem outside of superstar cities. According to the Eviction Lab research, eviction rates are higher in small and rural cities than in large cities; moreover, the large cities with the highest eviction rates are not the superstar cities that are the focus of the gentrification discussions.[15] It also misses the decades of exclusion, actual forced displacement, and discrimination caused by state-sanctioned and de facto racial segregation.

The deflation of the gentrification-based displacement claims does not mean there are no harms. According to the Urban Displacement Project report, neighborhood and housing conditions are connected to 48% of the moves in Bay Area neighborhoods. I criticized their definition of displacement; however, whether those moves are, in fact, instances of displacement or the result of growing housing unaffordability and precarity, it is a sign of the housing crisis.

Even in gentrification studies troubled by displacement, researchers find patterns of displacement that have less magnitude than was assumed. For example, in the report, *Mapping Susceptibility to Gentrification: The Early Warning Toolkit*, created for the Association of Bay Area Governments to track which San Francisco Bay Area neighborhoods were at risk of gentrification, the researchers found that just 7% of them are gentrifying (Chapple 2009, 21). Further, there is decent evidence of direct and indirect reinvestment displacement depending on the site; for example, Kathe Newman and Elvin K. Wyly, using some of the methods employed by Freeman and Braconi, but adjusting them to meet their methodological concerns, found that "displacement affects 6–10 percent of all rental moves within the city [New York City] each year" (Newman and Wyly 2006, 40), and that poor renters in gentrified neighborhoods in New York City have fallen by 30% since 1990 (Newman and Wyly 2006, 40). There has long been evidence that when the most vulnerable are displaced due to eviction or some other cause (e.g., forced removal from affordable housing), they are shuffled into other disadvantaged neighborhoods (Newman and Wyly 2006; Ding, Hwang, and Divringi 2015; Schlichtman, Hill, and Patch 2017, 121). This situation was starkly depicted in Matthew Desmond's *Evicted* (2016), which recounted the frustrations, trauma, and despair of poor blacks and whites experiencing eviction in Milwaukee, Wisconsin. On top of all this, research has linked rising rental costs with increases in homelessness (Glynn and Fox 2017). Increasing housing and rental costs, their links with increases in housing precarity, and enduring municipal resistance to dealing squarely with the housing shortage give us many serious reasons for attentive worry.

Harms and Inequality

Despite complications with the claims about gentrification-based or reinvestment displacement, there are serious normative concerns about gentrification, the effects of disinvestment displacement that led to our current situation, and the adverse effects of the other facets of the housing crisis. There are two main strains in objections to gentrification. The first concerns distributive inequality, and the second concerns the loss of community character or place-connected cultural loss. The latter is sometimes framed as cultural displacement and can also be understood as a variant of multicultural inequality. The bulk of the complaints about gentrification are devoted to the first two, with objections about the last one brought up to supplement or magnify the former. In the following chapter, I discuss those inequalities and distinguish them from two additional categories of harm: basic moral equality and social inequality. Social equality denotes an individual's standing as an equal citizen or resident, ultimately derived from their basic moral equality. Moreover, I argue that the focus on gentrification obscures larger injustices and inequalities tied to racial inequality. As I alluded to in the earlier sections, the focus on the experience of gentrification in modern American metropolises, and the opposition to it, obscures the consequences of the history of housing discrimination against blacks, Latinos, and Indigenous Americans. Nonideal accounts of the injustice of social-spatial arrangements must squarely confront this racist history and its enduring legacy to provide an accurate understanding of the injustice and to light the path toward its rectification and national reconstruction.

4

The Harms of Gentrification

The Harms

The United States is suffering from a severe housing crisis fundamentally linked to economic precarity and inequality and the enduring effects of racial segregation in housing and education. This has resulted in housing insecurity and homelessness in nearly every U.S. metropolis. Using the minimal definition of gentrification cited in Chapter 3 as "[t]he process by which central urban neighborhoods that have undergone disinvestments and economic decline experience a reversal, reinvestment, and the in-migration of a relatively well-off, middle- and upper-middle-class population" (Van Vliet 1998, 198), gentrification can be safely said to be a feature of this crisis. Therefore, what is commonly identified as the harms of gentrification are primarily a facet of the more significant harms of the U.S. housing crisis, whether they occur in small towns with high levels of eviction but no signs of takeover by the gentry or dense cities experiencing typical patterns of demographic and economic change. Those harms range from macro-level and mezzo-level processes (e.g., global or national economic conditions versus state and regional policies) to micro-level effects (e.g., local demographic and changes) visible from the street. The latter, micro-level effects are the ones most connected to gentrification.

These concerns lead to two categories of harm that provide a basis for objections to gentrification. The first concerns distributive injustice, while the second concerns community character loss. Most of the objections against gentrification are devoted to the former, with objections about the latter being brought up to magnify the former. I distinguish those harms from a third category, that of democratic inequality that might accompany gentrification.

In this chapter, I make the case that gentrification involves each of these harms but also that they are insufficient to capture the harm of gentrification in the American context of racial segregation. A singular focus on gentrification as a phenomenon obscures past injustices and their resulting inequalities in the geography of opportunity connected to unrectified historic racial wrongs. My position is similar to Jonathan Kaplan and Andrew Valls's (Kaplan and Valls 2007; Valls 2018) that the particularity of African American claims to rectify past racist harms can be lost in the scrum of arguments among diversity, multicultural rights, and distributive justice. The focus on gentrification in modern U.S. metropolises, and the opposition to it, obscures the consequences of the history of housing and land-use discrimination against African Americans, Latinos, and Native Americans.[1] To resist this obfuscation, I defend a liberal egalitarian critique of gentrification that prioritizes the needs of the poor, working classes, and those struggling with segregation, housing instability, and economic precarity. This response is reconstructive compared to this nation's history of milquetoast housing reform. Compared to calls for the decommodification of housing (a reasonable enough reform on a small and municipal scale), it is pragmatic. This is because it advocates for targeted rectification for those currently suffering from legacies of concentrated poverty, hypersegregation, and geographic immobility.

Distributive Injustice

Injustice in housing policy and inequities in housing patterns lead to disadvantages that negatively affect the well-being and the life chances of all affected households. These disadvantages include increased economic precarity, increased housing instability or homelessness, worsened educational stability of school-age children in the household, and the loss of communal networks and access to social services. They are unjust because they are the product of unjustified group-based inequalities and cause further harm. They set undeserved negative starting points in which individuals begin their lives that hamper or negate their development and life chances. Compounded on this individual harm, these disadvantages are attached to group-based, predominantly ethnic and racial inequalities, which generate further status inequalities that become concentrated in intergenerational burdens, all of which feed a systematic lack of fair and equal opportunity. If, and when, instances of gentrification participate in distributive injustice, either as a driver or vehicle of it, then it is unjust. Without these specific harms, gentrification is not a marker or a process of distributive injustice.

In *The Death and Life of the Urban Commonwealth* (2016), Margaret Kohn offers a broader categorization of gentrification's harms than this. She sorts the harms of gentrification into five types: (1) residential displacement; (2) exclusion of the former residents who desire to return to the neighborhood, and individuals who seek to live in the neighborhood but who do not fit the economic and demographic features of the place; (3) the transformation of the public, social, and commercial features of the neighborhood, such that those who remain but who do not match the characteristics of the incoming class, may experience alienation from the neighborhood and exclusion from those spaces; (4) the polarization of the neighborhood, in which it is starkly divided by race, ethnicity, or class, but it is not socially integrated; or its (5) homogenization into a middle- or upper-class or ethnic enclave, and its commercial and social spaces come to resemble the banal environment of American malls (Kohn 2016, 90–92).

All five of these categories involve distributive injustice insofar as they involve the unjust distribution of resources and lack of fair and equal opportunity to access the resources. Demographic polarization or homogenization of groups or populations is not an injustice as long as it is an expression of consensual group clustering. They are unjust when the clustering is affected through infringements of individual rights or are the results of distributive injustice, which are often connected to status inequality or mechanisms of group-based inequality. Polarization and homogenization, however, even if they do not involve injustices to individuals or groups, are harmful when they are demographically and geographically scaled up because they exacerbate political inequalities (Bishop and Cushing 2008; Enos 2017).

Margaret Kohn's analysis of gentrification is based on a vision of social equality that she calls "solidarism," which, roughly, considers all public property and an indeterminate amount of individual property, but especially the land, as common or social property, and holds that citizens have mutual obligations to care for the commonwealth and its members (Kohn 2016, 13–31). She calls any denial of commonwealth members' use and access to social property an act of dispossession, which is ethically akin to theft. In Kohn's view, gentrification is, at base, a form of such dispossession.

What Kohn's solidarism entails for individual property holdings, such as the extent and limits of its claims, is vague. It might justify the expropriation of private property in a manner that infringes on fundamental rights; this would be the case if it warrants the decommodification of all housing units. That goal, and any that linked decommodification to the expropriation of private property, would be plainly and dangerously illiberal. Or it could merely be a call for a shift in valuing public resources, such as land and housing stock, as social goods rather than commodities whose distribution is entirely at the mercy of market forces. This could involve decommodifying affordable housing units that are currently administered by public–private partnerships (through legal market-based means) and building more public or "social" housing. Another option is to view Kohn's solidarism as akin to what Gerald A. Cohen identified as a principle of community that affirms the mutual provisioning of resources and services as a fundamental marker of mutual respect and care (Cohen 2009). Despite concerns about the normative basis of Kohn's conception of justice and social-spatial arrangements, her categorization of the harms of gentrification is helpful because it alerts us to the features of the harms caused by injustice in housing policy.

Margaret Kohn's critique of gentrification also draws on the radical egalitarian approach of Cohen for satisfying preferences that others might consider "expensive tastes." In Cohen's radical egalitarianism, Kohn sees a way to meet residents' desire to remain in gentrifying neighborhoods they cannot afford (Kohn 2016, 98). What is equalized in Cohen's theory is a mix of resources and access to opportunities and advantages, including the opportunities to satisfy one's preferences that do not infringe on the legal rights of others. Cohen supports providing basic needs for individuals so that they are at least at the point of marginal utility where their everyday well-being would be secure. Still, he goes beyond that by advocating for the provisioning of resources that allows for the satisfaction of their nonharmful (to others) or morally offensive preferences. This sort of radical egalitarianism leads to questions about costs because satisfying the needs, preferences, or access to opportunities of some will be more expensive than it is for others. This is called the problem of "expensive tastes" (Dworkin 2000, 48–59; Cohen 2011, 13–33 and 81–115).

A salient feature of Cohen's account is that it distinguishes individual or social circumstances, which he defines as largely undeserved and for which individuals are not responsible, from choices, which individuals bear some responsibility for, as long as their circumstances do not overly constrain their choices (2011, 5–9). Adverse involuntary circumstances result from "brute" or bad luck, and any negative outcomes that flow from them deserve compensation. This category includes the negative effects of responsible yet overly restrained choices. Adverse involuntary circumstances describe the situation of many, and possibly millions of Americans, whose lives are economically precarious and who experience housing instability. In contrast to those facing dire circumstances, in Cohen's account, individuals may be left to suffer, but only to a humane degree, the adverse effects of their bad choices or the bad option luck due to their choices. This view of bad choices justifies, for example, "housing first" policies that prioritize the provision of shelter for the sake of individuals' basic well-being and society's general social and economic benefit.[2]

Cohen's distinction between circumstances and choices reflects the logic embedded in Rawls's second principle of justice, especially the ideas of fair equality of opportunity and democratic equality. Still, his linking the provision of social benefits to that distinction runs into profound metaphysical problems (e.g., the free will problem; Cohen 2011, 31–33) or psychological problems (e.g., cognitive scarcity; Mullainathan and Shafir 2013), social and cultural problems, or plainly bureaucratic ones. Furthermore, racial, ethnic, and gender biases in society easily distort the division between choice and circumstance; for example, the African American "welfare queen" is the racialized icon of irresponsible choice that implicitly stigmatizes black and brown poor women as dangerous, lazy, and careless (Hancock 2004).

In addition to concerns about responsibility, which Cohen is wary of, the framing of preference satisfaction under the rubric of expensive tastes trivializes them. It obscures relevant nonideal and historical reasons some preferences were blocked from being satisfied in the first place. Much of the philosophical literature draws on examples from antiquated, aspirational, and idiosyncratic tastes of philosophers, which then frame the debate; for example, inexpensive lentils versus plover eggs. These examples trivialize the issues. In contrast to those trivializing and morally obscuring examples, Cohen provides a nontrivial example relevant to its application to housing precarity and inequality in his discussion of heating subsidies. He wrote, "think of poor people in Britain who suffer discomfort in the winter cold. The egalitarian case for helping them with their electricity bills is partly founded on that discomfort. It does not rest entirely on the disenablement which the cold, both through discomfort and independently, also causes" (Cohen 2011, 17). Cohen's point is that egalitarians would compensate poor people who suffer from inadequate heating because the cold causes discomfort and disenables their normal range of functioning. He states, "[p]eople vary in the amount of discomfort which given low temperatures cause them, and consequently, in the volume of resources which they need to alleviate their discomfort. Some people need costly heavy sweaters and a great deal of fuel to achieve an average level of thermal well-being" (Cohen 2011, 17). He adds that such individuals would prefer their tastes were not so expensive, all the better to satisfy those tastes, so the bad luck they experience is not about their choices, which are not wanton, but the price. Such individuals can be said to suffer from "bad price luck," a variation on the idea of bad or brute luck that affects circumstances (Cohen 2011, 81–116).

Cohen's example is easily extended to housing subsidies (Kohn 2016, 106–110). Individuals need housing, and it is, as I argue, a civil right. A desire, however, to live in a particular location is a preference, which can be more or less costly depending on the location. Let us say that society recognizes the right to housing, and the government provides every qualified individual or household with a housing allowance. A household's preference to live in a particular location, for example, within the boundaries of the City of Oakland in the early months of 2023, would cost them, on average, around $2,450. We might consider this cost an expensive taste because it exceeds a national or even regional household allowance, especially because less costly rental rates are available in Bay Area locations proximate to Oakland. However, the well-being of the household might be linked to having a residence there for reasons involving discomfort (e.g., exhaustion caused by a two-hour or longer commute to a job) or disenablement (e.g., the cost of that commute). Likewise, we could apply the argument of expensive tastes to property owners who face the burdens of increased property taxes in gentrifying neighborhoods or who risk foreclosure because of predatory lending practices (Dwyer and Lassus 2015). Applying the argument of expensive tastes to housing precarity and inequality highlights the problem faced by the poor and working classes as they attempt to satisfy their preference for housing in their neighborhoods, which are experiencing the economic pressures accompanying neighborhood reinvestment due to undeserved and often unjust circumstances.

The labeling of the provisioning of necessities, such as heating or even health, nutrition, education, and housing, as expensive tastes is tone-deaf and inappropriate. In the case of housing, the preference for decent and affordable housing with equitable access to opportunity is not a "taste" but a demand for reciprocity, equality, and justice. This criticism reveals an additional problem: pushing back against the expensive taste frame calls into question the ability of social and political systems to reasonably determine what counts toward basic well-being versus mere preference satisfaction. And this is an inherent shortcoming of forward-looking theories of justice. Thus, by drawing on "expensive tastes" framing, Kohn repeats its tone-deafness and reproduces its historical blind spots. Kohn is aware of this deficiency but viewing the condition of the displaced or excluded through the lens of the argument of expensive tastes centers the problem on the preferences of the vulnerable rather than on the inequitable situation intentionally created and cultivated by state-sanctioned actors.

Furthermore, because Cohen's theory, as with Rawls's, is forward-looking, its application to housing precarity and inequality places the focus on the problem of the expense of the "taste" that the poor and working classes have for housing in their preferred neighborhoods rather than the social and economic consequences of the unjust circumstances that lie behind neighborhood disinvestment or reinvestment. This framing ignores the inequitable conditions intentionally created and cultivated by the state and state-sanctioned actors. Liberal egalitarians, or radical or socialist ones, such as Cohen or Kohn, should instead argue that present urban housing market conditions, its historical precedents, and its effects on the working classes and poor were unjust circumstances beyond the control of individuals. Those circumstances deserve an egalitarian distributive response. As Kohn recognizes, the residents of gentrifying neighborhoods are victims of this process and are not merely insisting on the satisfaction of their expensive tastes. Their typical, everyday taste, initially not preferred by the middle or upper classes because of class and racial segregation, has become unaffordable. So much so that they will lose their homes, neighborhoods, social networks, and routines embedded in the places they live. They did not choose to move into a gentrifying community that they couldn't afford. The gentry came to them, and the housing market responded or, as urban theorists have assumed, the landlords and real estate industry produced gentrification (Smith 1996, 3–29; Lees, Slater, and Wyly 2008, 39–86).

Therefore, Cohen's and Kohn's argument supports what Nancy Fraser called affirmative redistribution despite its radical pretensions. The problems of inequality in the geography of opportunity, including housing precarity, segregation, and inequality, should be faced head-on as a matter of structural circumstance instead of as a matter of choice sticky with moralism. In contrast to the ambiguous policy implications of the expensive taste arguments, the state should intervene. This affirmative approach does not affirm the present market-based housing system in the United States. It is reformist and broadly reconstructive. It justifies a range of policies that address housing precarity, mitigate displacement, support desegregation, and set a trajectory toward building more housing types and reimagining it all as a public good.

The problem of displacement and lack of fair and equal opportunity in the housing market should be faced head-on as a matter of distributive injustice. Displacement, whether caused by reinvestment or disinvestment, unjustifiably harms residents when they are subjected to displacement, assuming they have not broken the law or contractual obligation that would affect their claim. The possible harms include violations of contractual and other legal obligations, for example, the abuse of rent stabilization or eviction laws, such as California's Ellis Act,[3] and the failure of the federal and state governments to protect homeowners from predatory lenders who abuse foreclosure laws. Also included are governmental inaction to protect vulnerable renters and homeowners from the housing instability caused by property value increases and the lack of provision of affordable housing in metropolitan regions for residents across the income classes.[4] The housing market, under these conditions, does not offer middle and working classes and the poor fair and equal opportunities to live in regions that are reasonably proximate to their jobs and the educational institutions they depend on.

Left unaddressed thus far is an aspect of Kohn's third (exclusionary transformation), fourth (polarization), and fifth (homogenization) harms of gentrification; namely, the transformation of the public, social, and commercial features of the neighborhood. A liberal egalitarian response to gentrification and the two types of displacements may also extend to concerns about "commercial displacement." That type of displacement affects businesses that serve long-standing residents and are experiencing in gentrifying neighborhoods a rise in commercial rent or a fall in demand for their goods and services (Chapple and Jacobus 2009; Chapple and Loukaitou-Sideris 2019, 167–201). These challenges concern neighborhoods with a specific ethnic, racial, or religious identity, where those businesses are anchors for the community. Businesses rooted in neighborhoods are valued by their community members because they sometimes serve the community's commercial needs in a way that other businesses do not. Those shops and services are carriers of memory, local icons of ambition and success, and anchors for the community's identity, so their loss can be profound. That loss should not be trivialized as a mere feature of neutral market dynamics. Businesses, however, do not have a right to commercial success, but business owners have the right to equal treatment under the law and should expect that they will not be disfavored in policies set by different levels of government. Municipalities privilege some businesses over others, for example, through tax breaks or zoning policy, for the sake of some other greater good such as economic development or infrastructure investment. All the same, liberal egalitarian concerns may motivate some municipalities to protect businesses, faith communities, and nonprofit groups, including theater or gallery spaces, from commercial displacement through the use of land trusts and other policies to secure their tenancy and to stabilize the mix of shops, businesses, and nonprofit groups in cities.[5] Neighborhood groups can also use market-based strategies such as community benefit districts or business improvement districts to aid in the conservation and development of an ethnically identified district, such as a "Chinatown" or "Little Saigon," which might have the desired effect. Other policies may help, such as neighborhood-preference policies in the allocation of affordable housing or tactics like establishing land trusts that buy up several properties and preserve them for a specific group or use. However, those policies more directly address distributive inequality than cultural displacement. They mimic in a highly local, limited fashion the options individuals would have if there were distributive equality. Plus, there is no guarantee that the surviving enterprises will appeal to or even serve the segments of the community they were initially intended to cater to.

Treating citizens and residents with equal concern, which is the sovereign virtue of political community (Dworkin 2000, 1–3), means providing them with basic resources. Those resources are necessary to develop their capabilities and access fair, equal opportunity so that they might gain further resources to pursue their ambitions or life plans and to stand in equal relation as citizens and residents. The moral basis for this is captured in Dworkin's idea of equality as a sovereign virtue. Achieving this ideal requires distributive equality to undergird social and political reciprocity between society's members and citizens—relations emphasized by social egalitarians. Furthermore, in distributive schemes, society should give priority to the classes most at risk for displacement and unequal relations, but not only because, as with the "prioritarians" (Parfit 1997), they will, in balance, benefit more from resources than those who are better off, but because those resources are due to them as equal citizens (Anderson 1999, 326).

Cultural Loss

Distributive injustice captures a large portion of the potential injustice of gentrification but not the whole. Opposition to gentrification typically calls attention to how it changes and ruins community character, commodifies what was the community's character, and leads to the loss of long-standing local cultures. Narratives of cultural and community loss can be heard on neighborhood streets, seen in murals, or read in various accounts, such as the case with Harlem or the borough of Brooklyn in New York City or the Skid Row area in Los Angeles. In the San Francisco Bay Area, the rhetoric of invasion and loss is a significant feature of the concerns about the Mission neighborhood in San Francisco, Chinatown (in San Francisco and Oakland), West Oakland, and North Oakland (Chapple 2009; Rose and Lin 2015; Zuk and Chapple 2015; Dougherty 2020).

This objection is at the forefront of Rebecca Solnit's complaint about the "invasion" of San Francisco by Google Buses. The invaders are cast as hipsters, techies, and other middle- and upper-middle-class, highly educated, and often white white-collar workers (Solnit and Schwartzenberg 2000; Solnit 2013). The bite of the term "invasion" directly expresses local anxieties of displacement driven by the accurate perception of long-standing residents that there is a lack of substantial opportunity in the housing market and that their local networks of friendship and support will be scattered or dissolved. What is more, when gentrification occurs in neighborhoods that have endured the "de-'s" of segregation and disinvestment—especially in those whose communal life has managed to flourish despite discrimination and neglect—it adds to the bitterness of enduring injustice. Thus, the stories of residents who can no longer afford to live in their neighborhoods or face eviction express a loss of more than the simple loss of residence. It is about losing emplaced feelings, experiences, networks, and memories.[6] As one resident of the Mission district in San Francisco related to Solnit about the pending eviction of an old resident and Latino artist: "That's like evicting the history of the Mission" (Solnit and Schwartzenberg 2000, 105).

Another feature of the invasion language in anti-gentrification rhetoric is the view that urban gentrification results in "cultural displacement." This concern appears in objections to the use of pioneer, settler, and colonizer rhetoric by real estate developers and agents or as a self-description by newcomers to celebrate settling in empty, untamed, underdeveloped spaces (Smith 1996, 12–29). Plus, in an insulting twist, the cultural products (e.g., the cuisines, art, music, and festivals) produced by residents of these neighborhoods may be appropriated in the very process of gentrification that leads to the eviction of the people that created them in the first place. However, long-term residents also use colonizer rhetoric to accuse newcomers of having a sort of Christopher Columbus complex because they are perceived to be oblivious or hostile to the preexisting population and its practices, traditions, and mores (Schlichtman, Hill, and Patch 2017, 129–134).

The boosters of gentrification respond to such anecdotes by claiming that gentrification's "re-'s" promote racial and class integration. The increase, however, in cross-class or race mixing that incidentally occurs with gentrification or polarization does not necessarily generate or increase mixed networks (Walks and Maaranen 2008; Freeman 2006, 125–156; Tach 2009; Chaskin and Joseph 2013). The incidental mixing that occurs amid neighborhood or urban polarization is not evidence of substantial integration. While there is evidence of appreciation by long-standing residents for the improvements that the "re-'s" of gentrification bring (Sullivan 2006; Freeman 2006, 95–124), the evidence of division, suspicion, and anxiety in gentrifying neighborhoods is clear; long-standing residents may feel excluded by the changes, believing that they are being made solely for the benefit of the newcomers. They may also be resentful and outraged that society judges the new residents as worthy of amenities while the old residents have been neglected for so long (Freeman 2006, 95–124; Schlichtman, Hill, and Patch 2017, 129–174). These cultural and community-based criticisms of gentrification echo the harms of transformation, polarization, and homogenization that Kohn enumerated and contribute to the harm of exclusion—the erasing of the community anchor points that welcome and support those who identify with the original community, such as the adult children, extended relatives, or those that share in the identity that marks the community (Kohn 2016, 90–92, 102–106).

The objection to gentrification as a cause of unwelcome transformations of community character, local cultural loss, or cultural displacement can also be understood as state-sponsored "cultural inequality." This charge asserts that some cultural groups face unjustified discrimination and disparate outcomes caused by public policy. Using the phrase "cultural inequality," however, is unhelpful because it conflates a difference in the way that cultures are valued for their worthiness with differences in the treatment of groups affected by gentrification in such a way that it hinders their cultural expressions. The latter can be dealt with through distributive justice and democratic equality. However, the former is complex because there are few official systems or means of valuing cultures outside of public support for monuments, festivals, or holidays. The very idea of valuing or recognizing cultures is fraught with dangers to liberal and democratic values because liberal states are limited in their treatment of groups vis-à-vis other groups and their recognition of cultural, ethnic, or racial groups as official and

THE HARMS OF GENTRIFICATION 97

representative political units. Civil rights also allow individuals to precisely *not* value whole cultures or cultural products and express such nonvaluing (Barry 2001).[7]

Moreover, apart from thorny questions regarding cultural loss, the alteration of street life that results in demographic change, including instances where places become homogenized or polarized spaces, is not *necessarily* indicative of distributive inequality. Urban demographic change may occur for various distributive justice-neutral reasons, such as changes in taste, shifts in economic opportunities, or the desire for new or different amenities or environmental conditions in other locations. Therefore, the essential issue in complaints about cultural loss is that local life is being starkly transformed. The nub of the supposed harm is the loss of a community character upon which they have depended or enjoyed. This position privileges identity claims on some set of goods or places over individual rights. Specifically, it pits cultural claims over individual property rights and freedom of association or movement. This argument, which is thought to be an extension of civil rights claims, cuts against the grain of civil rights history in the United States. The U.S. civil rights movement has fought against race- and religious-based exclusion to public goods and services and public institutions and territory. The fight against racial segregation in education, employment, and housing has been a center point in the movement. The movement's most significant legislative achievements have explicitly struck against such exclusionary race-based claims.[8] The 1968 Fair Housing Act outlawed such claims. That same year the Supreme Court decided in *Jones v. Alfred H. Mayer Co.* (392 U.S. 409) that individual discrimination against property rights violated the Thirteenth Amendment. Anti-gentrification critics sometimes regard neighborhoods as sites that should have a right to cultural stasis or conservation. Those claims, in addition to being unconstitutional, depend on dubious and historically and ideologically selective conceptions of cultural authenticity. As Brian Barry has argued, they place cultural recognition over equality and undermine distributive justice (2001, 9, 317–328).

This point is deepened when sacred land claims are considered. For example, colonization of the Americas stripped indigenous peoples of their ancestral lands and subjected them to genocidal campaigns that resulted in deep and enduring injustices (Wilkins and Stark 2017, 22–54; Ostler 2019). As Barry Brian argued, the priority that individual rights are accorded in liberal systems leads to weakening claims of cultural recognition for the sake of liberty and distributive justice (2001, 9, 317–328). This makes liberalism and even the egalitarian sort incapable of dealing with enduring injustice tied to ancestral and sacred land claims, as with indigenous groups in Canada and the United States (Spinner-Halev 2012, 64–70). That is a serious limit to liberalism that exacerbates deep and enduring injustices and, at best, can only be partially dealt with through treaties and other forms of private and public contracts and market-based solutions. Additionally, objections to gentrification are not a reasonable extension of sacred land claims. Neighborhoods are precious to their inhabitants but not sacred in the same historical sense. Seeing them as such would be absurd and arbitrary because, at least throughout the Americas, the places experiencing gentrification have previous claimants that could claim ownership and control based on ancestral or sacred lands. The first claimants of, for example, the neighborhoods of North Oakland are the Ohlone people. Giving priority to any particular neighborhood composition after the Ohlone is to make either an arbitrary time-slice that subordinates, co-opts, or dismisses Ohlone ancestral claims, or, at best, does so based on some other normative standard; namely, distributive justice, social equality, and in some cases, rectification.

The priority of liberty, moral equality, distributive justice, and democratic equality over cultural claims is reflected in the ideals and achievements of the American struggle for civil rights. Freedom of mobility and desegregation has led to many instances of institutional and neighborhood change that we celebrate; for example, the shift of the Castro neighborhood in San Francisco from Italian-American to the residence of primarily gay men, who were also mainly white, the transformation of Harlem from an Anglo-Dutch neighborhood into a historic black metropolis, and the desegregation of the area in which I live, North Oakland, which comprises multiple neighborhoods, and was transformed from an Italian-American and Portuguese-American enclave to a racially mixed section of the city. In the history of American housing law, "community character" claims have been a tool in the arsenal of segregation and discrimination against Jews, blacks, Chinese Americans, Japanese Americans, and Latinos. The progress of desegregation comes with the price of periodic change to the community character of locales. This was true in the 1960s in Alabama as towns and cities across that state fought to resist school desegregation for the sake of preserving a white-dominated and segregated "community character"; a state of affairs that led to the 1963 Birmingham campaign, in which local civil rights activists, who were later joined by the national civil rights organization, Southern Christian Leadership Conference, to end the city's segregation practices. And it was true in 2011 when the state of Alabama passed State House Bill 56, an anti-immigration bill that would have excluded undocumented immigrants from participation in nearly all parts of social, political, and economic life.[9] Its implementation would have put undue and illegal pressure on legal immigrants who would inevitably be discriminated against by Alabamians who opposed their presence or feared interacting with anyone touched with the taint of migration. Some of the supporters of H.B. 56 engaged in racist and xenophobic rhetoric to advocate for its passage. Still, even among those who did not use the worst rhetoric to support the bill, there were white and black locals who supported it because they feared the loss of community character. This displays the double edge of the cultural displacement complaint; it often accompanies anxieties about demographic diversity resulting from neighborhood integration and immigration.[10]

Some might chafe at this comparison. After all, there is a historical asymmetry between the situation of Birmingham, Alabama, in 1963 and, for example, Oakland, California, in 2023. White Alabamians opposed to desegregation in 1963 hoped to preserve white supremacy, while in 2023, in neighborhoods like North Oakland or the Mission in San Francisco, it is poor and working-class residents, many of whom are Latino and black, who seek to prevent eviction and preserve their cultural spaces. It is correct that the comparison collapses when we focus on housing injustice rather than cultural displacement. This demonstrates, in contrast to Kohn's claims, that transformation and homogenization are not per se unjust. With the equitable systems of support for social institutions in place, the networks of each neighborhood community would progress through their own cycles depending on local interest and involvement. The cultural loss objection is at best an expression of the deeper distributive injustices, social inequalities, and unsatisfied demands for rectification; worse, it is an illiberal idea that undermines individual liberty and democratic equality.

Democratic Inequality

The value of social equality as a democratic virtue is crucial in reasonable objections to gentrification. Without social equality in mind, it would be easy to dismiss this discontent over the changes gentrification has brought if it is viewed as simply the result of market choices and the rightful exchange of property or as only a matter of distributive justice. Consider, for example, this statement on gentrification by Douglass S. Massey, a sociologist who produced influential research on residential segregation:

> On the one hand, liberal urban specialists rail against the sub-
> urbanization of America and the abandonment of the cities by
> the nation's whites. On the other hand, when a very few and

highly selected whites buck the trend and stake a claim in the city, they are berated as opportunists and decried for gentrifying the inner city. But liberals can't have it both ways. If the middle and upper classes are to remain in the city to shore up the tax base and play leadership roles in civic affairs, they have to live somewhere. . . . Another element in the hypocrisy pertains to the recent fascination of social scientists with the concentration of poverty—the social isolation of the poor in predominantly poor neighborhoods. If this is a bad thing—and much empirical evidence suggests that it is—then how can it be remedied without the presence of middle-class and affluent households in places also inhabited by the poor?[11]

The controversy over gentrification, according to Massey, is a stand-in for the "contestation of blacks and whites for urban space," which is a reduction of community character objections to a territorial dispute. Massey's reduction is wrong in three ways. First, at least in the Bay Area, gentrification is not just a black and white contestation but often one between primarily white (but also some Asians) wealthy or relatively wealthy professionals and poor and working-class blacks, Latinos, and even some Asians (Chinatown or Little Hanoi, the neighborhoods of first- and second-generation Asian immigrants). Second, his assumption of a role of leadership rather than equal civic partnership of the middle and upper classes in urban neighborhoods betrays a patronizing conception of integration that is retrograde and unnecessary. Third, although Massey is correct that the concern to preserve current forms of urban neighborhoods smacks against other legitimate concerns, such as concentrated poverty, segregation, and environmental sustainability, it is a mistake to dismiss gentrification controversies either because one thinks they mask territorial squabbles or that they divert from legitimate claims for distributive justice.

Complaints about cultural displacement indicate underlying concerns about group-based and status inequalities, and these disparities are signs of a lack of reciprocity and equal standing. The idea of democratic equality sheds light on the substantive concerns voiced by those gripped by the changes brought by gentrification and the threat of displacement. There is good evidence of division, suspicion, and anxiety in gentrifying neighborhoods (Freeman 2006, 95–124; Schlichtman, Hill, and Patch 2017, 129–174). Long-term residents feel excluded by the changes; they perceive their residency, belonging, and well-being threatened; and they are very aware of the class and race dimensions of these transformations and polarizations. Moreover, the context of gentrification can bring greater scrutiny and conflicts between long-term and new residents, who may possess a sense of entitlement and a willingness to call upon the aid of civic institutions such as the police, which increases the potential for conflicts between law enforcement and vulnerable populations. These conflicts include suspicious fear of new residents about the old ones and can extend to the enforcement of building codes and aesthetic standards that increase the unaffordability of the area for poor residents. And long-term residents are painfully aware that they have suffered years if not decades of neglect, only to see development return when middle- and upper-class residents, who are predominantly but not exclusively white, move in. They understandably feel that these improvements were not made for their sake and did not include or welcome them.

Tyler Zimmer uses a relational egalitarian framework in his analysis of gentrification that helps us understand such relational harms (Zimmer 2017, 53–54).[12] The features of gentrification that he addresses are rental costs and the power imbalances of tenant–landlord relations. Along with increased rental costs come other activities by landlords that are also open to normative criticism, such as purposeful neglect of properties or harassment to motivate or coerce tenants to leave and abuse municipal or state rental regulations to vacate rental units or buildings. There is also the removal of units from the rental markets—sometimes using illicit tactics mentioned to vacate them—to convert them into large single-family homes or condominiums, thereby diminishing the supply of available rental units, contributing to rising rents.

The potential inequities that Zimmer identifies in the landlord–tenant relationship are (1) economic exploitation, (2) economic marginalization, and (3) political subordination. Zimmer defines economic exploitation as the utilization of the tenant's vulnerability by the landlord as an "instrument" to exact a "net benefit" in the form of the "highest rent possible" from the tenant, regardless of the tenant's other basic needs. The landlord can also use it as leverage for extracting the highest rent possible from the tenants' potential attachment to their home, block, neighborhood, or community. This threatens the tenants' well-being, or even identity, that goes beyond economic aspects (Zimmer 2017, 56–61). Economic marginalization occurs, according to Zimmer, where the dominant party pushes the subordinate party to the "margins" and excludes them from the "center" (61). Relying on Iris Marion Young's conception of marginalization, Zimmer explains that "to be marginalized is, then, not to count, not to be someone who matters in a given arena. It is, we might say, to go unrecognized or to be misrecognized by others—to be invisible or belittled when one ought to have standing as a full partner in some sphere of social life" (61–62). The third harm that Zimmer identifies is political subordination, which he applies to the landlord–tenant relationship because the landlord can threaten the political membership of tenants by potentially threatening their residency in a city, municipal, or school district (65). Displacement from those political localities means that the tenant will have less or no voice in elections and even less influence than the little they may have had over the representatives of those localities (Schlichtman, Hill, and Patch 2017, 112). Housing crises are a regional phenomenon, and citizens' primary political membership is, in the American case, with the United States as a citizen, and secondarily with the state of residence and so on. But given that once a resident is forcibly displaced, say out of their former municipal district or city, that resident no longer has direct electoral connections to their former local representative or, possibly, the mayor of their former city. The former resident has less power to hold those officials accountable for displacement. A consequence of such displacement—in both residence and political membership—is that the displaced have no direct say on district concerns or the city or county housing policies that set the conditions for their displacement.

Zimmer's critique of the power asymmetries in the landlord–tenant relationship is instructive. The vulnerability and the potential exploitation and domination of the tenant are not indicative of equal standing as citizens, especially when regarding the fundamentals of well-being; this situation is magnified when we consider the vulnerability of tenants and the institutional challenges they face that go far beyond toxic or exploitative relations with landlords (Desmond 2016).[13] It is one thing to be condescended to because one's taste is thought pedestrian or too poor to afford the "best" goods and services. However, it is another when one's well-being, life chances, and fundamental attachments or identity are threatened. The type of rent control regulations he supports may address these concerns and are widely supported by fair and affordable housing advocates, but their efficacy is not firmly established.[14] All the same, Zimmer's categories of marginalization and subordination nicely capture the anxieties of displacement and replacement that the research about social mixing in gentrifying neighborhoods uncovers.

Concerns about cultural loss and social inequality have led some gentrifiers and would-be gentrifiers to develop a typology of their class: early versus late gentrifiers, and colonizers—the "true" gentrifiers—versus those who "respect" the neighborhood and its culture and who move in with the hope of belonging to, supporting, or preserving the neighborhood. Schlichtman, Hill, and Patch offer their own typology, dividing gentrifiers into groups characterized by their relation with their new neighborhood: conqueror,

colonizer/connector, consumer, competitor, capitalist, and cu-
rator (2017, 133–171). These noncomprehensive categories are
productively provocative. They uncover concerns about the ethics
of gentrification and reflect the role of race and class privileges in
urban life and the desire of some of the middle-class gentrifiers to
not contribute to the marginalization and subordination of long-
standing residents. The ethics of gentrification is an egalitarian approach to the division of moral labor on the problem of housing
inequality. This division roughly distinguishes between the duties
of the state to institute justice and the duty of individuals to support
those institutions (Scheffler 2010, 107–128). The attitudes of community members matter for building a public political culture that
affirms mutual social reciprocity and shared governance, and they
can be changed. The attitudes and "orientations" of new and long-
standing residents, as Schlichtman, Hill, and Patch recognize, can
be influenced, although not compelled, by neighborhood norms
(2017, 127). Neighborly norm building is valuable, particularly
when it increases collective efficacy and leads to positive neighborhood effects (Sampson 2015). However, it does not address
the injustice of displacement and the undermining of democratic
equality.

Pragmatic Rectification

The concern of social egalitarianism on relations and status is vital
for thinking about equality. It provides a check against the blind
spots of distributive justice and its tendency to reduce all inequality
to those material conditions or resources. Further, it provides a
framework to understand, for example, the importance of the value
of proximity to social institutions and the dynamics of community
and relations that feature in concerns about justice in social-spatial
arrangements. All the same, social egalitarianism prioritizes relational equality over distributional equality, to the point that social

egalitarians have been accused of being blasé about the required schemes of distribution to achieve social equality (Kymlicka 2006, 29). Inequalities of resources and how they connect with status inequality will not be solved by analyzing what resources are required by thinking about status equality alone (or vice versa) (Schemmel 2015). It may be that Elizabeth Anderson's or Samuel Scheffler's accounts of social egalitarianism, or Tyler Zimmer's critique of gentrification, if allowed to guide housing and social policy in general, would lead to a more egalitarian society, but absent a commitment to redress undeserved inequalities or to rectify or repair inequalities caused by oppressive circumstances, their view of sufficient distributive justice is insufficient.

The vulnerability of poor, working-class, and middle-class residents to the forces of gentrification is due to a patently unjust history of dispossession, exploitation, segregation, discrimination, disinvestment, and then in the twentieth century, redevelopment schemes that did not rectify past harms or compensate the ghetto poor for their continued displacement and dispersed them out of the bounds of their apparent responsibility. Those harms are ongoing for families who have not pulled out of intergenerational poverty and away from locales where that poverty is concentrated; indeed, the most vulnerable when they do move are typically excluded from gentrified neighborhoods and are more likely to relocate to other disadvantaged neighborhoods (Newman and Wyly 2006; Ding, Hwang, and Divringi 2015; Schlichtman, Hill, and Patch 2017, 121).

The particularity of this harm is lost when bundled with complaints about gentrification and the phenomenon of reinvestment displacement. Depending on the site, both types of displacement may be related, but treating them as fully coextensive obscures the past harms and the conditions of racial and ethnic discrimination that made the American ghetto and other sites of concentrated disadvantage. Egalitarian policies that mitigate reinvestment displacement are insufficient to address the past harms

THE HARMS OF GENTRIFICATION   107

and may include individuals and groups who were not subjected to disinvestment displacement. Addressing gentrification so that, for example, the economically struggling members of the creative class benefit does not make up for the harms done to the poor; indeed, the burying of those specific harms may result in benefits going to those who, while deserving, have not suffered the intergenerational consequences of concentrated poverty, hypersegregation, or context immobility.

The problem is seen in municipal strategies to address the loss of population of a minority population through its gentrification mitigation plans. For example, in the San Francisco Bay Area, municipalities are concerned about the drop in the African American population, which in San Francisco has fallen from 12.3% in 1990 to 5.2% in 2022, and in Oakland, from 43% in 1990 to 22% in 2022 (U.S. Census Bureau), but their proposed solutions do not target this situation.[15] The circumstances of impoverished and working-class African Americans are lost in political performative statements that are, in the end, not policies, even if they have an egalitarian intent.

This is not to say that means-based remediation of reinvestment displacement should be dismissed or necessarily made secondary because that is a social and distributive equality requirement. It does mean, however, that pragmatic forms of rectification are owed to those who suffered from race and ethnicity-based housing injustice and that this correction deserves priority. This priority results not just from utilitarian priority or the demands of status equality alone but because these enduring injustices are morally due rectification (Shelby 2004; Valls 2018, 16–43; Mills 2017, 201–215).

Rectification, in this case, could come in the form of programs for individuals whose families suffered from race- and ethnicity-based housing injustice and who are currently suffering the effects of intergenerational and concentrated poverty and hypersegregation. Programs could be envisioned to ameliorate the enduring harms that trace back to the state-based exclusion of Native Americans, blacks, and Latinos that affect current housing instability. They were not allowed to benefit from the programs and protections first instituted by the Federal Housing Administration in 1934. Native Americans specifically suffered from the harms of the American Indian Relocation Act of 1956. And all were negatively affected by the failure of federal and state governments to fully enforce the 1964 Civil Rights Act and the Fair Housing Act of 1968. These factors could be included in an algorithm for the egalitarian planners and require the vigorous enforcement of anti-discrimination and fair housing laws, the establishment of a reasonable right to housing, and the implementation of programs to address the enduring effects of past harms. This is a discomfiting demand. But it is the required price we must pay if we are committed, as a society, to moral and democratic equality and distributive justice.

5

Segregation and the Trouble with Integration

Know Your Place

The history of racial segregation in the United States is at the base of the spatial injustices scrutinized in the earlier chapters. State-sponsored and informal segregation affected the domains of education, employment, commercial activity, and residence, and extended to many other aspects of life, from those perceived to be most expressive of the society's core values, such as religious worship, to the mundane and private. The pattern of coerced exclusion and separation ran (and in some areas, still runs) through the history of class, race, ethnicity, and gender in the United States. It is a thick and toxic vein of experience that gives force to the commanding rebuke to "know your place."[1]

It is an old history. My analysis of it, however, only focused on a small yet determinative part; namely, the history of housing policy and state-sponsored housing segregation and discrimination in the post–World War II years. That period is key because it marks the point that the federal government instituted a series of policies that encouraged single-family homeownership, which built the wealth of the middle and upper classes that in turn was a central feature of the United States' postwar economic boom. Although the history of American racial segregation in housing, education, employment, commerce, and public space began long before the mid-1940s, that is the starting point for direct causal connections to contemporary patterns in housing and wealth disparities. My review of postwar housing policy and urban review in the earlier chapters highlighted the resulting harms: state-sponsored racial segregation and violation of basic equality and democratic equality, and racial and class distributive injustices. Those harms are the basis for the call for rectifying the resulting enduring injustice through the provision of a reasonable right to housing (and specifically corrective justice for those suffering from the effects of intergenerational poverty, concentrated disadvantage, and context immobility.

An appeal for spatial justice—for open communities and substantive opportunity—can be made without reference to that history and still support liberty, democratic equality, and distributive justice, including a reasonable right to housing. However, as beneficial as that would be, such an appeal would still fall short of reconstructive justice. It would leave a deep and enduring harm in American life unaddressed. Leaving it so leaves a rot in place that continues to compound and harm future generations. To address it, corrective justice is required.

But rectifying past harms does not answer questions about how to think and what to do about contemporary segregation patterns. Should we think of current patterns of segregation as *segregation*? What sort of demographic residential or social-spatial patterns should we as a nation promote? From the social sciences to philosophy and political theory, there is a host of excellent analyses and categorizations of the enduring injuries of the history of segregation that offer competing answers to those questions.[2] A broad consensus has recognized the assaults on moral and democratic equality and the distributive injustices rooted in de jure or otherwise coerced forms of segregation. Correspondingly, a consensus has formed in favor of desegregation, or instead, the formal opening of all public institutions, places, and opportunities to all—although significant differences about what counts as fair or equitable access endures. Nonetheless, despite the comprehensive agreement over those two broad issues, there is division over whether to support integration as a demographic goal and moral (both personal and public) ideal.

On one side of the debate, there has long been a call for integration of some form, including policies that aim to increase levels of it in schools, commerce, public institutions, and neighborhoods. Those programs, especially in education and housing, generally have had mixed results, so much so that Orlando Patterson called their legacy the *Ordeal of Integration* (1997). Nonetheless, because of the enduring damage done by segregation policies and the preservation of patterns of segregation through de facto practices (such as ongoing discrimination in the housing market) and seemingly race-neutral policies (such as exclusionary zoning), integration as a value of public morality and a policy goal remains a prominent position in education, housing, and social policy. Owen Fiss's position in *A Way Out: America's Ghettos and the Legacy of Racism* captures this view (2003).

The reaction to positions like Fiss's is to spotlight policies (such as the Moving Toward Opportunity demonstration project [MTO]) that unfairly burdens the poor and working classes and, often, people of color by further devaluing their neighborhoods and property (Merry 2013; Goetz 2003, 2018). Instead of being moved to sites of opportunity, affected residents are just cleared out of the way, and their former neighborhoods experience further disinvestment and sometimes are actually dismantled. All the while, those dispersed in the name of integration are simply concentrated in other underresourced communities. In reacting to this ordeal, advocates on the other side of the debate emphasize that voluntary separation is grounded in individual liberty, may result in a host of social goods, and is not necessarily harmful. This anti-integration-pro-separation camp values desegregation as a base value and advocates for community development as an alternative to failed integration policies.

This chapter joins the debate by first reexamining the idea of segregation and its harms, and considering how segregation is distinguished from other apparently more legitimate forms of separation, such as voluntary residential clustering. It assesses how the harms of state-sponsored segregation might still apply to voluntary arrangements. The chapter then turns to the question of what the idea of integration means, and the objections against it. Addressing these issues paves the way for the next and final chapter, which argues for retention of the ideal of integration, albeit in an alerted form. The shortcomings of past integration policies must be acknowledged, the blind spots of those policies should be exposed, and the undue burdens they put on disadvantaged communities rejected. However, doing so does not require jettisoning integration. Being forthright about integration's counterproductive and unjust costs is consistent with its retention as a political value that endorses and encourages intergroup exposure, interaction, and cooperation.

After the ordeal of integration, what it is and what it stands for need rethinking, and that process leads to the idea of reconstruction as an alternative. It makes little sense in liberal pluralist societies built on equality and liberty to abandon the value of integration. The view of integration *as reconstruction* is distinct from competing theories that reject integration in favor of solidarity built on a politics of difference and cultural revolution or that hitch integration to the expectation of personal transformation and affective conversion. The point of integration is open communities and opportunities, not conversion. From the vantage of reconstructive justice, the end of integration is equal liberty, democratic equality, and substantive opportunity, and not the troubled ends of policies that attempt to engineer demographic evenness, prioritize dispersion, and dismantle segregated neighborhoods.

The Concept of Social-Spatial Segregation

The imagining and drawing of territories has been an essential feature of human life and the history idea of race—the latter being a view of humans that falsely imagines our species naturally divided by spiritual essence, blood, character, or some other fundamental, perhaps biological aspect.[3] A constant feature of that history has been the social separation of groups carved out to correspond to those divisions, which was a way to make the invention of race appear to conform to the divisions of the natural world preordained by some divinity or natural law. These naturalized divisions were, in turn, expressed and enforced in various oppressive, dominating, and frequently brutal forms touching on every facet of human life; the world history of ghettos and other models of racial social-spatial exclusion segregation exemplifies this racist worldview (Goldberg 2002; Duneier 2016).[4] Let us start by examining how these divisions are conceived of, and measured in, empirical studies of segregation. Doing so prompts us to rethink blanket objections to segregation, helps us tease out the distinction between segregation and (perhaps, less injurious) forms of group self-sorting, and illuminates pragmatic and legitimate responses to segregation.

Segregation Measures Matter

Segregation measures pick out demographic patterns of residence of designated groups (e.g., race or class) in a demarcated area (e.g., zip code or neighborhood). The common expectation of racial residential segregation is that it will appear as ghettoization, or the concentration of one group in a particular area and their centralization, somewhere in an urban core. If so, one might prefer indices that capture the degree to which groups are concentrated or centralized in some urban area. However, patterns of concentration or centralization may not appear in cases where groups are unevenly spread or distributed across various clusters in a geographic area. Just as the concentration of a group in an area or their centralization in a city might be an indicator of disadvantage, so might unevenness or clustering.

These demographic complexities have led to the adoption of demographic evenness as a standard for measuring segregation and the use of what is called the "dissimilarity index," to statistically represent "the degree to which two or more groups live separately from one another, in different parts of the urban environment" (Massey and Denton 1988, 63).[5] The U.S. Census Bureau explains that the dissimilarity index "which ranges from 0 (complete integration) to 1 (complete segregation)," or from 0 to 100 depending on the study, "measures the percentage of a group's population that would have to change residence for each neighborhood to have the same percentage of that group as the metropolitan area overall."[6] Using this index to represent segregation on the national level in the United States through the mean metropolitan-level, black and white segregation in 2010 was 59.4%, down from 73.1% in 1980, and white and Hispanic segregation was 49.6%, down from 51.8% in 1980, and white and Asian segregation 41.5%, up slightly from 41.2% in 1980 (Ellen and Steil 2019, 9–10). Residential segregation, according to this index, has decreased over time. According to the analysis of Edward Glaesar and Jacob Vigdor, "American cities are now more integrated than they've been since 1910. Segregation rose dramatically with black migration to cities in the mid-twentieth century. On average, this rise has been entirely erased by integration since the 1960s" (Glaeser and Vigdor 2012, 1; Vigdor 2013).

However, the dissimilarity index reveals few details about the conditions in specific regions, cities, or smaller segments of metropolitan areas because it is an overly broad measure indicating national patterns at the mean metropolitan level. The dissimilarity index below the metropolitan level misses other potentially significant patterns, such as the concentration or centralization of groups. Douglass Massey and Nancy Denton addressed this problem in their research and compiled it in their now-classic book, *American Apartheid* (1993). They claimed that a richer sense of the degree of segregation in a locale is represented by considering several indices together. In addition to dissimilarity, they use the exposure, concentration, centralization, and clustering indices (Massey and Denton 1988, 74–78). When a group, neighborhood, or zip code is characterized by more than one of these, and to a great degree, it is said to experience "hypersegregation," which in America typically applies to segregated black neighborhoods. Additionally, those hypersegregated neighborhoods are also sites of concentrated disadvantage, which continues to fundamentally affect the lives and life chances of the segregated poor (Rugh and Massey 2014). Researchers tend to agree that multiple measures are needed to get an accurate picture of segregation, but there are around two dozen measures and there is an ongoing debate about which measures, and which combination of them, are best.[7]

All this research leads to the conclusion that old measures may not be adequate for measuring how segregation might appear in contemporary urban areas. Take, for instance, patterns of gentrification in the richly diverse neighborhoods of the cities of the San Francisco Bay Area in California. In those cities (which include San Francisco, Berkeley, Oakland, Richmond, and other municipalities) the wealthy reside near much poorer neighbors, including homeless residents living in tent encampments on the sidewalks, under overpasses, or on frontage streets bordering freeways. In those conditions, the demographic evenness of a city or an urban area does not say much about the levels of integration within particular neighborhoods. A city's relatively high level of demographic residential evenness might obscure deeper problems. Likewise, segregation can occur within cities and between them in a metropolitan area, such as between Ferguson and St. Louis, Missouri, or between Richmond and Berkeley in the Bay Area. San Francisco might have scored relatively well on the dissimilarity index, but that does not capture the social and economic disparity between that city and its less well-off neighbors. For example, a report from the Othering and Belonging Institute at the University of California in Berkeley makes a point to respond to the dominance of the dissimilarity index in its study of segregation in the Bay Area and the roots of structural racism in residential segregation by highlighting how older measures miss new forms of segregation in otherwise diverse regions. According to the study:

> A . . . problem with traditional perspectives and measures of racial residential segregation is that the form that racial residential segregation takes has evolved in critical respects. Whereas racial segregation once separated people of different races into different neighborhoods in the same cities (such as different neighborhoods in Oakland, Chicago, New York, or Detroit), racial residential segregation today is more "mobile" and regional. People of color have greater freedom to move to different communities than they did several generations ago, but those neighborhoods and communities are more likely to be struggling, either declining urban areas or struggling inner-ring suburbs or far-flung exurbs. In this sense, people of color are no longer locked into a small number of neighborhoods, but are channeled into certain types of often disadvantaged communities, like Ferguson, Missouri, or Vallejo, California.[8]

Segregation can occur in otherwise diverse metropolitan regions, cities, and districts. Understanding it requires shifting the scale from the regional level to the city level to the neighborhood or even the block level to reveal patterns that correspond to and are causal factors in disparities in residential stability and access to public resources and opportunities.

The Normative Implications of Segregation Measures

Debates around the various measures of segregation matter for the normative evaluation of it, because each measure captures distinct yet overlapping processes and outcomes. Objections to segregation (or, for that matter, integration) may hone in on one or multiple dimensions, but they should not prioritize a particular pattern and its corresponding dimensions for objection or defense. Such selections lead to blind spots in empirical and normative analyses. For example, defending residential clustering as an act of individual or group autonomy might neglect the potential negative effects of concentration or isolation. Likewise, objections to segregation may focus on outcomes, like the uneven spread of a group through a metropolitan area, but miss accounting for whether the process that led to that outcome was just or not.

The concerns about competing segregation measures also reflect a debate about the causality of and responsibility for segregation that has further normative implications. Tommie Shelby, for instance, considers "segregation" to be a morally neutral term while also recognizing that it is both the cause and effect of racially marked residential patterns in cities and towns and is associated with many harms.[9] He acknowledges the possibility of legitimate forms of residential separation, or what can also be called clustering or concentration, with the assumption that they result from voluntary choices and not discriminatory coercion.[10] It is for this reason that Ron Johnston, Michael Poulsen, and James Forrest briefly consider whether "concentration" should replace "segregation" because it implies choice, which characterizes the dominant processes leading to ethnic and racial residential segregation (Johnston, Poulsen, and Forrest 2014, 14).

Concentration (i.e., households from a particular group residing near each other in significant numbers in some part of the metropolitan area) and clustering (i.e., a group doing so across several clusters across a site) may happen voluntarily and through legitimate and lawful means and to good effect, but whether that is the case depends on local contexts and conditions. The distinction here is typically put in terms of de jure versus de facto segregation, or what the scholars mentioned earlier would instead label as separation or concentration. The fallout of this distinction is that although the state is responsible for ending and remediating the effects of de jure segregation, de facto segregation is not the state's responsibility. This position is evident in, for example, Supreme Court Justice Clarence Thomas's concurrence with the 2007 majority decision in the *Parents Involved in Community Schools v. Seattle School District*. Justice Thomas summed up the finding of the Court in his statement that the Supreme Court "holds that state entities may not experiment with race-based means to achieve ends they deem socially desirable."[11] On the state's lack of responsibility to intervene in de facto segregation, he wrote that "Racial imbalance is not segregation, and the mere incantation of terms like resegregation and remediation cannot make up the difference," and "[b]ecause this Court has authorized and required race-based remedial measures to address *de jure* segregation, it is important to define segregation clearly and to distinguish it from racial imbalance. In the context of public schooling, segregation is the deliberate operation of a school system to 'carry out a governmental policy to separate pupils in schools solely on the basis of race.' "[12] Based on this legal reasoning, Justice Thomas held, that racial imbalance "is not unconstitutional in and of itself," and school districts may not use race to prevent resegregation or remedy past segregation.[13]

Therefore, the distinction between de jure and de facto segregation rests on the presence or absence of segregationist intent backed up by state compulsion. We can admit that primary distinction and the idea that social-spatial concentration, clustering, separation, or imbalance all voluntarily occur. Accepting this is consistent (as Justice Anthony Kennedy recognized in his concurrence to *Swann*) with recognizing that complex ethnic, racial, and class histories condition choices that lead to social-spatial segregation patterns that create and reinforce disparities within contexts. This is what Maria Krysan and Kyle Crowder (2107) do in their research that identifies the social processes behind this conditioning leading to residential segregation patterns. They distinguish their view from three previous dominant explanations: first, that residential segregation is the result of residential racial preferences; second, that it is the result of social and economic resources; and third, that it is the result of "subtle but insidious forms of discrimination," or what we can see as unique acts of personal racism that conglomerate to form a pattern of structural racism. Krysan and Crowder agree that those three factors are in play. Still, they add that,

> while segregation in America was created out of a series of conscious efforts to ensure separation of the races, it is now maintained not just by overt segregationist efforts, socioeconomic differences, and racial preferences, but also by the social and economic repercussions of segregation itself. (Krysan and Crowder 2017, 5)

Essentially, local and national segregation patterns result from system-wide looping effects. Individual residential choices are conditioned by, among other things, perceptions of fit, welcoming or ostracizing behavior, and structures that perpetuate segregation, such as single-family zoning and the lack of affordable housing in neighborhoods. Further, many neighborhoods and residential developments throughout the United States were initially designed to be class and race exclusive. While it is the case that since the end of state-sponsored segregation, the policies that govern housing and land use are facially racial neutral, their economic and land-use restrictions maintain and promulgate racial residential and social-spatial segregation.

Segregation measures reveal these demographic-geographic divisions, but they can also obscure them when we view maps of residential patterns by race through choice-centric and invisible-hand explanations, such as Thomas Schelling's (1961, 1971). Those frameworks evade the historical contexts and political operations that lead to segregated social-spatial conditions. The state initiated the residential and community segregation that is playing out now in individuals' apparently voluntary housing choices. That starting point conditioned present segregated residential and educational segregation, the lack of fair access to housing opportunities, and resulting wealth disparities (Pietila 2010; Rothstein 2017). Certainly, multiple and overlapping factors lead to each household's circumstances, including fortunate and unfortunate choices and the vagaries of good and bad luck, but this history conditions residential choices.

The sorting of America into residential clusters that are or are nearly racially, ideologically, or class homogeneous, what Bill Bishop and Robert Cushing (2008) called the "big sort," is not accidental. The nation, as a whole, bears a political responsibility to rectify the harmful effects of past state-sponsored segregation and to mitigate its continuing harmful effects. For all the reasons stated, it is reasonable to label patterns of separation, clustering, concentration, and so on as segregation. Doing so is consistent with the ordinary usage of the term "segregation"—a setting apart of one thing from another—and does not evade the complexities of voluntary concentrations or clusters. Conserving this usage retains a solid link between present structural injustices linked to segregation and the long wake it has left through towns, cities, and institutions.

The Benefits of Segregation

As emphasized by those who would instead stress the voluntary-seeming ideas of clustering and concentration when considering segregation, segregation benefits those who seek it out or those who have only known and are supported by its confines. The lack of racial, ethnic, religious, or ideological diversity can comfort those whose locales are characterized by relative homogeneity or the demographic predominance of a preferred group.

Individuals and families who favor such demographic clusters, concentrations, or even isolation prefer them for various reasons. Places characterized by demographic concentrations can nurture networks that may have beneficial social, political, and commercial effects (Merry 2013, Goetz 2018, 57–58). Minority or otherwise marginalized communities sometimes cluster together for mutual defense against racism or xenophobia, to engage in mutually beneficial commercial activities, and to conserve and develop their cultural, religious, and ideological values and traditions. However, the potential benefits of group-sorting apply to a wide variety of groups, beyond numeral demographic minorities, from the racial to the ideological. When this occurs within the bounds of the law and as an expression of individual liberty, social-spatial segregation may have individual, group, and general societal benefits. Voluntary clustering, concentration, and isolation, all things considered, are entirely legitimate expressions of individual and group autonomy and are in keeping with the idea of democratic equality. What is it to those left behind? Why does it matter if a group takes the "Benedict" option and retires to a protective enclave or citadel, so long as the rights of others are respected?[14]

The primary problem with segregation is the conditions under which it occurs, such as forced exclusion or concentration. Even without explicit state or private coercion, significant negative results accrue from group sorting, such as opportunity hoarding or the stigmatization of exclusion; so while separation in and of itself may not be immoral or unjust, processes and disparate outcomes that result from it might be. This problem haunts the Benedict or "enclave" option and the comforting distinction between segregation and seemingly nonharmful instances.

The Harms of Segregation

The harms of segregation extend across society, differing in degree and effect depending on the individual, household, neighborhood, municipal, and regional conditions. They involve injuries to basic equality, democratic equality, and distributive justice. Growing up and living in segregated neighborhoods marked by such concentrations of disadvantage can have deleterious material consequences on individuals and households. Moreover, the harms of social-spatial segregation extend beyond those most immediately affected by it. Its injuries rise above low-level disconnection or friction in social communication and relations by diminishing the quality and possibility of democratic citizenship. Even within the confines of the citadels of the affluent, the harms of separation extend; although the residents of such places benefit from the concentration of wealth and advantages that brim over at those sites, they pay the price as citizens for the overall dysfunction and the social and political conflict and division that result from national patterns of racial and ethnic, economic, and ideological of social-spatial sorting.

The connections between segregation and distributive injustice are part of the history and continuing presence of disparities in access to fair and affordable housing and the geography of opportunity. They include the effects of state-sponsored segregation, the failure to fully enforce the Fair Housing Act, the continuing lack of substantive opportunities in housing, exclusionary zoning policies, and redlining in mortgage lending. Segregation exacerbates concentrated disadvantage, a condition that causes further disparities across a range of social indicators, including education, health, crime, and access to political power and economic opportunity.[15] Whether it is called segregation or separation, according to Elizabeth Anderson, it results in inequality through (1) spatial effects in access to goods, such as employment, retail and commercial services, and health-related goods and services; (2) capital-mediated effects involving financial, social, human, and cultural capital; and (3) state-mediated effects on access to public goods, which include public services, tax burdens, exposure to crime, decay, and police underenforcement and overenforcement (Anderson 2010, 27–43). These effects work together to create closed neighborhoods and communities in a process that sociologists call "social closure" (Anderson 2010, 7–16), which extends the mal effects across generations, showing up in a variety of disparities, such as educational attainment and wealth (Rothstein 2017; Shapiro 2017).

Social closure is an apt phrase for capturing the denial of effective liberties and substantive opportunity. It occurs through mechanisms involving, among other things, adaptation to and emulation of dominant group norms and practices of exclusion, which Charles Tilly (1998, 147–169) explained results in "opportunity hoarding." Opportunity hoarding is at the core of the distributive injustice of social-spatial segregation; as john a. powell (2008) wrote, "spatial segregation is opportunity segregation." Or, as crisply summed up in a report published by the Othering & Belonging Institute at the University of California:

> The best life outcomes are found . . . in highly segregated white neighborhoods, which is consistent with a theory of "opportunity hoarding" that predominantly white cities and communities have greater resources and often have the fewest people of color living in them. Household incomes in these neighborhoods are nearly twice those in segregated communities of color. That income differential contributes to wealth disparities, as home values are also nearly twice as high. Even life expectancy is four years longer in these neighborhoods than in segregated communities of color. But critically, these neighborhoods are difficult to access: monthly rents are more than $300 and $400 per unit higher than in either integrated or highly segregated P.O.C. neighborhoods, respectively. (Menendian Gailes, and Gambhir 2021, 17)

Furthermore, social-spatial distributive injustices have broader effects than the denial of resources and access opportunities. Talk of the harms of segregation tends to focus on its harmful distributive outcomes, but it is essentially an assertion of the lack of equal moral and political status in society. That denial of equal standing stigmatizes targeted groups and justifies exclusion, which is required to enforce and reproduce the stigma (Anderson 2010, 44–88). It is a public rebuke and declaration that stigmatized groups do not belong here, that they must "know their place."

Critically spotlighting the moral disrespect at the center of segregation, along with its social and political affliction, is an old insight that runs through the history of the African American intellectual tradition. The figures of the early civil rights movements, from Frederick Douglass to Ida B. Wells-Barnett to W. E. B. Du Bois, condemned it. Martin Luther King Jr., tapping into that history, and in the context of the midcentury civil rights movement, condemned segregation precisely on those grounds. As he wrote famously in the "Letter from Birmingham Jail,"

> All segregation statutes are unjust because segregation distorts the soul and damages the personality. It gives the segregated a false sense of inferiority. To use the words of Martin Buber, the great Jewish philosopher, segregation substitutes an "I–it" relationship for the "I–thou" relationship, and ends up relegating persons to the status of things. (King 1991, 293)

Moving beyond practices of coerced segregation, King held that what makes segregation laws unjust also applies to the de facto practices that support those laws and the resulting conditions.[16] King argued that the distortion of souls and the debasement of persons to things, drawing on the theologian Paul Tillich, is an "existential expression of man's tragic separation," of their "estrangement" from other persons from their personhood, and ultimately from God. From King's and Tillich's prophetic view, segregation is an act of separation from personhood and is fundamentally a sin (King 1991b, 295). For those compelled or given no substantive choice but to concentrate geographically or to cluster, it is an act of domination and a thwarting of choice. It is a civic "sin" as much as a grave failure within the context of King's liberal Christianity.

Further, the stigmatization that accompanies segregation (and reinforced by their material instantiations in the built environment) distorts our sense of place and, ultimately, ourselves. Research on "mental mapping" and the effects of social-geographic space on perceptions of others and social networks demonstrate these distortions. Mental maps are individuals' subjective mental representations of objective locations, their cities, neighborhoods, commutes, and all the space and places we inhabit or pass through (Golledge and Stimson 1996). Humans drape multiple layers of meaning over wild and urban spaces and places and invest them with their views about what is natural and beautiful versus what is foreign and ugly, what belongs, and, more to the point regarding segregation, who does and does not belong (Basso 1996). These mental maps are affected by and reinforce individual and group views about social identities. For example, women's spaces versus men's; areas demarcated by class status; and spaces and places with one or another racial, ethnic, or religious group. We inhabit spaces and places, so our mental representations of them and their effect on our lives influence how we see, understand, and move through the world.

Ryan Enos describes these effects by characterizing social-geographical space as an omnipresent demagogue (Enos 2017, 34). He has found through his research that geographic conditions increase the salience of group categories, that a group's "size, proximity, and degree of segregation" affects the salience of those categories, that the more salient a group category is, the more likely it will result in biases in attitudes and behavior, and that these group-based biases have political effects (Enos 2017, 33–34). Enos's research supports the view that spatial effects are causal and that segregation amplifies those effects. As I remarked in an earlier essay on segregation, "not only do we inhabit a divided America; divided America inhabits us" (Sundstrom 2003, 92). Segregation is an anti-democratic demagogue, even when it takes the form of seemingly voluntary concentration and clustering. It erodes or makes impossible moral and civic affinities that undergird the value of reciprocity and the ends of reconstructive justice.

Integration as Evenness and Mobility

When confronted by the harms of segregation, what seems to be called for is its opposite: demographic diversity throughout the nation's cities, towns, and neighborhoods. Neighborhoods should have levels of diversity proportional to their cities or towns, and cities should have levels balanced to their region. Balanced diversity across an area means more exposure and less isolation among individuals across the groups, less concentration of any group within any neighborhood, and less centralization or clustering. This is the desired outcome of desegregation or integration policies.

Roughly, desegregation is a process and outcome that ends or reverses policies and practices that generally enforce or otherwise uphold segregation. Integration is also a process and outcome that involves blending or distributing populations across institutions and locales, and it implies a degree of cooperation, interaction, and communication across groups. Those practices appear synonymous or on the flip sides of each other, and both appear consistent with moral and social equality, individual liberty, and distributive justice requirements. However, the long debate between those who emphasize one over the other reveals a misalignment between these terms' political and social meanings and goals.

King, for example, recognized a vital difference between calls for desegregation versus those of integration; for him, the difference was ethical, and it had vast implications not only for the rights and welfare of black Americans but also for the future of the country. The ethical difference he discerned came down to how Americans regarded each other, whether they saw each other as equally worthy of full moral dignity as persons and equal citizens. He held, therefore, that the mere formal ending of state-sponsored segregation through desegregation was not enough to provide democratic equality. It would offer only "physical proximity without spiritual affinity (King 1991a, 118). King voiced this view in his 1962 speech, "The Ethical Demands for Integration," wherein, after identifying segregation as essentially prohibitive and desegregation as merely eliminative and the negative of segregation, he stated,

> Integration is creative, and is therefore more profound and far-reaching than desegregation. Integration is the positive acceptance of desegregation and the welcomed participation of Negroes into the total range of human activities. Integration is genuine intergroup, interpersonal doing. Desegregation then, rightly, is only a short-term goal. Integration is the ultimate goal of our national community. (King 1991a, 118)

In his view, integration is more morally demanding than mere desegregation because it is ethically formative; it calls for recognizing the whole moral worth of persons, the requirement of freedom to live a dignified life as an equal citizen, and the solidarity of the human family.

A minimal, quantitative conception is a fine place to start to understand what such an integrated nation might look like. It might be initially understood as the opposite of what is revealed by multidimensional measures of segregation. For example, when the dissimilarity index is used, integration occurs when "every neighborhood has the same proportion of each group as the city as a whole" (Denton 2010, 36). Cities, towns, and neighborhoods would look like checkerboards. I call this view "integration as residential demographic evenness," or just "evenness" for short.

However, as soon as ethical ideas of integration, such as the one that King expressed, are translated into quantitative terms and policy outcomes, its animating ideals—equal personhood, liberty, citizenship—are diluted and distorted. Methods of measuring segregation, with their associated visible demographic presentations, fill in for its meaning and shape public understanding of integration, its point, and its appearance. Locales that attain such proportionality will score well on the evenness scale; however, it does not follow that they meet other criteria of justice or match common intuitions about neighborhood diversity. Further, judging the integration of locale solely by their demographic evenness may miss instances of segregation in other forms. In such cases, neighborhoods with a high degree of white and Asian American diversity also have high degrees of black or Hispanic and Latino exclusion or isolation. Residential demographic evenness, in that or similar scenarios, may be superficial and not that dissimilar from the cold desegregation that King judged as an insufficient response to the injustices of segregation. Integration as evenness, therefore, is not a sufficient remedy for the harms of segregation. It is not necessary either; this holds whether or not demographic evenness is a desirable aesthetic goal for particular communities. What is needed is securing equal liberties and access for individuals and families to public goods and substantive opportunity.

Relatedly, integration as evenness assumes that achieving an even demographic spread throughout urban areas results in increased access to place-based opportunities and the generation of social networks that buttress access to opportunity. I call this view "integration as administered mobility" or just mobility. Integration as mobility translated into policy has meant creating programs to relocate low-income families to better-resourced neighborhoods with lower poverty rates. Participants were supposed to be supported through direct housing subsidies (e.g., Section 8 housing vouchers) or placement in affordable housing developments. Plus, those programs sometimes came with promises to enforce fair housing laws and the hope that they would deconcentrate poverty in the neighborhoods that participating families moved from. Examples of such policies are the Gautreaux Assisted Housing Program in Chicago from 1966 to 1998 and the MTO Demonstration Project that sought to integrate families from poor neighborhoods into those with less poverty.[17]

The MTO project is what most new integrationists focus on in their defense of the ideal of integration. However, the results of that and other mobility programs are mixed, so much so that critics tend to dismiss their efficacy and moral legitimacy (Goetz 2003, 2018; Steinberg 2010). Programs, such as MTO, fetishized integrated demographic patterns and led to policies that were purportedly created to help families leave neighborhoods marked by concentrated disadvantage but ended up thwarting their mobility, educational, and housing preferences for the sake of attaining evenness (Goetz 2018, 102–108). These programs assumed, with little evidence, that the mere act of moving to a new neighborhood would increase participants' access to robust new social networks that would improve their access to opportunities. In doing so, policies motivated by the goals of evenness and mobility undermined the liberty of the affected families. They focused too much on a particular demographic outcome rather than the multiple other goods and motivations for integration, prioritizing moving families rather than supporting their ability to be mobile and reforming the processes they go through in accessing neighborhoods and opportunities (Denton 2010, 30; Goetz 2018).

Such objections are significant and point to real shortcomings and limitations in policy construction and implementation, but the wholesale rejection of mobility programs, in particular, is unwarranted. MTO programs have had, although they are limited, generally positive effects. Similar concerns have been registered about HOPE VI developments, but its effect on the quality of life in public housing and the reduction of concentrated poverty has been substantial (Cisneros 2009). Mobility programs can increase the quality of life and opportunities for participating families with young children. The younger the child and the longer they have been exposed to better-resourced neighborhoods, the better their long-term outcomes, including college attendance, earnings, and single parenthood rates (Chetty and Hendren 2015; Chetty, Hendren, and Katz 2016). These benefits should not be dismissed.

Some, like Owen Fiss, champion their expansion. Fiss argues that ghettos are sites of disparity and inequality that destroy the life chances of those trapped within them, so the best solution is to dismantle them:

> The only strategy with any meaningful chance of success is one that ends the ghetto as a feature of American life. Pursuing this remedy requires providing those who are trapped in the ghetto with the economic resources necessary to move to better neighborhoods—black or white—if they so choose. With the means to move, most will leave, and that will be enough to break the concentration of mutually reinforcing destructive forces—poverty, joblessness, crime, poorly functioning social institutions—that turn the ghetto into a structure of subordination. (Fiss 2003, 5)

Expanding mobility is a feasible way of providing the resources required by distributive justice, and it ties the economic fates of Americans across classes together. The policies he promotes to achieve this end all focus on voluntary relocation, including the creation of relocation programs, subsidizing rents of those relocated through the provision of housing vouchers, the rigorous enforcement of anti-discrimination in housing law, and expanding the MTO program (Fiss 2003, 28–33). He concedes that those who wish to remain should be allowed and supported, but the programmatic emphasis is on mobility (36). Likewise, he supports gentrification, which, if displacement can be mitigated, may support the efforts of community development of those who remain (117–118).

This view of integration, represented by Fiss, remains a critical facet of integration as mobility. It illustrates that integration as mobility is just as much a vision of integration as dispersion—a less appealing way of thinking about how societies get to demographic evenness—and, concerning the places left behind, this is a view of integration as disinvestment, departure, and demolition. All these "de-'s" come with the hope of reinvestment at some other time presided over by other people with better access to resources and opportunities.

Tearing down the walls of the ghetto will, as Fiss recognizes, disrupt community ties, but he claims the price is worth it because mobility programs deconcentrate poverty and give participating families new paths of access to resources and opportunities. The presumption is that doing this is a requirement of justice because of the demands of equality and distributive justice but also because the nation should address its significant role in establishing the inequities caused by generations of residential segregation. Mobility programs, accordingly, can be understood as an enactment of corrective justice but targeted not just to the former residents of projects torn down but to potentially all the residents of underresourced neighborhoods (Fiss 2003, 40).

In her *The Imperative of Integration*, Elizabeth Anderson offers a conception of integration that, like Fiss's, goes beyond mere physical proximity but, unlike his, is aimed at integration across several areas of common life beyond residence and access to opportunity. Anderson's defense of integration is egalitarian in intent and emphasizes civic participation and communication. According to Anderson,

> The ideal of integration . . . aims at the abolition of racial segregation and its attendant inequalities, not of racial identities. It permits the use of race-conscious policies to achieve racial integration and equality and accepts that some degree of racial solidarity and affiliation on the part of the racially stigmatized is needed to spur integrative policies and cope with the stresses of integration. Thus, integration should also not be confused with the dissolution of black institutions or with the absence of racial clustering in neighborhoods. It consists in the full participation

on terms of equality of socially significant groups in all domains
of society. (Anderson 2010, 113)

Notice that Anderson distinguishes integration from positions
associated with naive forms of colorblindness (reducing racial differences to irrelevant details that are to be ignored) and
disassociates it with naive versions of integration as simple demographic evenness across neighborhoods and cities. If desegregation
just requires demographic evenness, then it does not do enough to
disturb dominant racial patterns and practices, which Anderson
sees as the conditions for "group stigmatization, incompetence
and awkwardness in intergroup interaction, and ethnocentric and
bigoted politics" (Anderson 2010, 113). Integration goes further
than desegregation by upsetting those conditions and the social relations built on them. Because those conditions and relations undermine basic and democratic equality and distributive justice, we,
according to Anderson, have a moral and political imperative to
integrate.

Although Anderson promotes integration in education, political
representation, and employment, she gives particular attention to
residential mobility programs because the effects of those programs
can spill over into other domains of our common life. Integration
generally, and as attempted by mobility programs, is a requirement
of justice because it signifies the fair and equal distribution of social
goods and the benefits and burdens of society. Integration does not
boil down to demographic evenness or mere residential mobility.
However, individual and family mobility is a strong indication
of fair and equal access to the primary institutions of society and
the opportunities that flow from those institutions. It is an essential requirement for citizens to enjoy civic relations. It also benefits
the functioning of participating individuals and families and thus
supports their autonomy and freedom. Segregation has negative
consequences, so integration as mobility and access to networks
of opportunity has equally positive consequences in improving

the quality of life and opportunities for those who would benefit from greater access to education and housing resources. Moreover, integration in public life and the political culture benefits the individual and families and improves the democratic life of society. For these reasons, Anderson perceives integration as providing not only the opportunity for the development of the capabilities of individuals and increased access to further opportunities for them and their families but also more extensive social and political benefits (Anderson 2010, 2).

For its advocates, integration is a communicative and relational ideal, and it directs society to value civic friendship and keep in mind its binding force. Further, as Anderson indicated, it serves as a basis for cosmopolitan relations, which involves communication, interaction, cooperation, and reciprocity. Moreover, the latter idea, reciprocity, is at the core of the integration and egalitarian liberal theories of justice. Reciprocity characterizes relations between individuals engaged in social cooperation bounded by principles that derive from mutual agreement and benefit (Kymlicka 1995; Anderson 1999; Rawls 2001, 49; Dworkin, 2000, 233). Indeed, a high degree of integration is required, across the basic institutions of society, for the successful enactment of reciprocity.

To reject the idea of integration, from the perspective of integrationists, like Fiss and Anderson, is to dismiss a central value that promotes moral and democratic equality, justice, and reciprocity, which are fundamental features of a society marked by cooperation and mutual respect. To turn our backs on integration is a dangerous rejection of social and political virtue. It promotes citizen interaction and develops mutual understanding and ties, which builds bonding social capital and opens the possibility of bridging social capital. From neighborhoods to the larger society, it can promote trust and feelings and practices of reciprocity. Dismissing integration is akin to passing aside the value of a common national life that promotes cosmopolitan identifications.

Integration Is Not a Proxy for Justice

Although mobility programs result in positive outcomes for some participants, their efficacy is disputed. In addition to that are the ethical concerns about how they are administered; for example, there are objections about whether they respect individual autonomy or, in simple terms, whether they respond to their participants' actual (rather than assumed) preferences. Advocates of integration as evenness and mobility take up this condescending attitude and pair it with other assumptions about the automatic benefits of intergroup contact: that when black and brown folks move to better-resourced and predominantly white neighborhoods, they will absorb, through the magic of social osmosis, middle-class attitudes and comportment. Little to no thought is given to the effects of the neighborhoods left behind. But why spare a thought? Dismantling the ghetto is part of the point, correct?[18]

This set of concerns is crisply explained and put into the context of housing policy by Edward Goetz (2018). He elucidates the problematic implications of integration policies by showing how they overlay with the concurrent debate between, on the one hand, fair housing advocates and, on the other, community development advocates. He acknowledges that the knee-jerk answer to this division is simply "both." Both, however, is rarely an option in the nonideal world of practical federal, state, and municipal politics. Governmental entities that overlook housing and land-use policy have limited budgets, and they face local resistance to developing additional housing units due to the usual array of NIMBY exclusionary predilections or the fear of gentrification.

Goetz identifies what he calls the "three stations" of fair housing: (1) opening up exclusionary housing, (2) preventing further segregation, which may include "impaction" rules limiting subsidized housing in overly "impacted" areas (those places that are already racially "even"), and (3) dismantling poor communities of color through the use of redevelopment and mobility policies

(Goetz 2018, 11–14, 91–119). The first station is the only one that does not thwart the victims' preferences of segregation or add to the burdens of already underresourced neighborhoods. Given its focus on access to resources and the geography of opportunity, it is required to achieve open communities and is a positive step toward substantive opportunity; thus, it is a requirement of social-spatial justice and presents a broad conception of integration that has the potential to be reconstructive. There is an imperative to open communities and cities, and thus an imperative to integrate them.

On the other hand, policies motivated by the second station interfere with liberty and undermine opportunity when interpreted as justifying policies that attempt to achieve racial balance. The third station is inconsistent with moral and democratic equality and liberty; it justifies the destruction of communities and established social capital networks and the displacement and dispersion of populations without improving their lives. It amounts to policies mainly interested in "clearing the way" (Goetz 2003). American integration policies primarily aimed at the goals of the latter two stations, with the first station (open communities) supported through rhetorical posturing rather than actual enforcement—except for George Romney's brief tenure as the HUD Secretary;[19] the burdens of this policy and implementation priority fell mainly on the shoulders of poor, segregated, and black and brown communities without substantially improving the conditions of the segregated and is why the legacy of American integration policies has been, at best, mixed, and at worst, a failure.[20]

Therefore, while ameliorative in intent, the second and third undermine opportunity and, as such, are inconsistent with individual liberties, moral and democratic equality, and distributive justice. There is no imperative to thwart individual liberty, curtail opportunities for families to access neighborhoods, housing developments, and schools of their choice once some desired pattern or integration balance or tipping point has been reached, or dismantle neighborhoods without providing their residents substantive opportunity to access affordable, decent homes else-where. This insight leads to four distinct objections to integration as demographic evenness and mobility:

1. Desegregation is an imperative, but integration is not.
2. Compelling integration is morally and politically illegitimate.
3. The ordeal of integration magnifies its illegitimacy.
4. Integration focuses on the wrong problem.

As Michael Merry so succinctly put it: integration is not a proxy for justice (Merry 2013, 22). To explain these objections, we begin with desegregation as the normative baseline.

Desegregation Is an Imperative, but Integration Is Not

The minimal demands of a liberal approach to spatial justice start with desegregation because what is specifically required is access to resources and opportunities in keeping with the values of moral and democratic equality and distributive and corrective justice. Desegregation requires access to these goods but does not insist on the more extensive integration goals. Insofar as segregation is de jure, it is unjust because it fails to meet the demands of equal citizenship. However, insofar as separation is voluntary or de facto, the problem is the concentration of poverty and disadvantage generally rather than racial clustering, as long as ethnic and racial clustering does not negate or impede the rights of those outside the group. Sheryl Cashin gets directly at this point in her remarks about how widespread this view is among African Americans. Black people, according to Cashin, "have become integration weary. Most African Americans do not crave integration, although most sup-port it. What seems to matter most to black people is not living in a well-integrated neighborhood but having the same access to the good things in life as everyone else" (Cashin 2004, xii–xiii). Or, as Nina Simone declared in her song "Mississippi Goddamn": "You don't have to live next to me / Just give me my equality."

Iris Marion Young raised a similar point in her arguments against integration, which was part of her advocacy for a vision of urban life that she termed "differentiated solidarity." Young argued that emphasis on integration tends to leave dominant groups alone and instead supports moving the poor and segregated residents to middle-class neighborhoods. It places the burden of ameliorating segregation on the segregated, and it saddles them with the expectation that they should integrate and do the work of fitting in (Young 1999, 244–245; 2000, 216–221).

Tommie Shelby (2016) took this general point in his criticism of integration by explicitly challenging the moral and political legitimacy of integration policies that target the population he calls the black ghetto poor.[21] Contemporary (or "new," in Shelby's phrasing) integrationists identify patterns of residential segregation, especially among black and Latino poor, as the "linchpin" of segregation's harms. And this directly leads to conceptions of integration as demographic evenness and mobility. The problem with this viewpoint is that it fails to pick out the actual source of the problem (e.g., the lack of substantive access to fair and affordable housing) and fetishes residential patterns that may, with a closer look, be not just a sign of societal dysfunction but a pragmatic and normatively justified reaction to deeper problems (Shelby 2016, 49, and 51–57). Rejecting this ameliorative view, Shelby views residential segregation through a systemic-injustice framework that identifies the problem not with the symptom of residential clustering but as the result of, and a reaction to, unjustified discrimination, institutional racism, or structural injustices (Shelby 2016, 5). Thus, Shelby claims that not all residential self-sorting, clustering, or concentration is harmful, and much of it results from preferences, some of which are due to structural injustices. Although there may be social and political detriments to large-scale residential sorting by group identities, he argues that individual residential preferences are not overridden by the duties of justice and thus are not required by corrective justice. To do so would thwart individual choices and further undermine the liberty and autonomy of a population already burdened by poverty and other disadvantages.

Compelling Integration Is Illegitimate

Closely related to the first objection is the second, which argues that integration programs focusing on administered mobility are morally and politically illegitimate. It concerns the compulsion that the ghetto poor face in forming their housing preferences. The objection is that consent to participate in programs that superficially are about "moving toward opportunity" is manufactured, so choices are dominated (Imbroscio 2008; Steinberg 2010, 220). Thus, new integrationist policies compel participants who seek fair and affordable housing to participate in mobility programs. However, those programs do not allow them to stay in place in their neighborhoods, or they thwart the choice of program participants to move to their preferred locations due to impaction rules. Evidence of this type of domination was found in the aftermath of the MTO project; for example, a study of the Los Angeles MTO project reported that some residents would not have chosen the neighborhoods they were relocated to without being constrained in their choice (Hanratty, MacLanahan, and Petit 1998; Smith 2010). One lesson from this ordeal is that while family participation in MTO programs can be beneficial, as Janet L. Smith reveals in her study, "the means to the end requires constraining the choices that can be made by poor people and nonwhites" (Smith 2010, 236). On top of the illegitimate compulsion behind these programs, as Iris Marion Young pointed out, thwarting participants' preferences is tied to their potential dissatisfaction with the programs, and when the programs fail (partly because participants drop out), the program administrators blame the failure on the participants rather than the coercive system (Young 1999, 244–245; 2000, 216–221).

Additionally, and apart from the thwarting of participants' individual and familial preferences concerning their residence, integration as demographic evenness and mobility ignores the normative weight of the participants' potential preference to cluster with their groups. According to this view, the state is not justified in insisting on integration because individual conceptions of the good may resist or cut against more extensive contact with others outside the groups of one's life. The individual preference to separate may be due to their or their group's assertion of autonomy, including their commitment to comprehensive doctrines. They may seek to remove themselves from too much outgroup contact to conserve their distinct cultural practices or beliefs or protect themselves from the machinations of the majority.

By way of illustration, Du Bois, in 1934, took a position against unsophisticated claims of integration that denied the importance of racial solidarity, which ultimately contributed to his stepping down as the editor of *Crisis*, the NAACP's historical periodical and policy organ. Du Bois criticized the priority that black civil rights leaders placed on anti-segregation protests (which he considered an ultimately ineffectual spectacle) over the building of group solidarity and black institutions. Likewise, he warned against calls for "no segregation" rooted in shame and shirking duties to one's oppressed group. A month before he resigned, he remarked, "The real battle is a matter of study and thought; of the building up of loyalties; of the long training of men; of the growth of institutions; of the inculcation of racial and national ideals. It is not a publicity stunt. It is life" (Du Bois, 1996, 1259). According to this view, integration thins the group out, undermines social and political solidarity and cultural conservation (Du Bois's loyalties, training, institutions, and ideals), and presumes that the problem lies with the group— some minority—needing integration into the larger society. This line of criticism of integration parallels the criticisms of traditional conceptions of assimilation that held up as an ideal the "melting" of minority and foreign groups into the dominant Anglo-American society and their uptake of associated values, beliefs, and standards of taste and comportment. This is a serious objections grounded in individual autonomy and the freedoms of conscience and association, and the ideal of reasonable or egalitarian pluralism. One need not agree with Du Bois's pessimistic and black nationalist criticisms of integration to recognize this point.

The Ordeal of Integration Magnifies Its Illegitimacy

In addition to the political legitimacy objection to integration policies, a historically justified mistrust of the state is another reason to prefer desegregation. Indeed, the troubled legacy of segregation in America and the administration of its fair housing policies magnify the illegitimacy of the demand, especially among the urban poor, to integrate (Young 1999, 244–245; 2000, 216–218). The lack of trust in the state's integration programs is due to a range of causes, including historical crimes, abuses, or discrimination, such as the history of a state's institutional racism or history of its officials' racism or bias. Too often, pro-integration programs, as they played out in cities and urban neighborhoods, were carried out in the name of urban renewal but resulted in removal, dispersal, and increased housing precarity for those affected. The history of integration programs in American K–12 education tells a parallel narrative (Orfield and Eaton 1996; Merry 2013; Rothstein 2017). The black ghetto poor were simply relocated and concentrated in other impoverished neighborhoods, often sites of environmental and economic devastation and isolated from opportunities and public goods and services. Instead of integration, they received dislocation: the disruption of their local social networks and further removal of their access to the public goods and services they required and deserved (Wilson 1987; Massey and Denton 1988;

Pietila 2010; Sharkey 2013; Goetz 2018; Perry 2020). The results of those programs, including urban renewal, is what James Baldwin criticized as "Negro removal" in his criticism of urban renewal in San Francisco, and as he squarely pointed out, from the point of view of poor urban African Americans, delegitimizes the state (Clark 1989, 42). Furthermore, related to contemporary concerns about gentrification, that urban renewal project—an effort of mass dispersion and neighborhood disinvestment—set the stage for the steep decline in the African American population in San Francisco, falling from 12.3% in 1990 to 5.2% in 2022 (U.S. Census Bureau), and for decades of reinvestment displacement.[22]

The history of urban renewal provides a convenient point to respond to Anderson's view that ideologies that have given undue focus to celebrating (ideologically favored, and specifically non-white) identities have lost sight of the ideal of integration. She wrote, "in our preoccupation with celebrating our particularistic ethnic-racial identities, we have forgotten the value of identification with a larger, nationwide community. Integration in a diverse society expands our networks of cooperation and provides a steppingstone to a cosmopolitan identity, which offers the prospect of rewarding relations with people across the globe" (Anderson 2010, 2). Anderson's criticism resonates with typical liberal criticisms of multiculturalism and its role in the loss of a common national project and undermining moral universalism in favor of ethnic and racial particularism. And she is not entirely wrong; there are many prominent voices on the Left (some of whom were discussed in this chapter) that do not stop at criticizing troubled integration policies but go on to discard the idea of integration as an ideal. Indeed, some of their critiques embrace pessimistic attitudes toward all interracial relations that openly flirt with the reactionary position that interracial relations should be spurned.[23] Such extreme anti-integrationist views are illiberal and an insult to individual liberty and equal human dignity; they also dispense bad advice to people in need and in search of the potential opportunities that expanded social networks offer. However, contemporary expressions of this morally questionable view are not behind the diminishment of the idea of integration. Integration's undermining falls squarely on race- and class-segregated wealthier communities. They have fiercely resisted integration, and their politicians have abetted community resistance to just social-spatial arrangements. Wealthy and often overwhelmingly liberal municipalities have prioritized redevelopment and profit over housing justice. Likewise, wealthy regions have shirked their share of the responsibility to care for the residents of the cities and suburbs upon which they depend. What is more, all of this shirking of duty, this running away from the imperative of justice, has been aided by the federal government's tepid enforcement of fair housing laws (Pietila 2010; Lipsitz 2011; Rothstein 2017).

Integration Focuses on the Wrong Problem

Legitimacy objections to integration policy lead to another complaint. Those policies wrongly focus on the concentration of the non-white, and, in doing so, do not squarely address the lack of provision of primary goods or access to the institutions of the basic structure of society for displaced populations. By starting with integration, rather than the injustice in the spatial distribution of primary goods, integration as a guiding ideal for housing policy focuses on the wrong problem (Young 1999, 245; 2000, 217). Margery Austin Turner and Xavier de Souza Briggs make this point in their analysis of the results of the MTO demonstration:

A change of address alone will never compensate for the major structural barriers low-skilled people face in our economy: the absence of crucial supports for work, such as universal health care and high-quality child care, or persistent inequalities in public education. And initiatives that promote housing mobility should

not substitute for investing in the revitalization of distressed
communities; both place-based and people-based strategies
should be vigorously pursued. (Turner and Briggs 2008, 1)

The focus then on moving people and dismantling poor
communities is a serious distraction that creates what Andre
M. Perry calls a "deficit perspective." This perspective encourages
the attitude that people in an underresourced area, and the area
itself, are not worth investment or reinvestment. The attitude that
value cannot be added to a poor, segregated neighborhood and the
residents, most often poor Blacks and Latinos, are not worth the investment is encouraged (Perry 2020, 38–39). What this boils down
to, according to Perry's searing critique, is a racist devaluation of
people and the places they live (Perry 2020, 53).

What is more, for some of the individuals and families involved
in contemporary mobility programs, the promised benefits do not
pan out, and the opportunity costs for participation were too high
to participate (Briggs 2005c, 316–317). As a vision of integration,
demographic evenness and mobility are not moral imperatives.
As a policy, it is insufficient because it cannot help everyone who
is needful of fair and affordable housing and arguably contributes
to the deterioration of neighborhoods left behind (Goetz 2018,
59–61).

These views collect a variety of objections to the ideas of integration as residential demographic evenness and mobility. So why hold
on to the idea of integration? Visions of integration are alluring for
those peering in from the outside of communities marked by concentrated disadvantage and for those of urban elites who enjoy the
pleasures of a diverse urban environment—the food, public transportation, cosmopolitanism, progressive values and attitudes, and
the global, experimental mashups of music, art, and fashion that
result. These elites-*cum*-integrationists are situated to enjoy the
cultural products of the formerly marginalized as they lift them up
through the example of their middle-class bourgeois lifestyles. All

of this is unnecessary and not what one hears when one listens to
the demands of those facing eviction or the costs of unaffordable
housing; instead, one hears claims for affordable, safe, and decent
housing, community development, and equitable housing and
urban policy. The demand is a call for justice and reconstruction
and not the integration of housing policy bureaucrats.

What, then, is the alternative to integration? Integration is an inclusive but tainted ideal, while desegregation is flat and procedural.
It offers no more direction than a "We're Open" sign. It might be a
motivating ideal enough for those that prioritize liberty, equal opportunity, and at least formal democratic equality, but it does not
indicate support for corrective justice for the enduring harms of
state-sponsored residential segregation. This is a severe challenge
to the legitimacy and basic worthiness of the idea of integration.
Answering it is the task of the next chapter.

6

Reconstructing Integration

What Remains of Integration

What remains of the value and ideal of integration? The term has lost some of its resonance, except, perhaps, in debates about the ethnic and racial composition of K–12 schools. It was an appropriate demand in American civil rights movements from post-Reconstruction through at least a decade after the passage of the Fair Housing Act in 1968, when the United States struggled to end formal racial segregation across its major social, economic, and political institutions. Its appeal to the local communities that have borne the brunt of segregation has grown weak, and for some, it provokes cynical dismissal or even antipathy (Cashin 2004). This is the sentiment that James Baldwin communicated in his question, "Do I really *want* to be integrated into a burning house?" (1993, 94).

Instead of organizing under the banner of integration, civil rights proponents have focused on equal rights and protection, substantive opportunity, distributive justice, and rectifying deep and enduring injustice. Integration as an idea and value conceived in terms of demographic evenness, mobility, dispersion, and dismantling ghettos no longer fits—if it ever did—after the national ordeal over it. This is the conclusion that Paul C. Taylor arrived at, when he wrote that the idea of integration might be phenomenologically inadequate for our time. It falls flat and fails to represent our problems accurately and account for how we live our lives, how we collectively experience what he calls "shared problem-spaces," and what just social-spatial arrangements are required (Taylor

2013). Taylor captured its inadequacy; the term "integration" as a social virtue has dimmed in its contemporary fit, but despite his insightful diagnosis of the social life of the word, its pull has not entirely receded.

The inadequacies of past integration frameworks and policies should be acknowledged but call it what you will; the idea of integration directs our attention to a valuable ideal. Integration is not the bogus ideal of cities whose neighborhoods look like a demographic checkerboard or a chocolate chip cookie. It is not an urban version of Edward Hick's painting of the peaceable kingdom. Instead, it is a social and political value that signals democratic communication and open communities and opportunities. Integration as openness is consistent in a pluralist society with a wide range of forms of social organization, including group dispersion and clustering. It is compatible with individual and group-based preferences to stay put, insofar as the requirement of open communities tempers that right. The United States, and I would hazard any pluralist liberal democracy, ought not to quit the idea. Integration, however, needs reconstruction.

Indeed, suppose we reach back into the history of America's failures to deliver on the promise of equal rights, citizenship, and racial justice at the end of the Civil War. In that case, the idea of "reconstruction" represents a worthy but unfulfilled civic goal. Like "integration," "reconstruction" denotes a process, but one of transformation through repair, rebuilding, and public reaffirmation of the common good rather than demographic blending.[1] In the American context, reconstruction is as much backward-looking as forward-looking; the term rings with the remembrance of the consequences of national obligations compromised and abandoned during the Reconstruction era, the effects of which remain crucial to addressing injustice in social-spatial arrangements. For that matter, it is a suitable way to conceive of justice of social-spatial arrangements, and perhaps even social justice, in nonideal theory.

It is a reminder that integration for the black civil rights movement meant equal rights, fair access to opportunity, and political power. As Charles Hamilton and Kwame Ture wrote in *Black Power*, the meaning of integration was distorted by racist and sexualized fears of black people: "To many of them, it means black men wanting to marry white daughters; it means "race mixing"—implying bed or dance partners" (Hamilton and Ture 1992, 37). In their piercing critique, the fear of integration was a fear of blackness and racial replacement. However, as Hamilton and Ture note, integration "has meant," for black Americans, "a way to improve their lives—economically and politically" (37).[2] On the point of material conditions, and access to rights and resources, Hamilton and Ture's take on integration is consistent with King's call for an economic bill of rights for the poor. King's economic bill of rights included increases in school funding, apprenticeship programs for trades and vocational education, the creation of welfare and tenant unions, housing policy reforms to end discrimination and segregation, and the integration of neighborhoods and businesses so that black Americans could pursue their preferences and live where they liked.[3]

Therefore, understanding integration in light of the goals of reconstruction is a return to its liberal and democratic core. The reconstruction of integration must lock onto the deep and enduring injustices behind the history of social-spatial segregation and commit to a pragmatic approach that emphasizes reinvestment and rebuilding rather than dispersion and demolition of American communities.[4] It is a reinterpretation of an irksome term that meets Taylor's phenomenological adequacy condition; it addresses the present housing crisis while being aware of the enduring challenge of the past and the pressing needs of a just American future. This chapter spells out what that means, what integration as reconstruction entails, what it does not, and how it responds to objections motivated by the ordeal of integration.

Integration as Reconstruction

Integration, viewed as reconstruction, concentrates on individual liberty to access opportunity and to open all communities to support that broad normative and practical goal. It emphasizes the conditions under which integration might occur and be sustained. These conditions include equality in social-spatial arrangements, distributive justice, particularly in the form of open communities and substantive opportunity, and corrective justice. They are collectively consistent with individual liberty; indeed, they increase the worth of those liberties by enabling mobility to access opportunity in addition to equitable community development.

Integration as reconstruction contrasts with the conceptions of integration assumed by those Shelby calls the "new integrationists." It is not preoccupied with demographic evenness as a norm for spatial arrangements, and it certainly does not sanction the thwarting of the choices of those who suffer from economic and housing precarity to coerce them into participating in mobility programs. Nor does it hold that the term "integration" or the ideal it points to is magical, as if it were a special "catalyst for justice" to be wielded paternalistically in a cultural reformist cause, as Michael Merry criticized it (2021).

Additionally, integration as reconstruction agrees with the essential points that desegregation is imperative, but integration (as evenness and dispersion) is not, and the objection that compelling such a view of integration is illegitimate. However, it does not cede claim to the idea and ideal of integration to those grievances.

Compare this view of integration with Shelby's summation of his criticisms of integration. Concerning the question of whether black Americans specifically should integrate, Shelby writes that "blacks, including poor blacks, should be free to self-segregate in neighborhoods, and this practice is not incompatible with justice." His view leads to an endorsement of a position he calls "egalitarian pluralism" that, according to Shelby, "requires desegregation, social equality, and, importantly, economic fairness. It does not require residential integration. Nor does it oppose it. It does not proscribe voluntary self-segregation in neighborhoods. Nor does it call for it" (Shelby 2016, 67).

The reconstruction view of integration affirms individual residential choices and access to substantive opportunities to realize their preferences. It stands against civic exclusion. It reflects the egalitarian as well as pluralist features of Shelby's and Merry's positions. Likewise, it does not oppose voluntary clustering, concentration, or other place-based expressions of homophily. However, in contrast to Merry's view (2013, 2021), it does invite integration. This invitation recognizes the harms of segregation and the social, democratic, and economic benefits of increased opportunity, intergroup exposure, and democratic communication. Indeed, integration as reconstruction would be what john powell called *true* integration. Drawing on King's distinction between the mere physical proximity of desegregation and the spiritual affinity of integration, powell writes,

> True integration moves beyond desegregation—beyond removing legal barriers and simply placing together students of different races. It means bringing students together under conditions of equality, emphasizing common goals, and deemphasizing interpersonal competition. Because segregation creates a culture of racial hierarchy and subordination, true integration requires community-wide efforts to dismantle that culture and to create a more inclusive educational system and a more inclusive society in which all individuals and groups have real, equal opportunities to build and participate in the democratic process. (powell 2005, 297–298)

Powell's "true integration" affirms effective equal liberties, democratic equality, and open opportunity. The need and desire for the invitation to true integration, to integration as reconstruction, is

seen, for example, in community art projects such as the Folded
Map Project. That ongoing community-engaged art project
combines civic art, activism, and community building to illustrate
the social alienation and economic disparities wrought by social-
spatial segregation through literally folded maps of Chicago and related art projects.[5] Projects like that are examples of much-needed
civic rituals and shared spaces that conjure viable civic affinities.[6]

Community Development

Another option generally supported by neo-desegregationists is
prioritizing community development for locales negatively affected by discriminatory segregation policies and underinvestment and disinvestment. This is a sensible and necessary goal
for advocates of American reconstruction, but it cannot happen
without reconstructing cities and towns. Not every poor resident
of an area affected by hypersegregation and concentrated disadvantage can be relocated to a middle-class neighborhood. For
one thing, there is not enough affordable housing to accommo-
date such resorting; secondly, there is good reason to doubt the
political feasibility of such a policy, and, of course, it goes without
saying that it would be met with communal and national dissen-
sion (Goetz 2000, 2003; Ludwig et al. 2014). Mobility programs
are not the solution for most individuals and families seeking to
work their way out of integrational poverty and context immobility, and those programs do not address the needs of sites of concentrated disadvantage. If mobility solutions are the only solutions
the nation accepts, the result will be the continued abandonment
of people and places. Therefore, instead of pursuing integration as
individual mobility to opportunity, the goal of reconstruction and
integration through community development is to bring resources
and opportunities to communities guided by the ideals of moral
and democratic equality and distributive and corrective justice,

especially to those marked by concentrated disadvantage (Goetz 2018; Perry 2020).

As with all housing policies, there are real concerns about the efficacy of community development programs. Those shortcomings should be mitigated in the formulation of housing policy, which includes reasonable caveats about economic, demographic, and environmental sustainability connected to the necessities of shrinking cities. Nonetheless, for many practical reasons, including feasibility, affordability, and, most importantly, the preferences of some residents of segregated, underresourced neighborhoods to stay put, investing in people in their chosen communities is an element of spatial justice.

Shifting the focus to community development does not mean that "group empowerment" or "community-level" programs should replace mobility programs. Developing a neighborhood may improve local conditions, but those improvements would not necessarily benefit the needful individuals targeted in those neighborhoods because of general mobility patterns.[7] There has been significant demographic turnover in some neighborhoods that were formerly majority black and targeted by redlining, so much so that, in those areas, the black population is no longer the majority.[8]

These limits aside, Edward Goetz affirms the requirement of local development with his call for "affirmatively furthering community development," a play on the phrase "affirmatively furthering fair housing" from the second condition of the Fair Housing Act (Goetz 2018, 31). Goetz's call is consistent with new multimodal approaches to community development favored by housing and urban policy experts, such as participatory design, equitable development, and reinvestment (Briggs 2005b). It is a reasonable approach that reaches for reconstructive justice by caring for residents where they are and providing the basis for increased opportunity within neighborhoods and individual mobility for those that choose to move in search of other opportunities. Affirmatively furthering community development serves justice in social-spatial arrangements and is necessary for reconstructing neighborhoods, communities, and society.

An example of a set of policy recommendations that envision what such a reconstruction might look like is laid out by Andre Perry. He provides an example of a group of policy recommendations reimagining urban reconstruction, particularly in black neighborhoods. His view is striking and reflects Goetz's multimodal and powell's "targeted universalism" approach.[9] He urges planners and developers to go beyond the usual focus of developing places and instead invest in communities. Perry's focus on communities means turning away from only addressing "vacant lots, affordable housing, propping up storefronts, and creating bike lanes" (Perry 2020, 75). He writes that envisioning community development merely as "[r]ehabbing a bunch of buildings in the hope of prosperous tenants falls short of the kind of investments Black communities need, particularly in a business district" (75). Instead, he urges communities to "buy back the block" and invest in the community, which, in his view, "represents people who share a culture, history, traditions, all of which are held in neighborhoods, towns, and cities" (76). Doing so entails "constructing spaces that nurture human potential" through the development of the local economy and educational resources and opportunities and engaging "real estate developers and planners to think holistically about financing, self-determinism, and claiming space" (76). It is a pragmatic vision in keeping with the broad reconstructive view of justice in social-spatial arrangements mapped out in the first two chapters. Giving priority to equitable community development confronts the historical problems related to gentrification. Its recommendations offer an alternative to narrow conceptions of integration and the dismantling of communities. Doing so avoids the perils of the third objection to integration (that the ordeal of integration magnifies its illegitimacy) because it is responsive to those claims and does not conceive of integration as merely the achievement of demographic evenness or through the goals of mobility programs. Likewise, it learns from the fourth objection (integration focuses on the wrong problem) by linking integration to the possibilities that reconstruction opens.

Mobility

Just as integration as reconstruction does not deny the value of investing in communities, it does not deny the potential goods of greater diversity in neighborhoods and cities and the potential benefit of families in supporting their mobility. Mobility programs as a whole did not fail. The positive outcomes, while not overwhelming, are significant for the participating families, many of whom are eager and needful of high-quality housing in safer and better-resourced neighborhoods (Chetty and Hendren 2015; Chetty, Hendren, and Katz 2016).[10]

All the same, mobility programs have thwarted the choices of the ghetto poor. First, African Americans relocating were segregated into specific neighborhoods; in San Francisco, for example, this included the Western Addition, Fillmore, Bay View, and Hunters Point, and in Oakland, initially, it was West Oakland and then later into portions of East and North Oakland. Urban renewal projects of the 1960s and 1970s displaced many in those communities and pushed them into other ghetto neighborhoods or poor suburbs on the fringes of the Bay Area (Self 2003).[11] Mobility programs, then, using Section 8 vouchers, offered residents a way out of a set of limited choices that often pushed them into other poor neighborhoods, which then reinforced their experience of concentrated poverty—so much so that Rothstein labeled his study of this effect "moving to inequality" (Rothstein 2017; Sampson 2008). The agency of families involved in these programs was thwarted, and their autonomy undermined. Combine these offenses against agency and autonomy with the assumptions of those programs that the mere exposure of the ghetto poor to affluent neighbors along with mere access to more resources would benefit the families (which, again, they primarily do not experience), and what results is a patronizing and poorly administered amelioration that is demeaning and borders on the disrespectful (James 2013; Shelby 2016).

The illegitimacy that haunts mobility programs highlights how it is not integration per se that is the problem but a morally questionable and illegitimate process; indeed, the third and fourth objections are about processes. Opening more and better choices for participating families and providing further resources to assist in their integration into their new communities could improve the operations of mobility programs. Improving mobility programs would pressure cities, regions, and neighborhoods to adopt supportive and inclusive policies by enforcing anti-discrimination laws in housing rentals, sales, and finance. It would require confronting NIMBY resistance from local governments and predominantly white enclaves that fear and reject integration (Briggs 2005a, 2005b; Rosenbaum et al. 2005). This could be implemented with community development strategies to allow interested residents to stay put and access local opportunities. Once again, integration as reconstruction aims to desegregate the geography of opportunity and integrate it.

Opening up access to middle-class or affluent neighborhoods, in cities and suburbs, by fully enforcing fair housing laws and developing affordable housing for more individuals and families who desire to live in those locations is in keeping with the demands of equality and liberty of the participants. Opening communities is legitimate and does not run afoul of the four objections to integration. Moreover, the preponderance of the evidence shows majority support and preference among all Americans for diverse neighborhoods (Ellen 2001; Charles 2005; Turner and Ross 2005; Apgar and Calder 2005; Reardon et al. 2015).[12] This attitudinal trend reflects, by some estimations, decreasing levels of segregation in American communities (Glaeser and Vigdor 2021). Giving individuals who seek to leave sites of concentrated disadvantage or even less affluent areas for places with more wealth and opportunities hardly thwarts their choices. Opening such neighborhoods to desegregation integrates all involved through ordinary processes.

Civic Affinities

Making social-spatial arrangements more just, opening up communities, and increasing the ability of individuals to pursue their preferences and access more opportunities are necessary elements of any scheme of reconstruction. Likewise, it increases the likelihood of building and repairing civic affinities across a wide swath of society. Integration as reconstruction applies across a large number of American cities and towns, and it envisions open communities and increased access to opportunity and conditions for democratic communication. It responds to standard objections to integration by recommending a wide array of solutions, including community development and support for mobility through its focus on open communities and substantive opportunity. The reconstruction of social-spatial arrangements in the United States paves the way for the future of whatever integration might be or mean for America.

As such, a large portion of the benefit of integration as reconstruction is distributive: access to institutions, primary goods, the means for individuals and families to engender basic and advanced capabilities, and the opportunities that flow from such access. But its value also rests in the interpersonal and transpersonal connections that support social capital building (Putnam 2007, 2015; Enos 2017).[13] Although mobility-focused integration programs have mixed results, participating individuals and families experience improved access to economic opportunities and educational outcomes (Briggs 2005a; Rosenbaum, De Luca, and Tuck 2005).

These improvements are evidence of the positive consequences of integration programs and their potential for bolstering civic communication and democratic culture (Jois 2007). We should not be numb to those benefits. Liberal democratic societies are systems of social cooperation. As such, they have an interest in encouraging integration and arranging, through policy and material design, its social spaces in a manner that buttresses liberal and democratic values (Rawls 1999a, 17; 2001, 5; Anderson 2010a, 112–117). While there may be no imperative to achieve patterns of demographic evenness in residence, it is imperative to reconstruct our social-spatial arrangements to meet the requirements of justice.

A benefit of this position is that it recovers integration from narrow conceptions of the term without abandoning the obvious social benefits of a broad open vision of the society it communicates. Interpersonal and group integration as interaction or blending may happen, or not, under these conditions. But first, open up communities and opportunities, and then integration will occur among those who choose it. Thus, integration as reconstruction strikes a laissez-faire position on the deeper, more interpersonal, and affective forms of integration. Still, it is reasonably confident that the generation of interpersonal or even spiritual affinities will generally occur as a function of individuals enacting their liberties and freely making market choices under just conditions. Integration as reconstruction is expressly not a zero-sum political aspiration, and it demands outcomes concerned with moral and democratic equality and distributive and corrective justice.

Outcomes, Not Conversion

Integration as reconstruction pragmatically concentrates on outcomes rather than conversion. Reconstructing the United

States' social-spatial arrangements for democratic equality and distributive and corrective justice should not wait on society-wide attitudinal shifts or the generation of spiritual affinities. The demand for justice and equal citizenship should not tarry on the mass conversion of any particular group of Americans. Voluntary shifts in attitudes about race and class that support justice in social-spatial arrangements, for example, on the right to housing or access to affordable housing, would without a doubt be valuable in support of the full enforcement of the Fair Housing Act, open communities and substantive opportunity, a right to housing, and corrective justice. Likewise valuable is moral suasion by civil society groups urging supportive attitude shifts concerning reconstructive reforms. Yet the pursuit of integration and justice in social-spatial arrangements should not hinge on the conversion of Americans. As Samuel Beckett so entertainingly taught us, expecting otherwise is absurd and is a setup for cynicism and despair, or worse, unconstrained illiberal demands for ideological conversion.[14]

Integration in the reconstructive view is motivated by respecting the autonomy of those suffering economic inequality and housing precarity. That regard for individual liberty does not dissipate in advocacy for open opportunities and communities, even, for example, in the face of objections concerning cultural loss. Citizens should have access to public resources, be treated equally in the housing market, and expect that their cities and neighborhoods will not be subjected to race-based disinvestment. They should be able to exercise their right to move, and, if needed, receive aid from mobility programs to secure decent housing fit for human life. None of these things should hinge on their affirmation of any creed, ideological or otherwise; likewise, neither should it be linked to the ideological conversion of others.

One might have good reason to be skeptical that reconstruction will work without such conversions, that we will not have "true" integration or reconstructive justice without a tremendous, supportive shift in public and political culture about racial identifications in the United States. Integrationists cannot easily dismiss the urge to call for the sort of deeply personal moral integration that conversion invites, because of the nearness in connection of social relations to civic goods and virtues.[15] Indeed, a high degree of moral recognition and integration across the primary institutions of society may be required for the successful enactment of reciprocity, but the attitudes, affectations, and rites associated with conversion, a practice most associated with the Abrahamic faiths, is materially irrelevant to achieve justice. A call from the moral heights to repent of one's sins and alter one's view of goods and ends—including conceptions of identity thick with controversial ontological claims about race, ethnicity, and culture—has the additional flaw of being perceived as an arrogant imposition by other groups (or, worse, the state) on privately and closely held conceptions of the good and comprehensive doctrines. Such altar calls have the associated vices of being patronizing and condescending, and the epistemological presumptuousness that one possesses the gospel truth about the ethical, social, and political matters that divide the nation. This is not a winning strategy—one that will result in reconstructive justice, much less integration—in appealing to those whose cultural and moral references are not those of the progressive Left (Haidt 2012, 297).

Conversion can be understood in several ways. It can be an epistemological process where the subject accepts a set of dogmas, or they have a profoundly moving affective experience that leads them to embrace some ideology or practice. Both are characterized by inward and outward volition, a will to believe, feel, or even simply practice. Religious or quasi-religious conversions, such as these, are a legitimate matter of private and communal life, to be freely chosen or declined, but it should not be set as a precondition for integration or any other facet of social justice. Alternatively, there is a type of conversion that does not involve the acceptance of dogma or assuredness of feeling but is instead a *metanoia* characterized by the realization of not knowing or lack of certainty, as is depicted, for example, in Plato's dialogue, *Laches*, that simply invites further inquiry for some yet-to-be-revealed ultimate truth.[16] Conversion as metanoia is a self-emptying of sorts, a *kenosis*, that opens one up to ongoing dialogue but does not demand the declaration of a credo.[17] It is a form of conversion congruous with liberal principles, from the egalitarian to the libertarian, for two reasons. First, some version of metanoic conversion is consistent with liberal theory in its most basic form as an exercise of public reason and moral suasion. Second, the crucial epistemological humility associated with metanoic conversion within social contexts intrinsically involves recognizing fundamental moral equality.

The position taken here contrasts with those who link integration, as King and Baldwin did, to the transformation of Americans' attitudes (or souls), particularly of white Americans.[18] Iris Marion Young's politics of difference with its call for a cultural revolution and Sharon Stanley's explicit call for conversion reflect this position (Young 1990, 238–241; Stanley 2017, 61–62). If conversion is materially irrelevant, politically imprudent, and its requirement by the state is normatively illegitimate, then what is left to say? The argument for conversion is worth an extended analysis because it casts a stark contrast between the reconstruction view and the postures taken by what the journalist Matt Yglesias has arrestingly labeled as the "great awokening."[19]

In the book *Justice and the Politics of Difference*, Iris Marion Young offered up an ideal of city life that has been influential in urban theory, just as her critique of the distributive paradigm has been prominent in debates about theories of justice (Young 1990, 238).[20] Young envisions city life as brimming with different activities and different people, interacting and intersecting, in common conditions where each affects the lives of all in some measure.[21] Her idea of the city, which she initially called the "being together of strangers," emphasizes a general idea of mutual togetherness and solidarity, which she later relabeled as "together in difference" and then as "differentiated solidarity" (Young 1999, 245; 2000, 221).

She argues, drawing heavily on Jane Jacob's *The Death and Life of Great American Cities*, that city life approximates an ideal version when it features four virtues: (1) social differentiation without exclusion, (2) variety, (3) eroticism, and (4) publicity (Young 1990, 238–241).

Those virtues help explain what is off about a view of integration too tied to evenness and mobility. The first virtue, social differentiation without exclusion, is about affirming group differences that are not expected to be, in Young's words, "dissolved" into the whole while not excluding others from passing through, enjoying, or sharing the space a group inhabits. In her ideal of difference and ethnic neighborhoods, or neighborhoods marked by some other difference (e.g., religion, gender, race, sexuality), the borders between groups and communities are "open and undecidable" (Young 1990, 239). The second virtue, variety, is about precisely that in shops, offices, parks, bars, and so on. It also would feature and emphasize diversity in population, so her ideal is not consistent with segregated neighborhoods or cities. It gets at what urbanists hope to achieve in promoting inclusionary zoning and multiuse spaces. The third virtue, eroticism, simply reflects the experience and pleasure of being around others.[22] Her final virtue, publicity, is about being seen, interacting, and being among each other in a wide variety of public spaces. Young's take on publicity is the activity of the flaneur. It makes their sauntering a public virtue. Her idea of publicity is not about a unification in a common and rational deliberative space focused on civic affairs or incorporation of the public into some ideal civic body that we are metaphysically transported to when we reflect on the political; or in her words, it is not about "becoming unified in a community of 'shared final ends'" (Young 1990, 240). In contrast to the idea of national or civic unity, it is about being seen, interacting, and being among each other in public and within our differences in public spaces.

Likewise, Young is remarkably silent on whether all that being together of strangers will make those strangers more familiar and whether the eros that motivates or results from that being together will lead to the intersecting, blending, or even erasure of differences. She presumes that differentiated solidarity will preserve differences and thus concludes that being among each other within our differences does not require integration and that integration is inconsistent with differentiated being together. However, Young objects to integration as residential demographic evenness and, to some degree, the superficial ends of mobility programs (Young 1999, 243; 2000, 216). She did not consider alternative conceptions of integration, so it may very well be that her concept of differentiated solidarity is consistent with alternative versions, such as the reconstructionist view, but only insofar as it is separable from her overall politics of difference with its call for the cultural revolution that infringes on individual liberties.[23]

Overall, Young's "differentiated solidarity" ideal is best-suited for proponents of the politics of difference who focus on city life to the exclusion of a more comprehensive view of justice and social-spatial arrangements. However, spatial justice is not and should not be primarily about city life, and its demands are not satisfied by related calls for the "right to the city." Additionally, Young's differentiated solidarity primarily addresses the flaneur class, the "creative class," and what David Goodhart called the "anywheres" as opposed to "somewheres," whose mobility choices were more constrained (Goodhart 2017). Taking the concept of differentiated solidarity as a whole and as a normative claim, only the first (social differentiation without exclusion) and the fourth (publicity) are requirements of social-spatial justice. Indeed, those two ideas do not put distance between "differentiated solidarity" and integration; instead, they are consistent with Anderson's, if not Fiss's, vision of integration. What "differentiation without exclusion" and publicity look like in open communities is an integrated community that respects liberty and democratic equality and strives for substantive opportunity and the provision of resources necessary for justice in social-spatial arrangements.

In contrast with Young's version of solidarity, integration as re-construction shares much with Stanley's view of integration despite the difference over conversion. As discussed in this book, Stanley holds that society has an imperative to establish a just society but that groups do not have an imperative to integrate. However, Stanley goes on to argue that for integration to work, what is required is conversion on the part of white Americans, and the process she has proposed has more in common with the creedal sort than *metanoia* and involves intensive interrogation of white-ness and the relinquishment by white Americans of racial privilege and supremacy.[24]

The model of integration that Stanley settles on is understood as a process rather than an end state and has five elements (Stanley 2017, 121):

1. It does not insist on assimilation.
2. Nor does it demand the dissolution of groups, and specifically black spaces and institutions.
3. It requires the establishment of mutual respect that is more than what she calls a "veneer" of politeness that protects "mythic white innocence."
4. It requires conversion on the part of whites, which means that they are called to "transform" themselves and "relinquish" their claim to "superior citizenship."
5. And it reconciles group (largely black) power with integration.

Stanley's model's first, second, and fifth elements are consistent with the reconstruction view. However, on the final point regarding "group power," there is reason to doubt that we can talk coher-ently about the power of any ethnic or racial group in a manner that assumes it is singular, that obscures cross-cutting interests and perspectives, or that casts the issue in dichotomous black-white terms (Sundstrom 2008). The fifth element is unobjectionable when applied to private associations. However, it does not assume that ethnic or racial groups are effectively unified and possess and express a singular power. Integration as reconstructive justice is consistent with forming associations, parties, and sects. The third and fourth elements are remarkable, however, because they are politically perfectionist.[25]

Stanley draws on Baldwin's view of white racial innocence and his stark demands of recognition to tie the social and political goal of integration to what she calls the "psychic transformation" of white people. The psychic transformation she imagines, in turn, supports and makes way for the other elements of her model, such as the redistribution of power, as seen in the other items of her model. Stanley characterizes the process of psychic conversion like this:

> By internal transformation, I mean that individuals in a truly integrated society would experience a new sense of self, and a new relationship to other, particularly others from whom they had previously felt great social distance. I use the concept of conversion to capture the profundity and radical nature of this transformation. (Stanley 2017, 42)

She elaborates on this conversion experience by drawing on Danielle Allen's (2004) analysis of Elizabeth Eckford's experience integrating Little Rock High School in 1957 and agreeing with Allen's view that successful integration necessitates that whites surrender their "posture of dominance" and recognize blacks as equal participants in the school and society (43). The conversion process obligates whites (based on the demands of justice) to relinquish their claim to and posture of superior citizenship. It requires blacks to accept this relinquishment (50–56, 61–66). Whites are obligated to relinquish white power, and blacks are not bound to accept their conversion in Stanley's account. That acceptance needs, I take it, to be earned. Substantial majorities of whites and blacks need to be involved for true integration to proceed. Stanley calls for even more.

She agrees with Kaplan and Valls's argument for national civic recognition of the United States' racial wrongs, but she calls for internal transformation along with rightful behavior. Conversion for whites, according to Stanley, involves the following:

> to cease to demand abjection and humiliation from others is simultaneously to abandon one's own pose of arrogance and domination, of isolation and sovereignty. It is to recognize, furthermore, how the experience of freedom and self-sovereignty felt by many whites was essentially built upon the denial of those very possibilities to blacks, how white security depended upon black insecurity. (63)

And this conversion is to be followed by whites taking steps to show blacks that they have relinquished their white privileges (64). These steps include "seeking out black testimony, listening sincerely and actively to it, and making affirmative statements that they have learned from it and been changed by it," joining "movements committed to black equality," and "actively and openly seeking to educated and ultimately convert the not-yet-converted" (64).

If by internal or psychic transformation or conversion, Stanley means *metanoia* with whites accepting the status and political equality of racial others through moral suasion or witnessing stark racial injustice and the rise of a protest movement to counter that injustice, I concur with her. Optimistically, there is evidence of such transformation in attitudinal surveys that show a decline in race-based antipathy or beliefs about racial inferiority. However, there is wide disagreement about the state of racial equality and the incidences, depth, and causes of inequality.[26] Stanley, however, means more than a general improvement; she means psychic conversion. However, given the particular content of her version of true integration, conversion involves affirming contestable attitudes and beliefs about the nature of racial identity. It also requires accepting and experiencing a type of guilt that is even more demanding than what is asked for by actual faith-based calls for coalition politics and national reconstruction.[27]

Such altar calls for "true integration" and conversion are not realistic or even worthy as a goal. Stanley is correct, however, that most degrees of integration, and even desegregation, require lessening implicit and absence of explicit hostility and intense distrust. The expectation of moral recognition and reciprocity is consistent with integration as reconstruction. It is concordant with Ture and Hamilton's clear conception of integration as access to power and a wary version of Baldwin's integration: we can proceed with broadly social integration without having ceremonies of public confession and conversion (Hamilton and Ture 1992). National narratives of national historical wrongs, responsibility, and progress are valuable, and the elements outlined in the reconstruction view of justice in social and spatial arrangements are required. Still, expressive and performative bonfires of guilt are not. If white people who are into that sort of thing want to have a collective come-to-Jesus moment, more power to them, but it should not be coerced and should not undermine the goals of justice for all.

As stated earlier, perfectionist political demands are hubristic, irrelevant, illiberal, and likely ineffectual. Additionally, the call for conversion has three additional flaws. It centers on whiteness, is reactionary, and is insufficient. First, hinging integration to the mass conversion of white people puts them back into the center of the United States' racial life. White people are obviously important to the future of U.S. racial politics; saying otherwise would be silly, but they and their attitudes are not the only factors. Whether whites "convert" or blacks "accept" any conversions will be affected by the public stances of leading figures of other groups in the United States and the attitudes of those groups. As I noted elsewhere about the black-white binary:

The future of race in the United States, or elsewhere, will not be determined solely through the American instinct to return to black-white politics—as if the questions of the conservation or elimination of race and racial justice is in the hands of whites and blacks who need to hash out their issues for the sake of all of us. That somehow American racial problems are primarily black and white problems is the conceit of too many Americans.[28]

Many possible scenarios play out interracial and interethnic alliances and conflicts, which may result in varied integration patterns. What blacks and whites do will be very important. Still, they are not the only actors in this drama—and it will play out at the day-to-day and national level not only in the domain of affect, expressions of sincerity, and the recognition of embodied knowing but primarily in the realm of individual and local group interests. This is unavoidably clear if one considers this issue from the political realities of California and other states that reflect its demographic diversity. Thinking otherwise reduces other groups to passive witnesses on the sideline of the white-black struggle.

Second, the call for conversion is reactionary in a way that connects to its illiberalism. To ask the fallen or strayed to convert to the truth-the-light-and-the-way (whichever ideology or system one plugs into that variable) is all well and good. But asserting that the integration of groups into national life hinges on the conversion of whites is illiberal. It is not technically illiberal since Stanley is *not* promoting the compulsion of conversion. But Stanley's formulation of white conversion is cause for concern because it runs against the grain of liberal and republican conceptions of reasonable pluralism and the recognition of personal and, to a lesser extent, group autonomy. Talk of conversion moves the discussion from politics to the ontological claims about racial identity and thus makes political agreement less realistic, overlapping, and intellectually appetizing. It carries the political discourse away from public reason and to *gnosis* and, in doing so, is admittedly exciting and attractive to radical-purist-absolutist temperaments. It falls, however, into the trap of what Eric Voegelin criticized as eschatological political theory and ersatz religion (Voegelin [1968] 2012).[29]

An ersatz religious liturgy of white conversion would be entertainingly performative, but building a political theory of integration on that demand would land that theory in the realm of perfectionist political theory built on the politics of white guilt. Focusing on the state of conversion, its degrees, and its authenticity is a distracting sideshow or, worse, a distorting exercise of what Olúfẹ́mi Táíwò (2022) named elite capture. Although it might appeal to a type of progressive white elite, it distracts from the principal work of distributive justice, building egalitarian conditions, and the procedural and bureaucratic policy and legal work such amelioration would require.

Consider, for example, the comments of former mayor of Minneapolis, Minnesota, Betsy Hodges, after the protests reacting to the murder of George Floyd. She stated that the white liberals she represented favored performances of solidarity—what she calls "illusion of change"—over systemic reforms. On questions relating to policies that would lead to more inclusion—or integration by any other name—in schools and housing, those same white progressives, who would trip over themselves responding to an antiracist altar call, say "not in my backyard":

> In Minneapolis, the white liberals I represented as a Council member and mayor were very supportive of summer jobs programs that benefited young people of color. I also saw them fight every proposal to fundamentally change how we provide education to those same young people. They applauded restoring funding for the rental assistance hotline. They also signed petitions and brought lawsuits against sweeping reform to zoning laws that would promote housing affordability and integration.[30]

White support in those cities for Black Lives Matter, insofar as it is indicative of conversion, does not represent the necessary transformative or reconstructive reform. How often must predominantly white liberal elites in superstar cities convert to change housing or education policy? Instead of waiting for a Fourth Great Awakening, the imperative for reconstruction ought to be pursued through law and policy for open communities, opportunity, and society.

The reference to Voegelin's concept of ersatz religion was not just to bolster my concern that conversion politics is perfectionist and illiberal; my point is that it is classically reactionary. It is reactionary not because it calls for a return to simpler times but because it shares the same fatal flaw that reactionary political nostalgia has: a *gnostic* understanding and appreciation of some assumed set of ideas, values, and beliefs. It views epistemological conformity and purity (e.g., the shared consciousness of the proletariat and their solidarity) as the key to political harmony. I suspect that white conversion demands not only the rejection of white innocence from political responsibility but also agreement with a particular Left progressive ideological viewpoint and its favored remedies and movements. Such an imagined agreement does not conform to the actual complicated—and often conflicting—interests of blacks, Latinos, Asian Americans, and Native Americans.

Finally, even as Stanley recognizes, white conversion is insufficient. The four other parts of her model are needed and are reflected in the reconstructive view of integration. The point about insufficiency, however, is deeper than that. The Bay Area, for example, has plenty of progressive and liberal whites that agree with at least the rough outlines of the ideas required to mark an authentic white progressive internal transformation. But these same good white people oppose practical policies that would benefit the poor or are essential to black people because of their other progressive principles, not despite those principles. For example, it is the "woke" population in blue states and deep blue districts that fill the ranks of squadrons of Left-NIMBY activists who prevent the building and spread of affordable housing and housing for the homeless in our cities.[31] They seek to prevent shadows from falling on their community gardens or stop the development of high-rise rental units for the sake of their community's character. They do this to mitigate gentrification and fight capitalism and neoliberalism but end up engaging in their versions of Left-progressive exclusions hampering the provision of affordable housing in the Bay Area and other metropolitan areas.[32] The same dynamics can play out in progressive communities around school districts—middle-class families, regardless of race or politics, do not, to paraphrase the cliché, *put their children's future where their mouth is*.[33] These are just examples but serve to illustrate the point that the sort of conversion that Stanley advocates may not help to forward the other elements that make integration possible, and worse, the call to conversion (replete with yard signs, t-shirts, and themed consciousness-raising wellness retreats for affinity groups) may serve as a distraction or provide moral license not to support practical policies that clash with their interests and values. Outcomes in the form of reconstructive justice and actual progress are needed, not spectacles of conversion.

7

Conclusion

Discomfiting Justice

James Baldwin's evocative analogy of the "price of the ticket" to achieve justice is a sharp cue for the cost of achieving justice. For America, to draw on another of Baldwin's phrases, "achieving itself" comes at a discomfiting cost.[1] Project this idea on American neighborhoods, public spaces, towns, and cities, and then one gets a sense of the price of the ticket for justice in social-spatial arrangements.

The price of the ticket is discomfiting to a people who have prided themselves not only on what they build but who and what they keep out. Justice in social-spatial arrangements requires reforms that are discomfiting to those who think that among their rights is the prerogative to keep others out, including their fellow citizens. Justice might be sweet and musical, as Henry David Thoreau held, but it is vertiginously disconcerting when it is genuinely exacted.

Justice requires the recognition of moral and democratic equality of all citizens and legal residents in social-spatial arrangements. Citizens and residents should have the right to housing and, with that, the liberty to move and have equal access to public spaces and fair and equal access to opportunities to move into or stay put, within reasonable limits, in the locales of their choosing. Policies guided by the purposes of distributive justice should bolster the goals of opening communities and increasing fair and equal opportunity. Federal, state, and local governments should support policies that develop communities to meet the needs of people rather than lifestyle perks and accessories that exacerbate economic precarity and housing instability. Likewise, they should fully enforce fair housing laws and pressure every community that draws on public dollars and resources to provide their fair share of affordable housing. Furthermore, those agencies, along with local communities, and in keeping with the ethical and political goals of equal protection, should rectify the enduring effects of state-sponsored segregation.

What practical steps should be taken to satisfy these requirements and the multiple crises wrapped up in the housing crisis discussed in this book? *Just Shelter* focused on the core idea of justice and social-spatial arrangements and its application to gentrification, segregation, integration, and racial justice. It did not fully address every element and topic of justice and social-spatial arrangements that needs it, such as principles guiding environmental sustainability, the ethics of technology concerning urban planning, transportation justice, or the gritty details of policies on abating and addressing homelessness.[2] Those and other topics are legitimate areas of philosophical ethical and political inquiry that should be addressed and are being addressed by social scientists, public policy scholars, and even philosophers worldwide. Of particular importance are close and careful investigations of public policy that aim to address the concerns that I raised in this book.

There is a range of policy proposals and projects underway that deserve social and political support. Still, from the standpoint of ethical and political theory, that support should be tentative and ultimately deferential to assessments of the efficacy and feasibility of those policies and projects. The only policies worth investment, including the social and political as well as economic price, are policies that are efficient, data-driven, forward-leaning, focused on measured outcomes, resistant to ideological capture, and not subject to corruption at every level of government. That a policy seems to accord with the recommendation of a theory of justice is an insufficient reason for its advocacy. What a theory of justice in social-spatial arrangements can and ought to do, however, is provide, clarify, and justify principles that guide just policies and hopefully efficient ones. This pragmatic and experimental approach is responsive to the variability of local to national contexts and conditions. Favorable positions taken by political philosophers and theorists about policies and projects that have not yet been validated through empirical or economic assessment are, at best, a gamble and, worse, mere virtue signaling that could end up supporting ineffectual policy. This pragmatic tentativeness, for example, motivates my moderately negative view of rent control policies.[3]

There are, however, areas of housing policy that need specific targeting to achieve justice in social-spatial arrangements; these areas include fair and affordable housing, reforming land-use policies, the right to housing, homelessness, and rectification for past housing and land-use discrimination. Specific policies include building more housing and involve the vigorous enforcement of anti-discrimination and fair housing laws.[4] This should include a federal ban on discrimination against tenants who receive housing subsidies, such as those provided by the U.S. Section 8 program.

Beyond the building of more housing and the enforcement of fair housing policy, a reasonable right to housing needs to be established. In support of that right, several related policies should be implemented, such as public investment in social housing. Exclusionary zoning should be outlawed in the private housing market. In its place, up-zoning should be required, which would allow the development of multifamily and multistory housing and increase urban density. Also the housing supply should be increased using the tax credit to incentivize the building of affordable and low-income rental housing, the renovation of older properties, and the conversion of commercial buildings into residential ones.[5] And Community Development Block Grants could be used to develop affordable housing, including withholding those funds from communities that refuse or do not meet targets for developing affordable housing.[6] Related reforms should target the housing-lending industry to strengthen and enforce anti-redlining laws and the reform of Fannie Mae and Freddie Mac to serve primarily homeowners' interests rather than those of corporate investors. To help alleviate homelessness, emergency housing should be provided, and each neighborhood in metropolitan areas should be responsible for their fair share of that housing.

On the federal or state level, the state should provide subsidies to support individuals and their rent-burdened families, including those paying more than 30% of their income on rent. Subsidies could include providing tax credits to the poor, working, and lower-middle-class renters in a manner that matches subsidies that homeowners receive through mortgage interest deductions. Alternatively, or concurrently, the United States could experiment with canceling or reducing the mortgage interest deduction and channel the savings to subsidized housing or subsidies for renters. For renters facing eviction, establish the right of legal counsel and reform preexisting just-cause eviction laws.[7]

In addition to all these suggestions, it is necessary to rectify the harms caused by the history of state-sponsored segregation and state-condoned private discrimination in housing and land-use policy. My arguments support race-neutral laws and policies with positive race and class disparate effects to achieve this goal.[8] These policies and proposals exemplify the necessary steps a liberal democratic society that respects its citizens needs to take to reform its social-spatial arrangements to reconstruct a just society that treats its citizens as democratic equals.[9] What is required are practical, constitutionally sound solutions that serve all citizens and residents, reflect the demands of justice, and support local and national structures that will allow the nation to reconstruct America for the good of all.

The need for justice in social-spatial arrangements, particularly the need for fair and affordable housing, is imperative. According to the National Association of Realtors, the United States has built up a 5.5 million housing unit shortfall over the last twenty years. This shortfall affects renters, affordable housing, infrastructure, and the capability of communities to be open and inclusive. To meet this need, the United States, according to that report, needs to build around "550,000 additional new housing units would need to be constructed per year over and above the historical trend of 1.5 million new units annually."[10] Americans need homes, and we have failed to provide them.

What is more and worth repeating is that economic inequality and precarity, and enduring racial injustices, are tied to the housing crisis and that connection reverberates back through centuries of official U.S. racist policies and practices motivated by white supremacy and domination over American Indians, black Americans, and Asian Americans, and other groups that were, with the full knowledge and consent of the government, purposefully denied their basic and civil rights and excluded from equal citizenship and compelled to live apart. While the totalizing barriers of state-sponsored segregation have, for the most part, fallen, the effects are enduring in wealth gaps and rates of economic inequality. Without exaggeration, this history of racist segregation appears in most other indicators used to track individual life chances. There is a geography to opportunity, and in America, race and class overlay that geography. Again, racial segregation is opportunity segregation (powell 2008).

Accommodating this need is a daunting demand. Justice in social-spatial arrangements opens communities to greater pluralism. And that makes some profoundly uncomfortable. Meeting this need is not an essentially discomfiting social demand, although it will be economically and politically costly to society. It will be discomfiting to those who think not only do they have a right to determine the private affairs in their homes but the prerogative to determine who else gets to access their neighborhoods, towns, and cities.

Their discomfort of others does not, however, trump the fundamental dignity of others, even if embedded in concerns about property values, traffic, group preferences or power, and aesthetic matters. This imperative will only become more demanding and more present in everyday lives as global climate change worsens. Each nation will face massive internal migration and international immigration as human beings move in reaction to changing conditions brought on by climate change.[11]

In the face of this present and growing imperative, justice in social-spatial arrangements, when applied to the housing needs of others, requires the implementation (if not the full-throated affirmation) of Yes-In-My-Back-Yard to fair and affordable housing. After decades of concerns about eviction, displacement, and lamenting that the "rent is too damn high," Americans are starting to agree with the sentiment.[12] From the need for inclusive zoning and affordable and fair housing to the burgeoning homelessness, it is a promising but still too quiet omen that more Americans see the need to address these crises.[13] If the grand idea of an American Reconstruction means anything, it means this.

Notes

Introduction

1. Freddie Mac, "The Major Challenge of Inadequate U.S. Housing Supply," December 2018, http://www.freddiemac.com/research/insight/20181205_major_challenge_to_u.s._housing_supply.page.

2. For accounts of the housing crisis in the United States, see Florida, *The New Urban Crisis* (2017). For accounts about the San Francisco Bay Area, see Dougherty, *Golden Gates* (2020); Shellenberger, *San Fransicko* (2021); and Bowles, "How San Francisco Became a Failed City," *The Atlantic*, June 8, 2022, https://www.theatlantic.com/ideas/archive/2022/06/how-san-francisco-became-failed-city/661199/.

3. To understand the overall effects of this housing injustice, especially concerning its connections to policing and unfairness in the criminal justice system, see Rothstein, "The Making of Ferguson: Public Policies at the Root of Its Troubles" (2014).

4. Although the shortage of affordable housing is one part of the homelessness crisis, it is not the only significant factor in that crisis, which involves policy problems and failures relating to mental health treatment, narcotics policies, and addiction treatment. See, for example, the debate about the effectiveness of Housing First programs when used in conjunction with Harm Reduction programs and to address addiction and mental health issues (Kertesz et al. 2009; Tsai 2020; Shellenberger 2021).

5. Rose Kalima and Margaretta Lin, "A Roadmap toward Equity: Housing Solutions for Oakland, California," Policy Link and City of Oakland Department of Housing & Community Development's Strategic Initiatives Unit (2015), https://www.policylink.org/resources-tools/roadmap-toward-equity.

6. I explain the origins of my use of the term "reconstruction" in Chapter 6 (fn. 1) and what I mean by it in Chapters 2 ("Reaching for Transformation") and 6 ("What Remains of Integration"). "Reconstruction" refers, in the U.S. context, to the postbellum era roughly spanning 1863–1877, and I intend that reference and its civic connotations. However, I also draw on

ideas about the normative purpose of social and political reconstruction advanced by W. E. B. Du Bois and John Dewey.

7. On the role of ideal theory in political philosophy, see Rawls, *A Theory of Justice* (1999, 4–5) and Rawls, *Justice as Fairness* (2001, 5 and 24–25). For criticism of ideal theory and advocacy of a nonideal approach, see Anderson, *The Imperative of Integration* (2010, 1–22), and Mills, *Black Rights/White Wrongs* (2017, 72–90).

8. See also Thomas Shapiro, Tatjana Meschede, and Sam Osoro, "The Roots of the Widening Racial Wealth Gap: Explaining the Black-White Economic Divide," Research and Policy Brief (Waltham, MA: Institute on Assets and Social Policy, February 2013), https://heller.brandeis.edu/iere/pdfs/racial-wealth-equity/racial-wealth-gap/roots-widening-racial-wealth-gap.pdf.

9. See Dougherty's *Golden Gates* (2020) and Bowles, "How San Francisco Became a Failed City" (2008) for a depiction and explanation of NIMBY-ism and the rise of the Yes-In-My-Backyard (YIMBY) movement in the San Francisco Bay Area that struggles against local NIMBY politics. See also Macedo (2011), Monkkonen (2016), and Scheutz (2022) for studies of the effects of NIMBY-ism.

Chapter 1

1. This question was Justin Williams's, which he poised in this paper "Shrinking Equitably? Spatial Justice as an Analytic Approach," presented at a workshop on "Justice in the City" hosted by the Philosophy Department at the University of San Francisco in August of 2016. His criticisms of the idea of "spatial justice" influenced my skepticism about the value of the term.

2. Casey J. Dawkins, in *Just Housing* (2021), provides, among other things in his excellent book, a useful explanation and defense of the concept of housing justice. He recognizes that housing justice as a branch or application of distributive justice, as applied to housing, but he also provides a detailed analysis of its history in the United States and its specifics elements.

3. Wacquant's idea of "advanced marginality," from his *Urban Outcasts* (2008), also captures the force and effects of injustice in social-spatial arrangements. That phrase is evocative, but that does not mean that Wacquant's hypothesis about the structural function of the ghetto is correct. Not all the places that are colloquially labeled "ghettos" have the same level of concentrated poverty or disadvantage, nor do they have all the negative social dynamics that he associates with them.

4. Rawls's initial definition of the idea of the basic structure of society was, "By major institutions I understand the political constitution and the principal economic and social arrangements. Thus, the legal protections of the freedom of thought and liberty of conscience, competitive markets, private property in the means of productions, and the monogamous family are examples of major social institutions" (1999, § 2.6, 6–7). In *Justice as Fairness: A Restatement*, he demotes the reference to competitive markets to just an example, and he drops the narrow definition of the family. His revised definition is, "The political constitution with an independent judiciary, the legally recognized forms of property, and the structure of the economy (for example, as a system of competitive markets with private property in the means of production), as well as the family in some form" (2001, §4.1, 10). Rawls also defines "background justice" thusly: "The basic structure is the background social framework within which the activities of associations and individuals take place. A just, basic structure secures what we may call background justice" (2001, §4.1, 10). The idea of the basic structure of society has been the subject of debates about its coherence and limitations. See, for example, Samuel Scheffler's "Is the Basic Structure Basic?" (2010, 129–159).

5. The conception of dignity here is normatively constructivist and is consonant with Waldron's view that it is a status term and "refers to the standing of human beings in the great scheme of things, their status as persons who command a high level of concern and respect" (2017, 3).

6. It is tempting to conceive of the relationship among basic equality, relational equality, and distributive equality as stepped in that order (Scheffler 2003, 31). As Waldron argues, however, this assumption is a mistake because basic equality has distributive implications on its own, as is the case with the right to basic but decent housing (Waldron 1993; 2017, 12, and Chapter 2). My linear ordering of those concepts does not assume that that ordering, in itself, signifies a necessary conceptual dependence.

7. This distinction comes from the fourth point of the Black Panther Party's 10-point program, "What We Want—What We Believe," https://oac.cdlib.org/ark:/28722/bk001532b1j/?brand=oac4. See also Dawkins (2020, 2021) for helpful discussion of *sufficientarian* versus an *egalitarian* view of a right to housing.

8. UN General Assembly, "Universal Declaration of Human Rights" (December 10, 1948), https://www.un.org/en/about-us/universal-declaration-of-human-rights. See Article 25, where it states that housing is one of the things persons must have for an adequate standard of living. See also Waldron, "Homelessness and the Issue of Freedom" (1993); Bratt,

Hartman, and Stone, "Why a Right to Housing Is Needed and Makes Sense: Editors' Introduction" (2006b); Hartman, "The Case for a Right to Housing" (2006); and Dawkins, *Just Housing* (2021).

9. National Housing Task Force, "A Decent Place to Live" (Washington, DC: Department of Housing and Urban Development, 1998). Cited in Bratt et al. (2006b, 4).

10. Anderson writes, "Positively, egalitarians seek a social order in which persons stand in relations of equality. They seek to live together in a democratic community, as opposed to a hierarchical one. Democracy is here understood as collective self-determination by means of open discussion among equals, in accordance with rules acceptable to all. To stand as an equal before others in discussion means that one is entitled to participate, that others recognize an obligation to listen respectfully and respond to one's arguments, that no one need bow and scrape before others or represent themselves as inferior to others as a condition of having their claim heard" (1999, 313). For comparison, see the accounts of social egalitarianism by David Miller (1997), Samuel Scheffler (2003, 2015), and Christian Schemmel (2015).

11. The aspects of equal relations that are concentrated on here are equal concern and status equality, and that legitimate differences in status must be justified in light of equal concern. As Scanlon argues, equal concern is about reasons and not attitudes, because differences in levels of concern must be justified by the affected parties (2018, 21). Justice-based relational equality has implications for affective and psychological relations, but such relations are not subject to governmental administration, unlike the status of equal citizenship, which is legitimately administered.

12. In "What Is the Point of Equality?," Anderson claims that egalitarians should look to Amartya Sen's capabilities approach when thinking about the level of equality that citizens require (1999, 316). In *The Imperative of Integration*, she adopts a pragmatic approach, writing that "ideals," which I understand to include principles of justice, should be considered as "hypotheses, to be tested in experience" (2010a, 6).

13. Dworkin adds, "The integrated liberal will not separate his private and public lives in that way. He will count his own life as diminished—a less good life than he might have had—if he lives in an unjust community, no matter how hard he has tried to make it just" (2000, 233).

14. Rawls's conception of reciprocity is vulnerable, despite his repeated clarifications otherwise, of being associated with an instrumental regard for others that arises as a feature of contractual obligation by parties acting

reasonably and rationally. See, for example, his comments in *Justice as Fairness* that reciprocity is justified as *modus vivendi* but that it can shift overtime into a stable overlapping consensus (2001, 195–196). See also Anderson's "The Fundamental Disagreement between Luck Egalitarians and Relational Egalitarians" (2010b), for an explanation of why justice as fairness is based in relational equality.

15. Egalitarian schemes, however, that aim to fulfill some given pattern of distribution untethered to fulfilling the demand of equal concern, status equality, and procedural fairness might go too far (Anderson 2010b). Even Rawls's conception of distributive justice, which will be discussed in the next section, may be too demanding and thereby vulnerable to leveling-down objections. Anderson, for example, argued that this might be the case with Rawls's conception of justice as fairness if the transfers of primary goods that it requires to the least well-off are trivial and not needed to achieve relational equality. When it comes to housing, community, and educational equality, however, which differences are trifling are to be determined through democratic deliberation mindful of democratic equality. See Rawls, *A Theory of Justice* (1999, 88–89 and 434–449) and his *Justice as Fairness* (2001, 5–8, 132, and 195–196).

16. Hansberry captured the racist motivations behind segregation in the North through her rendering of the casual racism of the character Karl Lindner, who sought to discourage, through petty bribery and serious threats, the Younger family from moving into his neighborhood, Clybourne Park. Particularly striking is Hansberry's depiction of how institutional racism is often disguised as paternalistic benevolence and expressions of liberty and choice. Here are Lindner's key lines: "Well—you see our community is made up of people who've worked hard as the dickens for years to build up that little community. They're not rich and fancy people; just hard-working, honest people who don't really have much but those little homes and dream of the kind of community they want to raise their children in. Now, I don't say we are perfect and there is a lot wrong in some of the things they want. But you've got to admit that a man, right or wrong, has the right to want to have the neighborhood he lives in a certain kind of way. And at the moment the overwhelming majority of our people out there feel that people get along better, take more of a common interest in the life of the community, when they share a common background. I want you to believe me when I tell you that made prejudice simply doesn't enter into it. It is a matter of the people of Clybourne Park believing, rightly or wrongly, as I say, that for the happiness of all concerned that our Negro

families are happier when they live in their *own* communities" (Hansberry 1994, 119; original italics).

17. See also Peter Marcuse's "To Control Gentrification" presentation at the Resourceful Cities presentation, RC21 International Conference, August 29–31, in Berlin, Germany. And see Mary Patillo's "Housing: Commodity versus Right" (2013) for a survey of different approaches to the right to housing, and an account of the basis of their claims.

18. Despite the normative connections between the ideas of equality and equity, the latter is increasingly used in policy and legal discussions to refer to the required level of provision of some resource to achieve some justice goal, while equality is taken to be an abstract moral category that is distant or divorced from the idea of equity, or at least an unnecessary distraction. Fainstein's definition of equity reflects this disconnection with its normative roots (2010, 36). She provides two reasons for this preference: "First the goal of equality is too complex, demanding, and unrealistic to be an objective in the context of capitalist cities" and "Second, equity is the term used in policy analysis for describing the impacts of a program" (ibid.). So equality attracts or depends upon overtheorized and infeasible demands of justice and societal transformation, such as a radical amount of redistribution or leveling of resources. In contrast, equity is the industry standard and is associated with systems of evaluation and pragmatic reform (ibid., 36–37). Fainstein's conception of equity associates it with the view of political theories that insist on strict equal shares or outcomes, such as with the historical movements of the Levellers and Diggers or in the theoretical imaginings of Marxism. In doing so, her analysis adds to the confusion over the terms and unnecessarily disconnects it from its normative grounding in basic moral and democratic equality. Summoning the idea of equity does not extract us from philosophical debates over the right to primary goods or disagreements about who needs or deserves subsidies, what counts as a subsidy, what sort of subsidies are required, or where they should be applied. Substituting equity for equality is a conceptual sleight of hand that does not clarify controversies over equal treatment, access to primary goods, or opportunities. For a useful discussion of the evolution of this practice within social policy, see Österle (2002), and for an example of the explicit move from "equality" talk to that of "equity" in public and social policy, see Young (1994). And it is always a good idea to check in with Aristotle about such things (2014, Book 5, Section 3). Additionally, the term has a history in British and American common law, where its

evolving use displays some parallels but also differences from contemporary popular usage (Goldberg, Smith, and Turner 2019).

19. See the HUD's "A Decent Place to Live," a report of the National Housing Task Force (Washington, DC: 1988, p. 3). Additionally, recognizing housing as a primary good that has profound social consequences does not mean that it is a "public good." The latter are goods that are largely managed by the state and generally are available to and benefit all within the state, e.g., infrastructure and the military. Thank you to Tim Iglesias for pushing me on the importance of this distinction.

20. See Williams and Seichnaydre's "The Legacy and the Promise of Disparate Impact" (2018), for how Title VII of the Civil Rights Act of 1964 has been interpreted to include disparate impacts on protected groups, defined in terms of race, color, religion, sex, or national origin in U.S. law.

21. See also Hayward and Swanstrom's *Justice and the American Metropolis* (2011) and Davoudi and Bell's *Justice and Fairness in the City: A Multi-Disciplinary Approach to "Ordinary" Cities* (2016).

22. The principles of justice are as follows: (1) "Each person has the same indefeasible claim to a fully adequate scheme of equal basic liberties, which is compatible with the same scheme of liberties for all," and (2) "Social and economic inequalities are to satisfy two conditions: first, they are to be attached to offices and positions open to all under conditions of fair equality of opportunity; and second, they are to be to the greatest benefit of the least-advantaged members of society" (Rawls 2001, 41–42).

23. *Justice as fairness* and its principles are derived within the context of five ideas that capture liberal democratic ideals and thus make the theory itself ideal: "from society as a fair system of cooperation to the idea of a well-ordered society, to the idea of a basic structure of society, the idea of the original position, and finally to the idea of citizens, those engaged in cooperation, as free and equal" (2001, 24–25). All apply fully only in an ideal society. The idea of a well-ordered society, in particular, illustrates this. A well-ordered society is one "in which (1) everyone accepts and knows that the others accept the same principles of justice, and (2) the basic social institutions generally satisfy and are generally known to satisfy these principles" (Rawls 1999a, 4–5; see also, Rawls 2001, 5).

24. This is specifically Charles Mills's analysis in his "'Ideal Theory' as Ideology" (2017, 72–90). As Mills acknowledges, this argument was also made by Susan Moller Okin in *Justice, Gender and the Family* (1989) and Carole Pateman in *The Sexual Contract* (1988). A version was also made by Iris Marion Young in *Justice and the Politics of Difference* (1990). See *Justice*

as Fairness (2001, 64–65 and 162–168), for Rawls's replies to objections like these.

25. The difference principle states that "[s]ocial and economic inequalities are to satisfy two conditions: first, they are to be attached to offices and positions open to all under conditions of fair equality of opportunity; and second, they are to be to the greatest benefit of the least-advantaged members of society" (Rawls 2001, 41–42). See also Rawls, *A Theory of Justice* (1999a, 57–65) and *Justice as Fairness* (2001, 43–44).

26. I draw on T. M. Scanlon's conception of substantive opportunity, which he defines as a part of a three-part way to gauge whether an objection to some inequality is justified. Under his definition, substantive opportunity holds when "There is no wrong involved in the fact that the complainant did not have the necessary qualifications or other measures to do better in the process" (Scanlon 2018, 41). The operative term in this definition is "wrong," as in there is no wrong in the lack because the party would have had a fair opportunity to gain the required qualifications or other measures. Scanlon explains the idea of substantive opportunity by comparing it to James Buchanan's (1986) interpretation of Rawls's requirement that inequalities must be "open to all." Scanlon explains that Buchanan "thought that this requirement of justifiability is not met if desirable positions in the society are not 'open' to all members, regardless of the family into which they are born. One cannot ask individuals to accept and abide by the rules of a 'game' that they did not have a fair chance of playing" (ibid., 55–56).

27. On the idea of "social closure, see Elizabeth Anderson's relational theory of group inequality. To explain the generation of group inequalities through distorted social relations, Anderson draws on Max Weber's (1968, 341–342) idea of "social closure" and Charles Tilly's (1998, 10) idea of "durable inequalities." Her relational theory of group inequality lists as mechanisms of group inequality Tilly's ideas of "opportunity hoarding, emulation, and adaptation," along with "violence, leverage, political power, and psychological mechanisms," which were in part drawn from Iris Marion Young's (1990, 48–62) account of the fives faces of oppression: economic exploitation, social and economic marginalization, lack of power over one's work, cultural imperialism, and systemic violence (Young 1990, 48–62).

28. For more on the method and applications of opportunity and an example of the method applied to the social indices in California, see California's Department of Housing and Community Development (HCD) and the California Tax Credit Allocation Committee (TCAC) opportunity area

maps: https://www.treasurer.ca.gov/ctcac/opportunity.asp. How exactly the idea of the geography of opportunity should be conceptualized is a matter of debate within geography. See Casey J. Dawkins's, "Putting Equality in Place: The Normative Foundations of Geographic Equality of Opportunity" (2017) for his discussion of geography as opportunity as "geographic equality of opportunity" versus it as geographic equal resources. My discussion of the geography of opportunity involves elements of both views, although it hews closer to Dawkins's view.

29. Sampson writes on neighborhood effects that "differentiation by neighborhood is not only everywhere to be seen, but that it has durable properties—with cultural and social mechanisms of reproduction—and with effects that space a wide variety of social phenomena. Whether it be crime, poverty, child health, protest, leadership networks, civic collective efficacy, or immigration . . . the city is ordered by a spatial logic ('placed') and yields differences as much today as a century ago. The effect of this is not just geographical but simultaneously social. . . . Spatially inscribed social differences, I argue, constitute a family of "neighborhood effects" that are pervasive, strong, cross-cutting, and paradoxically stable even as they are changing in manifest form" (Sampson 2011, 6). These neighborhood effects have, as Rawls put it, profound effects on individual development. Sampson reviews the findings of this research in his "Individual and Community Mobility in the Great Recession Era: The Spatial Foundations of Persistent Inequality" (2015, 262–264).

30. Robert Sampson, for example, wrote that despite some disagreement in the research, "comprehensive reviews of the literature have nonetheless identified credible evidence of the deleterious effects of concentrated disadvantage on a number of individual outcomes relevant to understanding economic mobility, especially with respect to longer-term or developmental neighborhood influences" (2015, 263). One of the many sources he cites is the work of Raj Chetty, which can be viewed on the website of his Opportunity Project at https://opportunityinsights.org/.

31. See https://www.zillow.com/orinda-ca/home-values/.

32. See Harvey (2005) and Dawkins (2021, 122–125).

33. The longer form of this maxim states, "From each according to what he chooses to do, to each according to what he makes for himself (perhaps with the contracted aid of others) and what others choose to do for him and choose to give him of what they've been given previously (under this maxim) and haven't yet expended or transferred" (Nozick 1974, 65). Different forms of libertarianism, in contrast to Nozick's view, could

accept a vigorous enforcement of civil rights and equal protection that would, theoretically and to various degree of efficacy, blunt the effects of the social and economic discrimination that libertarianism would permit.

Chapter 2

1. The liberal egalitarian account that I present in this and the previous chapter is meant to be an alternative to neo-Marxist approaches to justice in social-spatial arrangements that are dominant in urban theory (Harvey 2009; Lefebvre 1996). Even so, a full critique of Marxism and its application to urban policy is not the domain of this work. Excellent critiques of Marxism by economists and political philosophers are available elsewhere (Kołakowski 1978). The theory-heavy and vague application of neo-Marxism in urban theory is straightforwardly rebutted, for example, by Susan Fainstein's (2010, 40–42) focus on practical reforms that do not depend on complete solidarity of the working classes, the supposition that there is an identity in their social-political-economic interests, and that they will work together for a "revolution" that brings an end to capitalism. Influenced by Eric Voegelin's *Science, Politics, and Gnosticism* (1968), I think of such national or global calls for social and political revolution to be eschatological in character and vision. In addition to those and standard critiques of Marxism, additional valuable criticisms are offered by Tony Judt's *Past Imperfect: French Intellectuals, 1944–1956* (2011) and its extension to some utopian conceptions of liberalism and neoconservativism in John Gray's *Black Mass: Apocalyptic Religion and the Death of Utopia* (2007).
2. I am thinking here of issue 10 of the magazine *Jacobin* (Spring 2013) for its depiction of a guillotine in the manner of an IKEA-like instruction manual. See also James Wolcott's (2020) penetrating analysis of the magazine, its politics and audience, in "Futilitarianism, or To the York Street Station."
3. Fainstein, for example, reiterates this criticism (2010, 4).
4. Charles Mills's analysis of this criticism and his defense of a nonideal approach, and really a Black radical nonideal liberal account of justice, are valuable and have shaped my analysis of the issue. See Mills's "Contract of Breach: Repairing the Racial Contract," in *Contract and Domination* (Pateman and Mills 2007, 106–133) and "'Ideal Theory' as Ideology," "Rawls on Race/Race in Rawls," "Retrieving Rawls for Racial Justice?," and "Epilogue (as Prologue): Toward a Black Radical Liberalism," in *Black Rights/White Wrongs* (2017, 72–90, 139–160, 161–180, 201–215).

5. In addition to Rawls's (1999a) original position, see Dworkin's (2000) resource auction or Cohen's camping trip (2009). They are all thought experiments about ideal initial distribution of primary goods and schemes of social cooperation.

6. Harvey (1973) claims that at best Rawls's theory of justice as fairness endorses a welfare-state capitalist system, and Soja (2010) opines that it would support neoliberal systems. Both positions are markedly incorrect and inaccurately depict Rawls's account (Rawls 2001, 133–140).

7. Their objection is correct about versions of egalitarianism, such as basic resource egalitarianism or prioritarianism that is ameliorative in the way that Marcuse criticizes. See, for example, Parfit's "Equality and Priority" (1997).

8. Relevant to Marcuse's goal of having policy with an overriding concern for the needs of residents and users of a neighborhood, Rawls writes of property rights that "The first principle of justice includes a right to private personal property, but this is different from the right of private property in productive assets" (Rawls 2001, 138).

9. See Longfellow's "The Great Metropolis," in *The Works of Henry Wadsworth Longfellow*, Vol. 7, ed. Samuel Longfellow (New York: Houghton, Mifflin, and Company, 1886), 367–368. The article was originally published in 1837. Its second paragraph makes Longfellow's point clear, and it is echoed in the polygon of the mural: "And more than all this, in great cities we learn to look the world in the face. We shake hands with stern realities. We see ourselves in others. We become acquainted with the motley many-sided life of man, and finally learn like Jean Paul, to "look upon a metropolis as a collection of villages; a village as some blind alley in a metropolis; fame as the talk of the neighbors at the street door; a library as a learned conversation; joy as a second; sorrow as a minute; life as a day; and three things as all in all, God, Creation, Virtue" (368). Although the mural remains, the Longfellow passage was covered over at some point in 2020 or 2021.

10. My adoption of the phrase "open communities" is a direct evocation of George Romney (former governor of Michigan from 1963 to 1969, and HUD Secretary from 1969 to 1973). In 1970 he attempted to implement a plan he called "Open Communities" to force suburbs to desegregate by denying them HUD funds if they failed to comply. His plan was thwarted by the Nixon administration. See Rothstein (2017, 201–202) and Edward J. Blum and Paul Harvey's "How (George) Romney Championed Civil Rights and Challenged His Church," *The Atlantic*, August 13, 2002, https://www.theatlantic.com/national/archive/2012/08/how-george-rom ney-championed-civil-rights-and-challenged-his-church/261073/, and Nikole Hannah-Jones's "Living Apart: How the Government Betrayed a

Landmark Civil Rights Law," *ProPublica*, June 25, 2015, https://www.pro
publica.org/article/living-apart-how-the-government-betrayed-a-landm
ark-civil-rights-law.

11. Section 808(d) mandates that "All executive departments and agencies
shall administer their programs and activities relating to housing and
urban development (including any Federal agency having regulatory
or supervisory authority over financial institution) in a manner affirmatively to further the purposes of this title and shall cooperate with the
Secretary to further such purposes." And 808(e)(5) states that all executive departments and agencies will "administer the programs and
activities relating to housing and urban development in a manner affirmatively to further the policies of this title." The Affirmatively Furthering
Fair Housing Rule of 2015 defines the second mandate thusly, in Section
5.152: "Affirmatively furthering fair housing means taking meaningful
actions, in addition to combating discrimination, that overcome patterns
of segregation and foster inclusive communities free from barriers that restrict access to opportunity based on protected characteristics. Specifically,
affirmatively furthering fair housing means taking meaningful actions
that, taken together, addresses significant disparities in housing needs and
in access to opportunity, replacing segregated living patterns with truly integrated and balanced living patterns, transforming racially and ethnically
concentrated areas of poverty into areas of opportunity, and fostering and
maintaining compliance with civil rights and fair housing laws. The duty to
affirmatively further fair housing extends to all of a program participant's
activities and programs relating to housing and urban development."

12. The summary of the Affirmatively Furthering Fair Housing Act in part
reads, "Pursuant to the affirmatively furthering fair housing mandate in
section 808(e)(5) of the Fair Housing Act, and in subsequent legislative
enactments, the purpose of the Affirmatively Furthering Fair Housing
(AFFH) regulations in §§ 5.150 through 5.180 is to provide program
participants with an effective planning approach to aid program participants
in taking meaningful actions to overcome historic patterns of segregation,
promote fair housing choice, and foster inclusive communities that are free
from discrimination." Department of Housing and Urban Development, 24
CFR Parts 5, 91, 92, 570, 574, 576, and 903 Federal Register v.80, n.136 (July
16, 2015): 42272. The Trump administration rescinded the rule in 2018, and
the Biden administration restored it in 2021.

13. This view is illustrated by the 2017 decision in *Open Communities Alliance
v. Ben S. Carson, Sr* (Civil Action No. 17–2192). The U.S. District Court

for the District of Columbia decided against Carson, the director of HUD in the Trump administration, in his decision to suspend the Small Area Fair Market Rent Rule, which mandated the use of zip codes to measure housing costs to determine the level of Section 8 benefits. The rule allowed families receiving subsidies to access neighborhoods with more resources and opportunities.

14. The Trump administration weakened the Fair Housing Act by limiting lawsuits against communities and institutions, such as banks, for policies and practices that lead to disparate impact against protected classes, and it has promoted lies about the AFFH rule by labeling it as an attack against the suburbs. The first mandate of the Fair Housing Act, guiding by the Civil Rights Act, counts disparate impact as discrimination. On this issue, see Jonathan Zasloff's "The Price of Equality: Fair Housing, Land Use, and Disparate Impact," *Columbia Human Rights Law Review* 48, no. 3 (2017): 99–153. On Trump's attack against the AFFH rule, see Glen Thrush's "Trump Attacks a Suburban Housing Program: Critics See a Play for White Votes," *New York Times*, July 1, 2020, https://www.nyti mes.com/2020/07/01/us/politics/trump-obama-housing-discrimination. html. For the announcement of is reinstatement by the Biden administration, see HUD Public Affairs, "HUD Restores Affirmatively Furthering Fair Housing Requirement," Washington, DC, June 10, 2021.

15. See Baldwin's "Introduction: Price of the Ticket," in *The Price of the Ticket: Collected Nonfiction, 1948–1985* (1985, ix–xx); and *Baldwin: Collected Essays* (1998, 830–842).

16. Treating substantive inequality or racial disparities that way is to use what Tommie Shelby calls the "medical model" (Shelby 2016, 2–4). The "medical model" is an often complained about methodological framework in medicine and psychology. It is complained about even by the technocratic bureaucrats who design and implement policies that can be associated with the model. The model is solution oriented; it calls for the identification of a specific problem and its key or "linchpin," and then for a specific, effective (including cost-effective) solution that should be applied to the problem with the expectation that the problem will eventually be fully addressed. In the best circumstances, such policies are "data-driven" and are subject to technical assessment or evaluation. The medical model approach, however, is prone to the technocratic fallacy, where it fails to see and address the problems outside of the purview of its assumptions. The medical model, according to Shelby, admits of a "status quo bias," "downgrades" the agency of individuals, and suffers from an "unjust-advantage blind-spot problem."

17. I follow Rothstein (2017) in recommending *rectification* rather than *reparations* for social-spatial injustice; the former is a form of corrective justice meant to signal a practical approach that is distinct from a purely normative call for reparations that does consider practical restraints against the idea.

18. See the Universal Declaration of Human Rights, General Assembly Resolution 217 (1948). See also Dawkins (2021, 159–192) for an insightful analysis of the history of the idea of a right to housing and for his positive argument for that right.

19. The United States is not a signatory to this Covenant. See the International Convent on Economic, Social and Cultural Rights, General Assembly Resolution 2200A (1966).

20. The article was approved by the state's citizens and adopted by the 1938 New York State Constitutional Convention. See https://dos.ny.gov/sys tem/files/documents/2022/01/Constitution-January-1-2022.pdf.

21. See The Coalition for the Homeless basic facts sheet: http://www.coalitio nforthehomeless.org/basic-facts-about-homelessness-new-york-city/.

22. A basic right to housing would be at least consistent with the sufficiency benchmark of Harry Frankfurt's account of egalitarianism (1987). On the limitations of sufficientarianism in relation to the right to housing, see Dawkins (2020, 24 and 142).

23. Cited in Bratt, Stone, and Hartman's "Why a Right to Housing Is Needed and Makes Sense" (2006b, 1). See also Hartman (2006).

24. Black Panther Party, "What We Want—What We Believe," https://oac. cdlib.org/ark:/28722/bk001532b1j/?brand=oac4.

25. Paragraph 7 of the Committee's "General Comment 4 on the Right to Adequate Housing," states that "In the Committee's view, the right to housing should not be interpreted in a narrow or restrictive sense which equates it with, for example, the shelter provided by merely having a roof over one's head or views shelter exclusively as a commodity. Rather it should be seen as the right to live somewhere in security, peace and dignity. This is appropriate for at least two reasons. In the first place, the right to housing is integrally linked to other human rights and to the fundamental principles upon which the Covenant is premised. This 'the inherent dignity of the human person' from which the rights in the Covenant are said to derive requires that the term 'housing' be interpreted so as to take account of a variety of other considerations, most importantly that the right to housing should be ensured to all persons irrespective of income or access to economic resources" (U.N. Office of the High Commissioner for Human Rights 1991).

26. Egalitarian schemes that aim to fulfill some given pattern of distribution untethered to fulling the demand of equal concern, status equality, and procedural fairness may go too far (Anderson 2010b). Even Rawls's conception of distributive justice may be too demanding for Anderson if the transfers of primary goods that it requires to the least well-off are trivial and not needed to achieve relational equality. When it comes to housing, community, and educational equality, however, what differences are trifling are to be determined through democratic deliberation mindful of relational equality. This point reflects the "leveling-down" problem within egalitarian theory. In "What Is the Point of Equality?," Anderson writes, "Would democratic equality support a wage-squeezing policy as demanding as Rawls's difference principle? This would forbid all income inequalities that do not improve the incomes of the worst off. In giving absolute priority to the worst off, the difference principle might require considerable sacrifices in the lower middle ranks for trifling gains at the lowest levels. Democratic equality would urge a less demanding form of reciprocity. Once all citizens enjoy a decent set of freedoms, sufficient for functioning as an equal in society, income inequalities beyond that point do not seem so troubling in themselves. The degree of acceptable income inequality would depend in part on how easy it was to convert income into status inequality—differences in the social bases of self-respect, influence over elections, and the like. The stronger the barriers against commodifying social status, political influence, and the like, the more acceptable are significant income inequalities" (1999, 326). Compare that with Anderson's discussion of Rawls in "The Fundamental Disagreement between Luck Egalitarians and Relational Egalitarians" (2010b).

27. See South Burlington County NAACP v. Mount Laurel, 67 N.J. 151 (1975): 174.

28. See the 1985 New Jersey Fair Housing Act, N.J.S.A. 52:27D-301, Section 2a.

29. For a comparison of the costs of the mortgage interest deduction versus Section spending, see Andrew Woo and Chris Salviati's report on the "Imbalance in Housing Aid: Mortgage Interest Deduction vs. for Apartment List, a Rental Brokerage Company," https://www.apartmentl ist.com/rentonomics/imbalance-housing-aid-mortgage-interest-deduct ion-vs-section-8/. For analysis of this imbalance, see Matthew Desmond's "How Homeownership Became the Engine of American Inequality," *New York Times*, May 19, 2017, https://www.nytimes.com/2017/05/09/magazine/how-homeownership-became-the-engine-of-american-inequality.html.

30. For a discussion of the link between zoning and the provision of fair and affordable housing, see Zasloff (2017). On the discrimination against housing vouchers, such as the Section 8 program, see Kriston Capps's "See How Landlords Pack Section 8 Renters into Poorer Neighborhoods," for *Bloomberg's* City Lab. January 19, 2019, https://www.bloomberg.com/news/articles/2019-01-09/where-section-8-renters-face-housing-discrimination, and Alicia Mazzara and Brian Knudsen's "Where Families with Children Use Housing Vouchers," Center on Budget and Policy Priorities, January 3, 2019, https://www.cbpp.org/research/housing/where-families-with-children-use-housing-vouchers.

31. See Kukla (2021) for the opposite view. They hold the view that some communities, especially those who are historically marginalized and vulnerable to oppression, should be able to form spaces that exclude others.

32. See supra fn.18. A purely normative approach to corrective justice will lead to a more forceful advocacy of reparations for slavery or state-sponsored segregation and other forms of discrimination in the United States than the pragmatic form of rectification I argue for here (Kaplan and Valls 2007; Valls 2007, 2018). Although, once the costs and other potential moral conflicts are included in the moral calculation, others reasonably question whether reparations are straightforwardly morally sanctioned or even wise (Loury 2000, 2007). This is a work of nonideal theory, so I do not take a pure normative approach on this question. Plus, the need to address housing crisis is so pressing that arguments of favor of corrective justice should take practical constraints seriously and temper their arguments accordingly.

33. Despite these challenges, some state and local governments are sponsoring initiatives to study, sponsor, and administer reparation polices. See, for example, California's Assembly Bill 3121 Reparations Task Force and its report, https://oag.ca.gov/ab3121, and Evanston's, Illinois, local reparations "Restorative Housing Program," https://www.cityofevanston.org/government/city-council/reparations. There is also, on the federal level, the House Bill (HR 40), first introduced in 2017, that would establish a "Commission to Study and Develop Reparation Proposals for African-Americans," https://www.congress.gov/bill/117th-congress/house-bill/40/text.

34. Coates indicates support for U.S. House Bill 40 (see supra note 32). But he also indicates support for Charles J. Ogletree's more pragmatic proposal that includes all of the poor. See Ogletree's "Litigating the Legacy of Slavery," *New York Times*, March 31, 2012, https://www.nytimes.com/2002/03/31/opinion/litigating-the-legacy-of-slavery.html.

35. There is an expansive debate over whether Rawls's system is compatible with arguments for reparations that I cannot resolve here. Charles Mills has pointed out that Rawls did not seriously consider the role of race and racism in any of his works, that he gravely underestimated the harm of racial oppression and the potential for those harms to be reproduced even in a well-ordered polity, and that justice as fairness does not offer a principle of rectification that is up to the task of dealing with past racial wrongs (Mills 1998, 2017; Pateman and Mills 2007). Other egalitarian philosophers have taken a different tack by noting that Rawls explicitly distinguished the difference principle from a *principle of redress* that would compensate individuals that have fewer native talents, suffer from disabilities, or have been disadvantaged by past injustices through the provision of more resources to equalize their welfare (Scheffler 2010, 192–193; Cohen 2011, 111; Rawls 1999a, 87; 1993, 185n; 1999c, 371). I have argued throughout this chapter that rectification is not achieved with forward-looking principles alone; however, a serious commitment to forward-looking reforms justified by the difference principle would address many disparities in the provision of primary goods and the opening up of fair equal opportunity. Additionally, there is no reason to presume that justice as fairness is necessarily opposed to rectification in local justice or in nonideal situations. Despite Mills's criticisms, or as he illustrates in his version of Black radical liberalism, a liberal egalitarian account of justice could explicitly build in a sensitivity to the harms of racism, either in the form of direct discrimination or disparate impacts, and accept a principle of rectification to address past wrongs (Mills 2007, 106–133; 2017, 201–215).

Chapter 3

1. Solnit's statements regarding othering of the Google Bus riders is not based in race, religion, or nationality; nevertheless, it is xenophobic in that it is an expression of civic exclusion. See my "Sheltering Xenophobia," *Critical Philosophy of Race* 1, no. 1 (2013): 73–85, and with David H. Kim, "Xenophobia and Racism," *Critical Philosophy of Race* 2, no. 1 (2014): 20–45.
2. See also "Confronting California's Rent and Poverty Crisis: A Call for State Reinvestment in Affordable Homes" (Sacramento: California Housing Partnership, 2016). The U.S. Department of Housing and Urban Development defines low-income families as families "whose incomes do not exceed 80-percent of the median family income for the area." The

relevant income level for "very low-income families" is 50% and 30% for "extremely low-income families." See https://www.huduser.gov/portal/datasets/il.html#2022_faq.

3. For more on context immobility, see Sharkey (2013, 16–20, 91–116). The concept of concentrated poverty, from the research of William Julius Wilson (1987), describes an area (neighborhood, zip code, or census tract) where a high proportion of the residents (for Wilson it was up to 40%) fall under the poverty line. Context mobility captures the ability of an individual or household to move from one geographic context, marked by social and economic features, to another; ideally, a household with positive context mobility would have the ability to move from a poorer neighborhood, with less access to social goods, to another that is better off and with more access to social goods.

4. See also Beauregard (1986), Vigdor (2002), Freeman (2006), and Schlichtman, Hill, and Patch (2017).

5. Smith took inspiration from the term for the French reactionary movement that sought revenge (*revanche*) against the working class and the remains of the "discredited" royalty.

6. There is more than one cause of gentrification, and we may have distinct labels for each; this is a condition that marks many categories of people and actions in the human sciences, but because those categories are not completely nominal (a random category of things joined only by name), they have value in the social sciences. Ian Hacking argues that a dynamic nominalism better captures such social categories. Philosophers call such categories "kinds," and they distinguish between natural kinds and other sorts like social kinds (e.g., "American" or "bus driver") or artificial (e.g., "plastic" or "pianos"). Natural kinds are considered the gold standard because they, like the chemical elements—such as *gold*—are fully mind-independent, precisely definable, and unique. But even though social kinds lack, if you will, a molecular or genetic essence, that does not mean they do not have significant social presence and effect. See Hacking's "Five Parables" in *Ideas in Context* (1990, 122; 1999).

7. Both the *Encyclopedia of Housing* and the Hammel and Wyly definitions were cited by Lance Freeman (2005, 469). This minimal definition is consistent with the definition used by the Urban Displacement Project at the University of California Berkeley, authored by Miriam Zuk and Karen Chapple. See https://www.urbandisplacement.org/sites/default/files/images/urban_displacement_project_-_executive_summary.pdf. Chapple and Loukaitou-Sideris use two related definitions in their book

Transit-Oriented Displacement or Community Dividends? (2019). The first is minimal and states that gentrification is "urban transformation via flows of both capital and people" (2019, 39). The second longer version develops the first and is consistent with the definition from Chapple (2009, 1–2) cited earlier (Chapple and Loukaitou-Sideris 2019, 45–46).

8. I follow the account of the stages of gentrification given by John Joe Schlichtman, Marc Lamont Hill, and Jason Patch's *Gentrifier* (2017). They provide by far the best account and analysis of the stages of gentrification I have found.

9. See Kim-Mai Cutler's "How Burrowing Owls Lead to Vomiting Anarchists (Or SF's Housing Crisis Explained)," *TechCrunch*, April 14, 2014, https://techcrunch.com/2014/04/14/sf-housing/.

10. See Eric Rodenbeck, "Mapping Silicon Valley's Gentrification Problem through Corporate Shuttle Routes," *Wired*, September 6, 2013, https://www.wired.com/2013/09/mapping-silicon-valleys-corporate-shuttle-problem/.

11. Freeman used the Panel Study of Income Dynamics (PSID) in his research, which led him to, "consider as displaced all those respondents in the PSID sample who give as their reason for moving in the previous year that they wanted to consume less space, wanted to pay less rent, or moved in response to outside events including being evicted, health reasons, divorce, joining the armed services, or other involuntary reasons. Although this category includes some responses that might not be considered displacement, the PSID categorization of responses precludes separating them out. This measure will overstate the extent of displacement due to gentrification because this type of displacement is usually conceptualized as households moving because they were evicted or because their housing costs became prohibitive due to rising housing costs in their neighborhood. Nevertheless, this definition will reveal an upper bound on the extent to which displacement appears to be caused by gentrification" (Freeman, 2005, 469).

12. These points were assembled from the concerns expressed by urban affairs scholars Maureen Kennedy and Paul Leonard (2001), Frank Braconi and Lance Freeman (2002, 2004, 2005), and Jacob L. Vigdor (2002), and by legal scholar Peter J. Byrne (2003).

13. This conception of displacement and the method for measuring it is used by the Urban Displacement Project at the University of California Berkeley. Notably, that project does not strictly associate displacement with gentrification, because displacement can occur before or even

without gentrification. Nonetheless, they use a wide and perhaps too wide conception of displacement. In the executive statement about the project, they define displacement as occurring "when housing or neighborhood conditions actually force moves" (p. 2), and to measure displacement, they "calculated the loss of low-income households for each time period" (p. 4). The loss of low-income households alone, however, is not strictly indicative of forced moves. See https://www.urbandisplacement.org/sites/default/files/images/urban_displacement_project_-_execut ive_summary.pdf.

14. This approach contrasts with that of Margaret Kohn's in her book *The Death and Life of the Urban Commonwealth*. Kohn acknowledged the concerns raised by empirical research into gentrification, but she did not take on these findings (Kohn 2016, 91). She recognized that displacement is distinct from demographic replacement, or what the urban affairs literature calls succession, and asserted that both are harmful without delineating their separate harms. She focused on a normative analysis of those threatened with displacement by gentrification, without considering the distinction between disinvestment and reinvestment displacement, their distinct harms, and how the magnitude of the harm of reinvestment displacement was less than she supposed, or how its diffused causes affect her theoretical analysis.

15. The Eviction Lab is a team of researchers led by Matthew Desmond that publicly document eviction rates. See the Eviction Lab's rankings at https://evictionlab.org/rankings/#/evictions?r=United%20States&a= 0&d=evictionRate.

Chapter 4

1. Similar injustices were perpetrated against some Asian American groups, too, especially in the American West, from the period encompassing the Chinese Exclusion Act of 1882 through the internment of Japanese Americans starting in 1942 through 1944. The populations they affected were not as big and their effects not as enduring as segregation against blacks and some Latinos.

2. See, for example, the National Alliance to End Homelessness's definition of the housing first approach: https://endhomelessness.org/resource/hous ing-first/. As I noted earlier, however, the homelessness crisis involves other factors in addition to a lack of affordable housing (cf. Introduction, fn. 4).

3. The Ellis Act (Chapter 12.75: Residential Real Property) is a policy that allows, under specific conditions, for owners of rental units to evict residents so that the owners may occupy the units. See the statute at http://leginfo.legislature.ca.gov/faces/codes_displayText.xhtml?lawCode=GOV&division=7.&title=1.&part=&chapter=12.75.

4. See Zuk and Chapple (2015) and Rose, Kalima, and Margaretta Lin (2015), "A Roadmap toward Equity: Housing Solutions for Oakland, California," City of Oakland Department of Housing & Community Development's Strategic Initiatives Unit and Policy Link, https://www.policylink.org/sites/default/files/pl-report-oak-housing-070715.pdf.

5. See, for example, Ali Tadayon's "Bay Area Organizations Work to Protect Nonprofits from Displacement," *East Bay Times*, November 15, 2017, https://www.eastbaytimes.com/2017/11/15/bay-area-organizations-work-to-protect-nonprofits-from-displacement/.

6. August Wilson depicted an "eviction" of memory in his play *Radio Golf* (2007), which is the final piece of his ten-play Pittsburgh cycle. It occurs in the same neighborhood, the Hill District, that serves as the setting of the other plays in the cycle. The house (at 1839 Wylie Avenue in Pittsburgh, PA) at the center of *Radio Golf* had a role in the first play of the cycle, *Gem of the Ocean*. From the 1900s to the 1990s, that home and district were the loci of the drama in those plays. In the final play, it is slated for redevelopment into a mixed-use high-rise. What is lost in its erasure can only be grasped through recognizing the history it contained and the people, pain, joy, and overcoming it sheltered.

7. In Will Kymlicka's account of multicultural liberalism, some national groups are recognized and granted a form of group rights (Taylor and Gutmann 1992; Kymlicka 1995). Some nations, such as Canada, recognize a degree of multicultural rights, which would affect the applicability of cultural equality arguments in relation to gentrification. In the United States, the basis of group rights consists of treaties and not cultural claims, as is the case with Native Americans. It is perhaps the only case where multicultural group rights claims are relevant in the United States. In addition to the limited applicability of multicultural citizenship in the United States, there are several other problems with Kymlicka's theory that limit its acceptability or applicability, such as serious concerns about how states institutionalize recognition fairly, questions about which groups would be recognized, or how regimes that accepted multicultural citizenship could even possibly instrumentalize the equal valuing of cultures or balance recognition with individual rights of expression and association. Plus, there

are concerns about its application in societies that do not already have the recognition of established national minorities built into their political constitutions (Kelly 2002). Questions about groups' rights and multicultural citizenship cannot be addressed here; however, the concerns about gentrification and cultural loss, changes in community character, or cultural displacement can be addressed through liberal egalitarian theories of distributive justice and social equality without appealing to the fraught ideas of cultural equality or cultural group rights. Further, due to the history of the American Indian Relocation Act of 1956 that compelled Native Americans to resettle into urban areas, such as San Francisco and Oakland, affected tribal members could offer a group rights–based argument for displacement mitigation programs (Fixico 1986; Wilkins and Stark 2018; Keeler 2016).

8. See Quill R. Kukla's *City Living: How Urban Dwellers and Urban Spaces Make One Another* (2021), for an illuminating analysis of gentrification and cultural loss that, in contrast to the view I uphold, advocates for the right to exclude to protect the marginalized groups from cultural loss.

9. For the text of Alabama H.B. 56, see http://immigration.alabama.gov/ Immigration-Act-No-2011-535-Text.aspx. Most but not all of its controversial components were blocked by legal suits. For the Southern Poverty Law Center's report on the aftermath of the law, see https://www.splcen ter.org/news/2021/06/25/cruel-legacy-alabama-anti-immigrant-law-rem embered.

10. See Rachel Lienesch, Daniel Cox, and Robert P. Jones, "Beyond Economics: Fears of Cultural Displacement Pushed the White Working Class to Trump," Public Religion Research Institute, 2017, and *The Atlantic*, https://www.prri.org/research/white-working-class-attitudes-economy-trade-immigration-election-donald-trump/.

11. Douglass S. Massey, "Comment on 'Does Gentrification Hurt the Poor?'" in Vigdor (2002).

12. See also Daniel Putnam's "Gentrification and Domination" (June 2021).

13. See also the work of Desmond's eviction lab, https://evictionlab.org/.

14. Rent stabilization ("control") is a key idea in mitigating reinvestment displacement, but it is not clear which policies should be favored (Desmond 2016, 293–313). The effects of rent stabilization on the development of new rental units, how it may disincentivize repairs or capital improvement by landlords, and the inability of such policies, thus far, from targeting the poor and working-class residents, however, are worthy reasons to hesitate on his recommendations (Freeman 2006, 171). Rent stabilization alone will not address concerns about marginalization and stabilization; rather,

policies should be put in place that make sure renters have equal political say and have the power to hold their city councilors and state representatives accountable to their interests.

15. For example, in the report, "A Roadmap toward Equity: Housing Solutions for Oakland, California," Oakland's former mayor, Libby Schaff, writes, "A growing number of Oakland residents cannot afford to buy or rent a home or move within their own neighborhood. This housing affordability crisis threatens to undermine the economic recovery of long-standing community members. . . . Facing a rising loss of families with children, and a dramatic loss of African American households, Oakland risks following in San Francisco's footsteps, and losing the intergenerational treasures of our community" (Rose and Lin 2015, 5).

Chapter 5

1. The chapter draws on my previous essays about segregation and integration, although my position on most of the issues and debates has changed substantially. See my "Race and Place: Social Space in the Production of Human Kinds" (2003); "Racial Politics in Residential Segregation Studies" (2004); and "Residential Segregation and Rethinking the Imperative of Integration" (2020).

2. See Fiss (2003), Kaplan and Valls (2007), Anderson (2010a), Merry (2013), Shelby (2016), Stanley (2017), and Valls (2018).

3. The view that I have defended is that racial categories are social, necessarily site-specific, and are a real social phenomena. For a survey of the contemporary debate in analytic philosophy about the nature of race itself, see Glasgow, Haslanger, and Jeffers (2019).

4. This sense of segregation was noted in, not incidentally, the first documented usage of the term "racism." *The Oxford English Dictionary* tells us that the first recorded reference to the term traces back to Richard Henry Scott Pratt's usage of it in a 1902 address to the Lake Mohonk Conference of the Friend of the Indian, in which he criticized the U.S. government's exterminatory policies toward Native Americans following the American Indian Wars and advocated for the forced assimilation of Native Americans into white American society through education. On that occasion, Pratt declared, "Segregating any class or race of people apart from the rest of the people kills the progress of the segregated people or makes their growth very slow. Association of races and classes is necessary to destroy racism and classism." See "Proceedings of the Twentieth

Annual Meeting of the Lake Mohonk Conference of Friends of the Indian, 1902," published by the Lake Mohonk Conference in 1903, p. 134.

5. See also Johnston, Poulsen, and Forrest, "Segregation Matters, Measurement Matters" (2014).

6. Iceland, Weinberg, Steinmetz, and U.S. Census Bureau, *Racial and Ethnic Segregation in the United States: 1800–2000* (2002).

7. Johnston, Poulsen, and Forrest's, "Segregation Matters, Measurement Matters" (2014); and Stephen Menendian and Samir Gambhir's "Racial Segregation in the San Francisco Bay Area" (2019).

8. See Stephen Menendian, and Arthur Gailes, and Samir Gambhir's "The Roots of Structural Racism: Twenty-First Century Racial Residential Segregation in the United States" (2021, 11). For a criticism of the methodology of that study, see Judge Glock's "An Advocacy Group Spins Diversity as Evidence of Segregation," *Wall Street Journal*, June 29, 2021, https://www.wsj.com/articles/an-advocacy-group-spins-diversity-as-evidence-of-segregation-11625004857?st=0aaqad3abwzjupa&reflink=desktopwebshare_permalink. Glock's point is that the study intentionally ignores overall increases in desegregation and integration by inventing a measure that overemphasizes the existence of pockets of group clustering. He writes, "So how can the institute claim that segregation is increasing? By creating yet another index, which it calls a "divergence index," and which adds together the difference between the proportions of all of the races in each neighborhood and their citywide average. Instead of looking at how much of each race in a city would have to move to be spread evenly across a city, the index calculates how different each neighborhood's racial percentages are from the whole city's."

9. See Shelby (2016), 39. In *Dark Ghetto*, Shelby's references to segregation are intentionally focused on residential segregation. He associates segregation with unevenness and clustering, which conforms to his focus on the "ghetto poor." Shelby distinguishes his view from the view that "segregation itself is a form of unjust disadvantage" (2016, 39–48). That was the position I defended in "Racial Politics in Residential Segregation Studies" (2004). In that article I held the view that segregation is a value-laden term because its social existence as a thing to be recognized is driven and made possible by human interest, and it is a "partisan" term insofar as it carries with it judgments about its connection to racism and distributive injustice. I no longer posit that social-spatial or residential segregation has an essential moral-ontological status. Voluntary segregation, if there is such a thing, that we might call separation or clustering is not in and of itself

morally bad or good. However, segregation at larger scales, even if it is
the result of voluntary behavior, indicates and leads to disparities that we
rightly consider a public moral failure and an injustice.

10. See Schelling (1961, 1971).

11. *Parents Involved in Community Schools v. Seattle School Dist. No. 1*, 551
U.S. 701 (2007, 1).

12. Ibid., 3.

13. Ibid., 3.

14. In using the terms "enclave" and "citadel," I draw on Peter Marcuse's
helpful distinction between ghettos, which in his definition are sites of
forced segregation, and ethnic enclaves, which are voluntary (Marcuse
2002, 109–111). Citadels, in his view, are sites of intentional exclusion. The
line, however, between enclave and citadel is not so clear and is subject
to ideological bias. An enclave to the person whose entry is frustrated is
a citadel. The "Benedict" option refers to the advice imparted by Alastair
MacIntyre at the end of his *After Virtue* (1984, 263). Retreat, into enclaves
or citadels, is an option for communities that seek to protect and preserve
their values and traditions in the face of the domination exerted by liberal systems of government. See "Integration and Reaction" (Sundstrom
2022), for my discussion of the idea of the Benedict option as it applies to
the segregation and integration debate.

15. See, for example, Oakes (2004), Orfield (1996), Massey and Denton
(1993), Hartman and Squires (2010), Reardon and Bishoff (2011a, 2011b),
Sharkey (2013), and Rugh and Massey (2014).

16. In "The Ethical Demands for Integration" (1962), King adds: "Segregation
stands diametrically opposed to the principle of the sacredness of human
personality. It debases personality. Immanuel Kant said in one formulation of the *Categorical Imperative* that 'all men must be treated as *ends* and
never as mere *means*.' The tragedy of segregation is that it treats men as
means rather than ends, and thereby reduces them to things rather than
persons. To use the words of Martin Buber, segregation substitutes an 'I–It'
relationships for the 'I–thou' relationship" (King 1991, 119). King's reference to Buber translates it into a statement of public reason that can stand
independently of King's theological commitments. Spiritual affinity is ethical affinity, the recognition of equal moral personhood.

17. Other initiatives that can be associated with mobility include the post-
1990 "Housing and Opportunity for Everyone" (HOPE VI) policy, the
Moving to Work (MTW) demonstration program, the Department
of Transportation's "Ladders of Opportunity," and the HUD Rule on

Affirmatively Furthering Housing Rule (AFFH) (§2.3.1). See the U.S. Department of Housing and Urban Development website on the MTO Project, http://portal.hud.gov/hudportal/HUD?src=/programdescript ion/mto, and the website on the HOPE VI, http://portal.hud.gov/hudpor tal/HUD?src=/program_offices/public_indian_housing/programs/ph/ hope6. For the AFFH, see https://www.hud.gov/AFFH.

18. For findings about the positive effects and also the limitations of mobility programs, see Chetty and Hendren (2015) and Chetty, Hendren, and Katz (2016).

19. For more on George Romney work for fair housing, see Rothstein (2017, 201–202) and Goetz (2018, 98–100).

20. For accounts of these failures, see Wilson (1987), Massey and Denton (1988), Orfield and Eaton (1996), Pietila (2010), and Sharkey (2013).

21. See also James (2013), Merry (2014, 67–91), and Stanley (2017).

22. See also "African American Citywide Historic Context Statement" (San Francisco: San Francisco Planning Department, January 2016), https://sfp lanning.org/african-american-historic-context-statement.

23. See, e.g., Matthew (2021) and my reply (Sundstrom 2022).

Chapter 6

1. In Chapter 2, I characterized the components of justice in social-spatial arrangements as providing a partial conception of reconstructive justice, but I think it most accurately applies in the reconstruction of the idea of integration. My adoption of "reconstruction" as a replacement for "integration" was inspired by Brandon M. Terry's use of the term in his analysis of Malcolm X's intellectual legacy. He used it in the second of two articles on works about Malcolm X. The first was "Malcolm's Ministry" (*The New York Review of Books*, February 25, 2021a), and the second was "What Dignity Demands" (*The New York Review of Books*, March 11, 2021b, 12–14). In the latter essay, Terry writes, "Malcolm's criticisms of so-called integrationism never adequately grappled with the leftist tenor of King's views, which could be better described as 'reconstructionist.' For King, authentic integration 'was meaningless without the mutual sharing of power.' King-inspired integration would involve the widespread redistribution of assets and real democratic participation in economic and political decision-making instead of allowing municipal borders, the dictates of private profit, and existing measures of 'merit' to unfairly disadvantage the life chances of so many Americans" (14). Terry compared the sort of

integration (as reconstruction) that Martin Luther King Jr. supported with Tommie Shelby's position of "egalitarian pluralism" as an alternative to the view of integration promoted by those who prioritize demographic evenness and mobility. For more on Terry's take of King and Malcom, see his "Requiem for a Dream: The Problem-Space of Black Power" (2018). Beyond Terry's use of reconstruction, it is used by others to frame the goals of their social justice movements; for example, see William J. Barber II and Jonathan Wilson-Hartgrove's *The Third Reconstruction* (2016). See also their "A Cry of 'I Can't Breathe' United a Generation in a Gasp for Justice," *New York Times,* March 21, 2021, https://www.nytimes.com/2021/05/21/opinion/george-floyd-death-william-barber.html.

2. Hamilton and Ture (formerly Stokely Carmichael) note that the "white" conception of integration as interracial social and intimate mixing had already come in their time in 1967 to dominate the popular meaning of the term. They also distinguish their view of integration, which was simply an expression of equal rights and access to opportunity that should be consistent with their black nationalist politics, from a view of integration understood as black assimilation into the white middle class, which was in their estimation not available to most black Americans (Hamilton and Ture 1992, 53–56).

3. Ture and Hamilton's view of integration is compatible with King's proposals, except that he emphasized the mutual recognition of the theological-ontological conception of personhood. How integration should occur, given King's view, is personal and communal, but it should also be mandated by law and policy and supported by government institutions and programs. His institutional recommendations are laid out in his economic Bill of Rights for the poor and disadvantaged in his *Where Do We Go from Here: Chaos or Community?* (King 2010). As to the ontological-theological basis of the mutual recognition required by integration, we can get a sense of its high demands from King's "Christmas Sermon on Peace." It is worth quoting at length because it provides a nontrivial depiction of what full integration would be like for King: "I have a dream that one day men will rise up and come to see that they are made to live together as brothers. I still have a dream this morning that one day every Negro in this country, every colored person in the world, will be judged on the content of his character rather than the color of his skin, and every man will respect the dignity and worth of human personality. I still have a dream that one day the idle industries of Appalachia will be revitalized, and the empty stomachs of Mississippi will be filled, and brotherhood will be more than a few words

at the end of a prayer, but rather the first order of business on every legislative agenda. I still have a dream today that one day justice will roll down like water, and righteousness like a mighty stream. I still have a dream today that in all of our state houses and city halls men will be elected to go there who will do justly and love mercy and walk humbly with their God. I still have a dream today that one day war will come to an end, that men will beat their swords into plowshares and their spears into pruning hooks, that nations will no longer rise up against nations, neither will they study war any more. I still have a dream today that one day the lamb and the lion will lie down together and every man will sit under his own vine and fig tree and none shall be afraid. I still have a dream today that one day every valley shall be exalted and every mountain and hill will be made low, the rough places will be made smooth and the crooked places straight, and the glory of the Lord shall be revealed, and all flesh shall see it together. I still have a dream that with this faith we will be able to adjourn councils of despair and bring new light into the dark chambers of pessimism. With this faith we will be able to speed up the day when there will be peace on earth and good will toward men. It will be a glorious day, the morning stars will together and the sons of God will shout for joy" (King 1991c, 257–258).

4. On the history of the Reconstruction, see Foner's *Reconstruction: America's Unfinished Revolution, 1863–1877* (1988) and Du Bois's *Black Reconstruction in America* (1935).

5. See Tonika Lewis Johnson's Folded Map Project: https://www.foldedmap project.com.

6. See, for example, the Reimagining Civic Commons Project and its initiatives included in its demonstration cities: https://civiccommons.us/ cities/. The justification and aim of the project are to counter the socially and politically corrosive results of separation by building assets open to the whole communities in their demonstration cities, or as they explain it, "As communities have segmented by income, technology has advanced and priorities have shifted, support for civic assets has declined. Due to underinvestment and apathy, our civic assets are no longer providing the connective tissue that binds us together and anchors neighborhoods. The result is more than overgrown ballfields and lackluster libraries: research shows that Americans spend less time together in social settings, trust each other less and interact less with others whose experiences are different."

7. As economist Jens Ludwig put it, "While one potential concern is that MTO might have less beneficial impacts on people's lives than would community-level interventions, given the potentially disruptive effects

of moving itself, this concern strikes me as less serious than it initially appears once we recognize the high rates of residential mobility that we see in general in the U.S. Typically around 18–22% of Americans change addresses each year. . . . Mobility rates are higher still among American renters, around 32.5% per year. If we implemented a community-level program in a sub-set of distressed urban neighborhoods, after a 10–15 year follow-up period a large share of the original residents would have turned over. A large share of the people who currently lived in the new-and-improved neighborhood would have moved in from somewhere else" (Ludwig et al. 2014, 19–20).

8. Andre M. Perry and David Harshbarger report that, "The University of Richmond's Mapping Inequality project has digitized scans of the HOLC redlining maps held in the National Archives. Examination of the maps, numbering over 200, reveals that approximately 11 million Americans (10,852,727) live in once-redlined areas, according to the latest population data from the Census Bureau's American Community Survey (2017). This population is majority-minority but not majority-Black, and, contrary to conventional perceptions, Black residents also do not form a plurality in these areas overall. The Black population share is approximately 28%, ranking third among the racial groups who live in formerly redlined areas, behind white and Latino or Hispanic residents." See Andre M. Perry and David Harshbarger, "America's Formerly Redlined Neighborhoods Have Changed, and so Must Solutions to Rectify Them" (Washington, DC: Brookings Institution, October 14, 2019), https://www.brookings.edu/research/americas-formerly-redlines-areas-changed-so-must-solutions/, and the University of Richmond's Mapping Inequality project, https://dsl.richmond.edu/panorama/redlining/#loc=5/39.1/-94.58.

9. To achieve integration, powell recommends a variety of approaches, involving both mobility and community development, to connect needful individual and families to public and private resources. He supports processes that adopt a "targeted universalism," or what most would identify as an equity approach. For example, he claims, "For any given issue—whether it is employment rates, housing, incarceration, or health care—the challenge is to appreciate how these issues interact and accumulate over time, with place as the linchpin holding these arrangements together. Universal policies that are nominally race-neutral and that focus on specific issues such as school reform will rarely be effective because of the cumulative cascade of issues that encompass these neighborhoods. What is required is a strategy of "targeted universalism." This approach

recognizes that the needs of marginalized groups must be addressed in a coordinated and effective manner. To improve opportunities and living conditions for all residents in a region, we need policies to proactively connect people to jobs, stable housing, and good schools. Targeted universalism recognizes that life is lived in a web of opportunity" (powell 2008), https://prospect.org/special-report/race-place-opportunity/.

10. See, for example, the article "A Year after Ferguson, Housing Segregation Defies Tools to Erase It," from the *New York Times* by John Elgion, of a family seeking to escape the gravity of segregated housing in Ferguson, Missouri, a year after the killing of Michael Brown on August 9, 2014, and of the history of discriminatory housing policy in the St. Louis metro area: http://www.nytimes.com/2015/08/09/us/a-year-after-ferguson-hous ing-segregation-defies-tools-to-erase-it.html?hp&action=click&pgtype= Homepage&module=first-column-region&region=top-news&WT.nav= top-news&_r=0.

11. See also "African American Citywide Historic Context Statement" (San Francisco: San Francisco Planning Department, January 2016), https://sfp lanning.org/african-american-historic-context-statement.

12. A Gallup poll from 2004, for example, reported that among non-Hispanic whites, 57% preferred a mainly mixed neighborhood versus 40% who preferred it to be primarily white; non-Hispanic blacks, in comparison, preferred mainly mixed neighborhoods by 78% versus 14% (with 4% preferring neighborhoods composed of mostly Hispanics and non-Hispanic blacks); and Hispanics preferred mixed neighborhoods by 61% versus 19% (with 11% preferring neighborhoods composed of mostly Hispanics and non-Hispanic blacks). See Gallup's "For Most Americans, Friendship Is Colorblind," https://news.gallup.com/poll/12349/Most-Americans-Fri endship-Colorblind.aspx.

13. The view of integration as reconstruction and tying it to the ideal of open communities is similar to Danielle Allen's idea of a "connected society" (Allen 2017, 2018).

14. On this tendency within strains of liberalism focused on identity politics and multiculturalism, see Brian Barry's *Culture and Equality* (2001). Thomas Sowell makes related claims about liberalism in general in his *A Conflict of Visions* (1987). Relevant to this tendency in American politics regarding race in the years during and following the Trump presidency, see Mark Lilla's *The Once and Future Liberal: After Identity Politics* (2018), and John McWhorter's *Woke Racism: How a New Religious Has Betrayed Black America* (2021).

15. The connection between reciprocity and ethical integration is explicit in Ronald Dworkin's egalitarianism, which demands equal concern and has implications for social-spatial integration. Moral integration, in Dworkin's theory, is the integration of the right and the good in the lives of individual moral agents, and the political community in which they abide, in his holistic political-ethical theory, is a mode of ethical understanding and way of living that communicates central lessons of both liberalism and civic republicanism. Dworkin wrote, "The integrated liberal will not separate his private and public lives [. . .]. He will count his own life as diminished—a less good life than he might have had—if he lives in an unjust community, no matter how hard he has tried to make it just. That fusion of political morality and critical self-interest seems to me to be the true nerve of civic republicanism, the important way in which individual citizens should merge their interests and personality into political community. It states a distinctively liberal ideal, one that flourishes only within a liberal society" (Dworkin, 2000, 233). The sort of integration that Dworkin was concerned about is contained in the requirements of basic and democratic equality that starts with the reconstructive conception of social-spatial justice.

16. The dialogue ends with Socrates responding to his interlocutors—Laches, Nicias, and Lysimachus—that they should continue their search for a teacher who has a proper understanding of the truth about the good for themselves and their sons and, with the usual irony, Socrates humbly asserting he is not the one (Plato 1992, 201a).

17. See Karen Armstrong's *The Case for God* (2009, 61–12). On the *Laches* Armstrong cites Pierre Hadot's *Philosophy as a Way of Life* (1995, 152–170).

18. See Chapter 5, fn. 15.

19. Matt Yglesias, "The Great Awokening," *Vox*, April 1, 2019, https://www.vox.com/2019/3/22/18259865/great-awokening-white-liberals-race-polling-trump-2020.

20. Young introduced her idea of city life in *Justice and the Politics of Difference* (1990) in a chapter on "City Life and Difference." That chapter was followed by an article on "Residential Segregation and Differentiated Citizenship," and an updated version of that article, now with the title "Residential Segregation and Regional Democracy" as a chapter in her book, *Inclusion and Democracy* (2000). For an example of the uptake of her work in urban theory, see David Harvey's and Cuz Potter's use of Young's theory of oppression in their analysis of the idea of the right to the city (Harvey and Potter 2009).

21. Young contrasts the ideal of city life she promotes with an alternative ideal of community life provided by communitarian theories of social organization, belonging, and justice (Young 1990, 227–236) that criticized standard liberal approaches and emphasized collective over individual or atomistic identities, and based respect not just in the enforcement of rights, but in "attending to and sharing in the particularity" of group needs and interests (228). Young shared these general communitarian criticisms of liberalism but identifies a set of problems with the community ideal which led her to reject it, such as its assumption of intersubjective transparency between its members and a common consciousness, its assertion of an exclusive group identity she criticizes as essentialist and as a metaphysical illusion, and its propensity to exclude and oppress those outside the group (227–236). These are concerns that were evoked in my objections to anti-gentrification arguments based on appeals to community character (see Chapter 5).

22. See Young (1990, 239). Young's criteria of eroticism are an instantiation of the reestimation, or in her terms the rescaling, of bodies that is required to end oppression and domination. Young views oppression and domination as the result of five elements or "faces" of oppression (48–62).

23. For Young's advocacy of cultural revolution, see *Justice and the Politics of Difference* (1990, 152–155), and for criticism of it, see Barry (2001, 9, 317–328).

24. Sharon Stanley, "Toward a Reconciliation of Integration and Racial Solidarity," *Contemporary Political Theory* 13, no. 1 (2014): 46–63; "The Enduring Challenge of Racial Integration in the United States," *Du Bois Review* 12, no. 1 (2015): 5–24; and. *An Impossible Dream? Racial Integration in the United States* (New York: Oxford University Press, 2017).

25. See the discussion in Chapter 1 regarding the relation between social egalitarianism and perfectionism. Stanley's version of perfectionism predicates the achievement of a political end (integration) with the adoption by agents of specific goods in the forms of ideas that go beyond general principles. This contrasts types of political perfectionism that argue for the adoption of a thinner set of civic goods and general principles as civic values (Galston 1991). Parts of her view compare with Christopher Lebron's democratic perfectionist view with its focus on improving the moral agency of subjects by calling on them to abandon negative social valuations of blackness and black people (Lebron 2013, Chapter 5). My prioritization of basic and democratic equality corresponds with Stanley's and Lebron's positions on the "social valuation" or normative status of all

persons. Therefore, the reconstruction view is perfectionist in the narrow or thin manner that Galston defends. Such a thin view, however, is not associated with political perfectionism, because perfectionists' views usually insist on the adoption of specific conceptions of the good or comprehensive doctrines. Stanley's and Lebron's views are perfectionist because they promote the adoption of specific content. Stanley does so with her claims about "whiteness" and Lebron does so through the content in his proposal of "The 'Real America' Re-Education" act. Although I cannot fill out my argument in this context, the problem for Lebron (and Stanley) is that their moral-agency perfectionism (which promotes civic virtues necessary to achieve justice) collapses into a perfectionism that demands the personal affirmation of particular goods and ultimate ends, which in their case is content related to contentious views about theories of race and racism. To put it bluntly, the reconstruction view does not require the personal repudiation of "color-" or "race-blindness," nor the adoption of critical ideas of white privilege and systemic racism. It does, however, require the acknowledgment of moral and social equality, the need for distributive justice to some degree, and the objective fact that some Americans, and in particular, black Americans, were subjected to state-sponsored segregation that has enduring material effects and that those effects require correction is some form.

26. Gallup, Race Relations: http://news.gallup.com/poll/1687/race-relati ons.aspx, and Pew Research Center, "On Views of Race and Inequality, Blacks and Whites Are Worlds Apart," http://www.pewsocialtrends.org/ 2016/06/27/on-views-of-race-and-inequality-blacks-and-whites-are-wor lds-apart/. Similar patterns are seen in the shifting attitudes toward the Black Lives Matter movement; see Pew's "Support for Black Lives Matter Has Decreased since June but Remains Strong among Black Americans," https://www.pewresearch.org/fact-tank/2020/09/16/support-for-black-lives-matter-has-decreased-since-june-but-remains-strong-among-black-americans/.

27. See, for example, the outcome-based demands of the Moral Mondays movement with its call for a "third reconstruction." See Barber and Wilson-Hartgrove's *The Third Reconstruction* (2016).

28. Ronald R. Sundstrom, "The Black-White Binary as Racial Anxiety and Demand for Justice," *The Browning of America and the Evasion of Social Justice* (2008, 65).

29. Relatedly, see also John McWhorter's *Woke Racism: How a New Religion Has Betrayed Black America* (2021).

30. Betsy Hodges, "As Mayor of Minneapolis, I Saw How White Liberals Block Change," *New York Times*, July 9, 2020, https://www.nytimes.com/2020/07/09/opinion/minneapolis-hodges-racism.html.

31. The urban Left-NIMBY activist is distinct from the typical Right-NIMBY activist that seeks to get the poor and dark out of their suburbs. They are also distinct from the Marin County Left-NIMBY activists that seek to prevent density so they can save open space and agricultural land.

32. See, for example, Connor Dougherty, "The Great American Single-Family Home Problem, *New York Times*, December 1, 2017, https://www.nytimes.com/2017/12/01/business/economy/single-family-home.html. See also Clayton Nall and William Marble, "Where Self-Interest Trumps Ideology: Liberal Homeowners and Local Opposition to Housing Development" (2021, forthcoming).

33. See the discussion of school choice and gentrification in Schlichtman et al.'s *Gentrifier* (2017).

Chapter 7

1. Baldwin used the term "price" in his writing to connote the social, political, and even economic costs of liberation, love, reciprocity, whiteness, and personal success in a racialized America. See, for example, *The Fire Next Time* (1993, 18, 87, and 102). See also his "The Price of the Ticket" in *Baldwin: Collected Essays* (1998a, 830–842). Baldwin writes of achieving our nation that "we, the black and the white, deeply need each other here if we are really to become a nation—if we are really, that is, to achieve our identity, our maturity, as men and women" (1993, 97). He was pointing out that racial separatism and an assumption of white racial supremacy operated in de facto white-majority conceptions of American nationhood and belonging of his time. He condemned racial nationalism and demonstrated through his writing that the idea of white supremacy assumed in American nationalism was no different and more harmful than the black nationalism of the 1960s that white intellectuals and politicians criticized.

2. On transportation justice, see Karel Marten's *Transport Justice* (2017) and Shane Epting's *The Morality of Urban Mobility*, and on technology and philosophy of the city, see Michael Nagenborg et al.'s *Technology and the City* (2021). On homelessness policy, see Bart van Leuween's "To the Edge of the Urban Landscape: Homelessness and the Politics of Care" (*Political Theory* 2018, 46, no. 4: 586–610) and van Leuween and Michael S. Merry's

"Should the Homeless Be Forcibly Helped?" (*Public Health Ethics* 2019, 12, no. 1: 30–43).

3. Rent stabilization policies or rent control policies are motivated by the concerns of justice in social-spatial arrangements and offer relief to current residents but may worsen housing affordability in their areas. For example, Diamond et al. conclude in "The Effects of Rent Control Expansion on Tenants, Landlords, and Inequality: Evidence from San Francisco," that "We find tenants covered by rent control do place a substantial value on the benefit, as revealed by their choice to remain in their apartments longer than those without rent control. Indeed, we find the vast majority of those incentivized to remain in their rent-controlled apartment would have been displaced from San Francisco had they not been covered. . . . However, landlords of properties affected by the law change respond over the long term by substituting to other types of real estate, by converting to condos and redeveloping buildings to exempt them from rent control. In the long run, landlords' substitution toward owner-occupied and newly constructed rental housing not only lowered the supply of rental housing in the city, but also shifted the city's housing supply towards less affordable types of housing that likely cater to the tastes of higher income individuals. Ultimately, these endogenous shifts in the housing supply likely drove up citywide rents, damaging housing affordability for future renters, and counteracting the stated claims of the law" (2–3). For a response to this, see Pastor et al.'s "Rent Matters: What Are the Impacts of Rent Stabilization Measures?" (2018). See also Chapter 4, fn. 14.

4. See my comment, "Build More Housing," in Olasov's "Cities after COVID" (2022).

5. This set of is from the report, "Housing Is Critical Infrastructure: Social and Economic Benefits of Building More Housing" (June 2021) prepared for the National Realtors Association, https://cdn.nar.realtor/sites/defa ult/files/documents/Housing-is-Critical-Infrastructure-Social-and-Economic-Benefits-of-Building-More-Housing-6-15-2021.pdf.

6. See, for example, Senator Cory Booker and Representative James E. Clyburn's proposed "Home Act," https://www.booker.senate.gov/news/ press/booker-clyburn-take-innovative-two-pronged-approach-to-tackl ing-affordable-housing-crisis.

7. For other recommendations regarding rental policy, see Matthew Desmond's *Evicted* (2106) and "How Homeownership Became the Engine of American Inequality" (2017).

8. The programs involve the right of return for residents who experienced housing discrimination and displacement because they lived in neighborhoods that were redlined and targeted for urban renewal, such as Portland's North/Northeast Preference Policy; see, for example, https://www.portland.gov/phb/nnehousing/preference-policy. The city of San Francisco implemented a similar project called the Neighborhood Preference Plan that is implemented through a lottery system; see, for example, https://projects.sfplanning.org/community-stabilization/lottery-preference-programs.htm and an SF Chronicle article about the program, https://www.sfchronicle.com/bayarea/article/Neighborhood-preference-program-for-affordable-13668858.php. Portland's and San Francisco's policies are consistent with constitutional equal protection standards. Evanston's reparations policy is directly targeted to black residents of the city, and the funds are dedicated to supporting home ownership, improvement, and mortgage assistance. See Evanston's Local Reparations Policy, https://www.cityofevanston.org/government/city-council/reparations.

9. For further policy proposals, see Sheryl Cashin (2004, 321–331), Xavier de Souza Briggs (2005c, 330), Angela Glover Blackwell, Judith Bell (2005), Edward G. Goetz (2018), and Andre Perry (2020).

10. Kenneth T. Rosen, David Bank, Max Hall, Scott Reed, and Carson Goldman, "Housing Is Critical Infrastructure: Social and Economic Benefits of Building More Housing," Rosen Consulting Group for the National Association of Realtors (June 2021), https://www.nar.realtor/political-advocacy/housing-is-critical-infrastructure.

11. See, for example, the World Bank's report, "Groundswell: Preparing for Internal Climate Migration," https://www.worldbank.org/en/news/infographic/2018/03/19/groundswell---preparing-for-internal-climate-migration.

12. "Rent is too damn high" was the motto and catchphrase of Jimmy McMillan, who ran for the mayor of New York City in 2005 and 2009 and for governor of the state of New York in 2010.

13. See, for example, the Vox and Data for Progress poll from February 2021, https://www.filesforprogress.org/datasets/2021/2/dfp-vox-multi-family-zoning.pdf, and Jerusalem Demas's "How to Convince a NIMBY to Build More Housing: A New Vox and Data for Progress Poll Suggests Voters Increase Support for Building More Homes When Presented with an Economic Case for It," Vox, February 24, 2021, https://www.vox.com/22297328/affordable-housing-nimby-housing-prices-rising-poll-data-for-progress.

Works Cited

Alexander, Lisa T. 2015. "Occupying the Constitutional Right to Housing." *Nebraska Law Review* 94, no. 2: 245–301.

Allen, Danielle. 2017. "Toward a Connected Society." In *Our Compelling Interests: The Value of Diversity for Democracy and a Prosperous Society*, edited by Earl Lewis and Nancy Cantor, 70–105. Princeton, NJ: Princeton University Press.

Allen, Danielle. 2018. "Integration, Freedom, and the Affirmation of Life." In *To Shape a New World: Essays on the Political Philosophy of Martin Luther King, Jr*, edited by Tommie Shelby and Brandon M. Terry, 146–160. Cambridge, MA: The Belknap Press of Harvard University Press.

Anderson, Elizabeth.1999. "What Is the Point of Equality?" *Ethics* 109, no. 2: 287–337.

Anderson, Elizabeth. 2010a. *The Imperative of Integration*. Princeton, NJ: Princeton University Press.

Anderson, Elizabeth. 2010b. "The Fundamental Disagreement between Luck Egalitarians and Relational Egalitarians." *Canadian Journal of Philosophy* Suppl. Vol. 36: 1–23.

Apgar, William, and Allegra Calder. 2005. "The Dual Mortgage Market: The Persistence of Discrimination in Mortgage Lending." In *The Geography of Opportunity: Race and Housing Choice in Metropolitan America*, edited by Xavier de Souza Briggs, 101–123. Washington, DC: Brookings Institution Press.

Armstrong, Karen. 2009. *The Case for God*. New York: Knopf.

Bagenstos, Samuel R. 2014. "The Unrelenting Libertarian Challenge to Public Accommodations Law." *Stanford Law Review* 66, no. 6: 1205–1240.

Baldwin, James. 1985. *The Price of the Ticket: Collected Nonfiction, 1948–1985*. New York: St. Martin's/Marek.

Baldwin, James. (1963) 1993. *The Fire Next Time*. New York: Vintage International.

Baldwin, James. 1998. *Baldwin: Collected Essays*. New York: Library of America.

Barber, William J., and Jonathan Wilson-Hartgrove. 2016. *The Third Reconstruction: Moral Mondays, Fusion Politics, and the Rise of a New Justice Movement*. Boston: Beacon Press.

Barry, Brian. 2001. *Culture and Equality: An Egalitarian Critique of Multiculturalism*. Cambridge, MA: Harvard University Press.

Basso, Keith H. 1996. *Wisdom Sits in Places*. Albuquerque: University of New Mexico Press.

Beauregard, Robert A. 1986. "The Chaos and Complexity of Gentrification." In *Gentrification of the City*, edited by Neil Smith and Peter Williams, 35–55. Boston: Allen & Unwin.

Bishop, Bill, and Robert G. Cushing. 2008. *The Big Sort: Why the Clustering of Like-Minded America Is Tearing Us Apart*. Boston: Houghton Mifflin.

Boxill, Bernard R. 1972. "The Morality of Reparation." *Social Theory and Practice* 2, no. 1: 113–123.

Brandon, Terry M. 2018. "Requiem for a Dream: The Problem-Space of Black Power." In *To Shape a New World: The Political Philosophy of Martin Luther King, Jr.*, edited by Tommie Shelby and Brandon Terry, 290–324. Cambridge, MA: The Belknap Press of Harvard University Press.

Brandon, Terry M. 2021a. "Malcolm's Ministry." *The New York Review of Books*, February 25, 2021. https://www.nybooks.com/articles/2021/02/25/malcolm-x-ministry/.

Brandon, Terry M. 2021b. "What Dignity Demands." *The New York Review of Books*, March 11, 2021. https://www.nybooks.com/articles/2021/03/11/malcolm-x-martin-luther-king-what-dignity-demands/.

Bratt, Rachel G., Michael E. Stone, and Chester W. Hartman, eds. 2006a. *A Right to Housing: Foundation for a New Social Agenda*. Philadelphia: Temple University.

Bratt, Rachel G., Michael E. Stone, and Chester W. Hartman. 2006b. "Why a Right to Housing Is Needed and Makes Sense: Editors' Introduction." In *A Right to Housing: Foundation for a New Social Agenda*, edited by Rachel G. Bratt, Michael E. Stone, and Chester W. Hartman, 1–19. Philadelphia: Temple University.

Briggs, Xavier de Souza, ed. 2005a. *The Geography of Opportunity: Race and Housing Choice in Metropolitan America*. Washington, DC: Brookings Institution Press.

Briggs, Xavier de Souza. 2005b. "More Pluribus, Less Unum? The Changing Geography of Race and Opportunity." In *The Geography of Opportunity: Race and Housing Choice in Metropolitan America*, edited by Xavier de Souza Briggs, 17–41. Washington, DC: Brookings Institution Press.

Briggs, Xavier de Souza. 2005c. "Politics and Policy: Changing Geography of Opportunity." In *The Geography of Opportunity: Race and Housing Choice in Metropolitan America*, edited by Xavier de Souza Briggs, 310–341. Washington, DC: Brookings Institution Press.

Bryson, David B. 2006. "The Role of the Courts and a Right to Housing." In *A Right to Housing: Foundation for a New Social Agenda*, edited by Rachel G. Bratt, Michael E. Stone, and Chester W. Hartman, 193–212. Philadelphia: Temple University Press.

Buchanan, James M. 1986. *Liberty, Market, and State: Political Economy in the 1980s*. New York: New York University Press.

Burkhart, Ann M. 2003. "The Constitutional Underpinnings of Homelessness." *Housing Law Review* 40, no. 2: 211–279.

Byrne, J. Peter. 2003. "Two Cheers for Gentrification." *Howard Law Journal* 46, no. 3: 405–432.

Cashin, Sheryll. 2004. *The Failures of Integration: How Race and Class Are Undermining the American Dream*. New York: Public Affairs.

Cervero, Robert. 1989. "Jobs-Housing Balancing and Regional Mobility." *Journal of the American Planning Association* 55, no. 2: 136–150.

Chapple, Karen. 2009. "Mapping Susceptibility to Gentrification: The Early Warning Toolkit." Berkeley, CA: Center for Community Innovation.

Chapple, Karen, and Rick Jacobus. 2009. "Retail Trade as a Route to Neighborhood Revitalization." In *Urban and Regional Policy and Its Effects*, edited by Margery Austin Turner, Howard Wial, Harold Wolman, and Nancy Pindus, 2: 19–68. Washington, DC: Brookings Institution.

Chapple, Karen, and Anastasia Loukaitou-Sideris. 2019. *Transit-Oriented Displacement or Community Dividends? Understanding the Effects of Smarter Growth on Communities*. Cambridge, MA: The MIT Press.

Charles, Camille Zubrinsky. 2005. "Can We Live Together? Racial Preferences and Neighborhood Outcomes." In *The Geography of Opportunity: Race and Housing Choice in Metropolitan America*, edited by Xavier de Souza Briggs, 45–80. Washington, DC: Brookings Institution Press.

Chaskin, Robert J., and Mark L. Joseph. 2013. "'Positive' Gentrification, Social Control and the 'Right to the City' in Mixed-Income Communities: Uses and Expectations of Space and Place: Mixed-Income Communities and Control of 'Public' Space in Chicago." *International Journal of Urban and Regional Research* 37, no. 2: 480–502.

Chetty, Raj, and Nathaniel Hendren. 2018. "The Impacts of Neighborhoods on Intergenerational Mobility I: Childhood Exposure Effects." *Quarterly Journal of Economics* 113, no. 3: 1107–1162.

Chetty, Raj, Nathaniel Hendren, and Lawrence Katz. 2016. "The Effects of Exposure to Better Neighborhoods on Children: New Evidence from the Moving to Opportunity Project." *American Economic Review* 106, no. 4: 855–902.

Cisneros, Henry, Lora Engdahl, and Project Muse. 2009. *From Despair to Hope*. Washington, DC: Brookings Institution Press.

Clark, Kenneth B. 1989. "A Conversation with James Baldwin." In *Conversations with James Baldwin*, edited by Fred L. Standley and Louis H. Pratt, 38–45. Jackson: University Press of Mississippi.

Coates, Ta-Nehisi. 2017. *We Were Eight Years in Power: An American Tragedy*. New York: One World.

Cohen, G. A. 2009. *Why Not Socialism?* Princeton, NJ: Princeton University Press.

Cohen, G. A. 2011. *On the Currency of Egalitarian Justice, and Other Essays in Political Philosophy*. Edited by Michael Otsuka. Princeton, NJ: Princeton University Press.

Collinson, Robert, Ingrid Gould Ellen, and Jens Ludwig. 2015. "Low-Income Housing Policy." Cambridge: National Bureau of Economic Research. https://doi.org/10.3386/w21071.

Darby, Derrick, and Richard E. Levy. 2016. "Postracial Remedies." *University of Michigan Journal of Law Reform* 50: 387–488.

Davoudi, Simin, and Derek Bell. 2016. *Justice and Fairness in the City: A Multi-Disciplinary Approach to "Ordinary" Cities*. Bristol, England: Policy Press.

Dawkins, Casey J. 2017. "Putting Equality in Place: The Normative Foundations of Geographic Equality of Opportunity." *Housing Policy Debate* 27, no. 6: 897–912.

Dawkins, Casey J. 2020. "The Right to Housing in an Ownership Society." *Housing and Society* 47, no. 2: 81–102.

Dawkins, Casey J. 2021. *Just Housing: The Moral Foundations of American Housing Policy*. Urban and Industrial Environments. Cambridge, MA: The MIT Press.

Desmond, Matthew. 2016. *Evicted: Poverty and Profit in the American City*. New York: Crown.

Desmond, Matthew. 2017. "How Homeownership Became the Engine of American Inequality." *The New York Times*, May 19. https://www.nytimes.com/2017/05/09/magazine/how-homeownership-became-the-engine-of-american-inequality.html.

Diamond, Rebecca, Tim McQuade, and Franklin Qian. 2019. "The Effects of Rent Control Expansion on Tenants, Landlords, and Inequality: Evidence from San Francisco." *American Economic Review* 109, no. 9: 3365–3394.

Ding, Lei, Jackelyn Hwang, and Eileen Divringi. 2016. "Gentrification and Residential Mobility in Philadelphia." *Regional Science and Urban Economics* 61 (November): 38–51.

Denton, Nancy A. 2010. "From Segregation to Integration: How Do We Get There?" In *The Integration Debate: Competing Futures for American Cities*, edited by Chester W. Hartman and Gregory D. Squires, 23–37. New York: Routledge.

Dougherty, Conor. 2020. *Golden Gates: Fighting for Housing in America*. New York: Penguin Press.

Duany, Andres. 2001. "Three Cheers for Gentrification." *American Enterprise Magazine* 12, no. 3: 36–39.

Du Bois, W. E .B. 1935. *Black Reconstruction in America: An Essay toward a History of the Part Which Black Folk Played in the Attempt to Reconstruct Democracy in America, 1860–1880*. New York: Oxford University Press.

Du Bois, W. E .B. (1903) 1999. *The Souls of Black Folk*. Edited by Henry Louis Gates and Terri Hume Oliver. New York: W.W. Norton.

Du Bois, W. E .B. (1899) 2014. *The Philadelphia Negro: A Social Study*. New York: Oxford University Press.

Du Bois, W. E. B., and Nathan Irvin Huggins. 1996. *Writings*. New York: Library of America.

Du Bois, W. E. B., Eric Foner, and Henry Louis Gates Jr. 2021. *W.E.B. Du Bois: Black Reconstruction: An Essay toward a History of the Part Which Black Folk Played in the Attempt to Reconstruct Democracy in America, 1860–1880*. Library of America 350. New York: Library of America.

Du Bois, W. E. B., Henry Louis Gates, and Terri Hume Oliver. 1999. *The Souls of Black Folk: Authoritative Text, Contexts, Criticism*. New York: W.W. Norton.

Duneier, Mitchell. 2016. *Ghetto: The Invention of a Place, the History of an Idea*. New York: Farrar, Straus and Giroux.

Dworkin, Ronald. 2000. *Sovereign Virtue: The Theory and Practice of Equality*. Cambridge, MA: Harvard University Press.

Dwyer, Rachel E., and Lora A. Phillips Lassus. 2015. "The Great Risk Shift and Precarity in the U.S. Housing Market." *Annals of the American Academy of Political and Social Science* 660: 199–216.

Ellen, Ingrid Gould. 2001. *Sharing America's Neighborhoods: The Prospects for Stable Racial Integration*. Cambridge, MA: Harvard University Press.

Ellen, Ingrid Gould, and Kathy M. O'Regan. 2011. "How Low Income Neighborhoods Change: Entry, Exit and Enhancement." *Regional Science and Urban Economics* 41, no. 2: 89–97.

Elster, Jon. 1992. *Local Justice: How Institutions Allocate Scarce Goods and Necessary Burdens*. New York: Russell Sage Foundation.

Engels, Friedrich. (1872) 1975. *The Housing Question*. Moscow: Progress Publishers.

Enos, Ryan D. 2017. *The Space between Us: Social Geography and Politics*. New York: Cambridge University Press.

Epting, Shane Ray. 2021. *The Morality of Urban Mobility: Technology and Philosophy of the City*. Lanham, MD: Rowman & Littlefield.

Fainstein, Susan S. 2010. *The Just City*. Ithaca, NY: Cornell University Press.

Fainstein, Susan S. 2011. "Redevelopment Planning and Distributive Justice in the American Metropolis." In *Justice and the American Metropolis*, edited by Clarissa Rile Hayward and Todd Swanstrom, 149–176. Minneapolis: University of Minnesota Press.

Fiss, Owen M. 2003. *A Way Out: America's Ghettos and the Legacy of Racism*.

Fixico, Donald Lee. 1986. *Termination and Relocation: Federal Indian Policy, 1945–1960*. Albuquerque: University of New Mexico Press.

Florida, Richard L. 2017. *The New Urban Crisis: How Our Cities Are Increasing Inequality, Deepening Segregation, and Failing the Middle Class—And What We Can Do about It*. New York: Basic Books.

Frankfurt, Harry. 1987. "Equality as a Moral Ideal." *Ethics* 98: 21–43.

Fraser, Nancy. (1996) 2009. "Social Justice in the Age of Identity Politics: Redistribution, Recognition, and Participation." In *Geographic Thought: A Praxis Perspective*, edited by George L. Henderson and Marvin, 72–91. New York: Routledge.

Fraser, Nancy. 1997. *Justice Interruptus: Critical Reflections on the "Postsocialist" Condition*. New York: Routledge.

Freeman, Lance, and Frank Braconi. 2002. "Gentrification and Displacement." *The Urban Prospect: Housing, Planning and Economic Development in New York* 8, no. 1: 1–4.

Freeman, Lance, and Frank Braconi. 2004. "Gentrification and Displacement: New York City in the 1990s." *Journal of the American Planning Association* 70, no. 1: 39–52.

Freeman, Lance, and Frank Braconi. 2005. "Displacement or Succession? Residential Mobility in Gentrifying Neighborhoods." *Urban Affairs Review* 40, no. 4: 463–491.

Freeman, Lance. 2006. *There Goes the 'Hood: Views of Gentrification from the Ground Up*. Philadelphia: Temple University Press.

Freeman, Samuel Richard. 2007. *Rawls*. New York: Routledge.

Foner, Eric. 1988. *Reconstruction: America's Unfinished Revolution, 1863–1877*. New York: Harper & Row.

Fulwood, Sam, III. 2018. "The Costs of Segregation and the Benefits of the Fair Housing Act (1966–1968)." In *The Fight for Fair Housing: Causes, Consequences, and Future Implications of the 1968 Federal Fair Housing Act*, edited by Gregory D. Squires, 28–39. New York: Routledge.

Galster, George C., and Sean P. Killen. 1995. "The Geography of Metropolitan Opportunity: A Reconnaissance and Conceptual Framework." *Housing Policy Debate* 6, no. 1: 7–43.

Galston, William A. 1991. *Liberal Purposes: Goods, Virtues, and Diversity in the Liberal State*. New York: Cambridge University Press.

Glaeser, Edward L. 2011. *Triumph of the City: How Our Greatest Invention Makes Us Richer, Smarter, Greener, Healthier, and Happier*. New York: Penguin Press.

Glaeser, Edward, and Jacob Vigdor. 2021. "The End of the Segregation Century: Racial Separation in America's Neighborhoods 1890–2010." Manhattan Institute's *Civic Report*, No. 66 (January). https://files.epi.org/2014/making-of-ferguson-final.pdf.

Glasgow, Joshua, Sally Anne Haslanger, and Chike Jeffers. 2019. *What Is Race? Four Philosophical Views*. New York: Oxford University Press.

Glynn, Chris, and Emily Fox. 2017. "Dynamics of Homelessness in America." *arXivLabs*. arXiv:1707.09380 [stat.AP].

Goetz, Edward G. 2000. "The Politics of Poverty Deconcentration and Housing Demolition." *Journal of Urban Affairs* 22, no. 2: 167–173.

Goetz, Edward G. 2003. *Clearing the Way: Deconcentrating the Poor in Urban America*. Washington, DC: The Urban Institute Press.

Goetz, Edward G. 2018. *The One-Way Street of Integration: Fair Housing and the Pursuit of Racial Justice in American Cities*. Ithaca, NY: Cornell University Press.

Goldberg, David Theo. 2002. *The Racial State*, Malden, MA: Blackwell.

Goldberg, John C. P., Henry E. Smith, and P. G. Turner, eds. 2019. *Equity and Law: Fusion and Fission*. New York: Cambridge University Press.

Golledge, Reginal D., and Robert J. Stimson. 1997. *Spatial Behavior*. New York: Guilford.

Goodhart, David. 2017. *The Road to Somewhere: The Populist Revolt and the Future of Politics*. London: Hurst & Company.

Gray, John. 2007. *Black Mass: Apocalyptic Religion and the Death of Utopia*. New York: Farrar Straus and Giroux.

Grier, George W., and Eunice S. Grier. 1978. *Urban Displacement: A Reconnaissance*. Washington, DC: Department of Housing and Urban Development, and Office of the Secretary.

Hacker, Jacob S., and Paul Pierson. 2010. *Winner-Take-All Politics: How Washington Made the Rich Richer—And Turned Its Back on the Middle Class*. New York: Simon & Schuster.

Hadot, Pierre. 1995. *Philosophy as a Way of Life: Spiritual Exercises from Socrates to Foucault*. Introduced and edited by Arnold I. Davidson and translated by Michael Chase. Malden, MA: Blackwell.

Haidt, Jonathan. 2012. *The Righteous Mind: Why Good People Are Divided by Politics and Religion*. New York: Pantheon Books

Hammel, D. J., and E. K. Wyly. 1996. "A Model for Identifying Gentrified Areas with Census Data." *Urban Geography* 17, no. 3: 248–268.

Hancock, Ange-Marie. 2004. *The Politics of Disgust: The Public Identity of the Welfare Queen*. New York: New York University Press.

Hanratty, Maria, Sara McLanahan, and Becky Pettit. 1998. "The Impact of the Los Angeles Moving to Opportunity Program on Residential Mobility, Neighborhood Characteristics, and Early Child and Parent Outcomes." Working Papers 990. Princeton University, School of Public and International Affairs, Center for Research on Child Wellbeing. https://Eco nPapers.repec.org/RePEc:pri:crcwel:wp98-18-hanratty.pdf.

Hansberry, Lorraine. (1959) 1994. *A Raisin in the Sun*. New York: Vintage Books.

Hartman, Chester W. 2006. "The Case for a Right to Housing." In *A Right to Housing: Foundation for a New Social Agenda*, edited by Rachel G. Bratt, Michael E. Stone, and Chester W. Hartman, 177–192. Philadelphia: Temple University.

Harvey, David. 1973. *Social Justice and the City*. London: Edward Arnold.

Harvey, David. 2005. *A Brief History of Neoliberalism*. Oxford: Oxford University Press.

Harvey, David. 2012. *Rebel Cities: From the Right to the City to the Urban Revolution*. London: Verso.

Harvey, David, and Cuz Potter. 2009. "The Right to the Just City." In *Searching for the Just City: Debates in Urban Theory and Practice*, edited by Peter Marcuse, James Connolly, Johanes Novy, Ingrid Olivo, Cuz Potter, and Justin Steil, 40–51. New York: Routledge.

Hayward, Clarissa Rile, and Todd Swanstrom. 2011. *Justice and the American Metropolis*. Minneapolis: University of Minnesota Press.

Iglesias, Tim. 2007. "Our Pluralist Housing Ethics and the Struggle for Affordability." *Wake Forest Law Review* 42 (Summer): 512–593.

Imbroscio, David. 2008. "[U]Nited and Actuated by Some Common Impulse of Passion: Challenging the Dispersal Consensus in American Policy Research." *Journal of Urban Affairs* 30, no. 2: 111–130.

James, Denise V. 2013. "The Burdens of Integration" *Symposia on Gender, Race and Philosophy* 9, no. 2: 1–5. https://web.mit.edu/sgrp/2013/no2/James0 913.pdf.

Jacobs, Jane. 1961. *The Death and Life of Great American Cities*. New York: Random House.

Johnston, Ron, Michael Poulsen, and James Forrest. 2014. "Segregation Matters, Measurement Matters." In *Social-Spatial Segregation: Concepts, Processes and Outcomes*, edited by Christopher D. Lloyd, Ian G. Shuttleworth, and David W.S. Wong, 13–44. Bristol, England: Policy Press.

Jois, Goutam U. 2007. "Affordable Housing and Civic Participation: Two Sides of the Same Coin." *Brigham Young University Journal of Public Law* 22: 1–41.

Judt, Tony. 2011. *Past Imperfect: French Intellectuals, 1944–1956*. New York: New York University Press.

Kaplan, Jonathan, and Andrew Valls. 2007. "Housing Discrimination as a Basis for Black Reparations." *Public Affairs Quarterly* 21, no. 3: 255–273.

Keeler, Kasey. 2016. "Putting People Where They Belong: American Indian Housing Policy in the Mid-Twentieth Century." *Native American and Indigenous Studies* 3, no. 2: 70–104.

Kelly, Paul J. 2002. *Multiculturalism Reconsidered: Culture and Equality and Its Critics*. Malden, MA: Polity.

Kennedy, Maureen, and Paul Leonard. 2001. "Dealing with Neighborhood Changes: A Primer on Gentrification and Policy Choices." Washington, DC: The Brookings Institution Center on Urban and Metropolitan Policy and Policy Link.

Kertesz, Stefan G., Kimberly Crouch, Jesse B. Milby, Robert E. Cusimano, and Joseph E. Schumacher. 2009. "Housing First for Homeless Persons with Active Addiction: Are We Overreaching? Housing First for Homeless Persons with Active Addiction." *Milbank Quarterly* 87, no. 2: 495–534.

King, Martin Luther, Jr. 1991. *A Testament of Hope: The Essential Writings and Speeches of Martin Luther King, Jr.* Edited by James M. Washington. New York: Harper Collins.

King, Martin Luther, Jr. (1962) 1991a. "The Ethical Demands for Integration." In *A Testament of Hope: The Essential Writings of Martin Luther King, Jr.*, edited by James Melvin Washington, 117–125. San Francisco: Harper & Row.

King, Martin Luther, Jr. (1963) 1991b. "Letter from Birmingham City Jail." In *A Testament of Hope: The Essential Writings of Martin Luther King, Jr.*, edited by James Melvin Washington, 289–302. San Francisco: Harper & Row.

King, Martin Luther, Jr. (1967) 1991c. "Christmas Sermon on Peace." In *A Testament of Hope: The Essential Writings of Martin Luther King, Jr.*, edited by James Melvin, 253–258. Washington, DC: Harper & Row.

King, Martin Luther, Jr. (1967) 2010. *Where Do We Go from Here: Chaos or Community?* Boston: Beacon Press.

Kohn, Margaret. 2016. *The Death and Life of the Urban Commonwealth.* New York: Oxford University Press.

Kołakowski, Leszek. 1978. *Main Currents of Marxism: The Founders, the Golden Age, the Breakdown.* New York: W.W. Norton & Company.

Krysan, Maria, and Kyle Crowder. 2017. *Cycle of Segregation: Social Processes and Residential Stratification.* New York: Russell Sage Foundation.

Kukla, Quill R. 2021. *City Living: How Urban Dwellers and Urban Spaces Make One Another.* New York: Oxford University Press.

Kymlicka, Will. 1995. *Multicultural Citizenship: A Liberal Theory of Minority Rights.* New York: Oxford University Press.

Kymlicka, Will. 2002. "Liberal Equality." In *Contemporary Political Philosophy: An Introduction*, edited by Will Kymlicka, 53–101. New York: Oxford.

Lebron, Christopher J. 2013. *The Color of our Shame: Race and Justice in Our Time.* New York: Oxford University Press.

Lees, Loretta, Tom Slater, and Elvin K. Wyly. 2008. *Gentrification.* New York: Routledge.

Lefebvre, Henri. (1968) 1996. "Right to the City." In *Writings on Cities*, edited by Eleonore Kofman and Elizabeth Lebas, 147–159. Oxford: Blackwell.

Ley, David. 1996. *The New Middle Class and the Remaking of the Central City.* New York: Oxford University Press.

Lilla, Mark. 2018. *The Once and Future Liberal: After Identity Politics.* New York: Harper.

Lipsitz, George. 2011. *How Racism Takes Place.* Philadelphia: Temple University Press.

Loury, Glenn. 2000. "It's Futile to Put a Price on Slavery." *New York Times*, May 29. https://www.nytimes.com/2000/05/29/opinion/it-s-futile-to-put-a-price-on-slavery.html

Loury, Glenn. 2007. "Transgenerational Justice—Compensatory versus Interpretative Approaches." In *Reparations: Interdisciplinary Inquiries*, edited by Jon Miller and Rahul Kumar, 87–113. New York: Oxford University Press.

Ludwig, Jens, Greg J. Duncan, Lisa A. Gennetian, Lawrence F. Katz, Ronald C. Kessler, Jeffrey R. Kling, and Lisa Sanbonmatsu. 2014. "Moving to Opportunity: The Effects of Concentrated Poverty on the Poor." *Third Way*. Washington, DC. https://www.thirdway.org/report/moving-to-opportunity-the-effects-of-concentrated-poverty-on-the-poor.

Macedo, Stephen. 2011. "Property-Owning Plutocracy: Inequality and American Localism." In *Justice and the American Metropolis*, edited by Clarissa Rile Hayward, and Todd Swanstrom, 33–59. Minneapolis: University of Minnesota Press.

MacIntyre, Alasdair C. 1984. *After Virtue: A Study in Moral Theory*. Notre Dame: University of Notre Dame Press.

Marcuse, Peter. 2002. "The Shifting Meaning of the Black Ghetto in the United States." In *Of States and Cities: The Partitioning of Urban Space*, edited by Peter Marcuse and Ronald van Kempen, 109–142. New York: Oxford University Press.

Marcuse, Peter. 2013. "To Control Gentrification." Presentation at the RC21 International Conference, "Resourceful Cities." August 29–31. Berlin, Germany.

Massey, Douglas S., and Nancy A. Denton. 1988. "The Dimensions of Residential Segregation." *Social Forces* 67, no. 2: 281–315.

Massey, Douglas S., and Nancy A. Denton. 1993. *American Apartheid: Segregation and the Making of the Underclass*. Cambridge, MA: Harvard University Press.

Matthew, Dale C. 2021. "Racial Integration and the Problem of Relational Devaluation." *Dialogue*, September, 1–43.

McCarthy, Thomas. 2002. "*Vergangenheirbewälatigung* in the USA: On the Politics of the Memory of Slavery." *Political Theory* 30, no. 5: 623–648.

McKinnish, Terra, Randall Walsh, and Kirk White. 2010. "Who Gentrifies Low-Income Neighborhoods?" *Journal of Urban Economics* 67, no. 2: 180–193.

McWhorter, John. 2021. *Woke Racism: How a New Religion Has Betrayed Black America*. New York: Portfolio.

Menendian, Stephen, and Samir Gambhir. 2019. "Racial Segregation in the San Francisco Bay Area." Berkeley, CA: The Othering & Belonging Institute. https://belonging.berkeley.edu/segregationinthebay.

Menendian, Stephen, Arthur Gailes, and Samir Gambhir. 2021. "The Roots of Structural Racism: Twenty-First Century Racial Residential Segregation in the United States." Berkeley, CA: The Othering & Belonging Institute. https://belonging.berkeley.edu/roots-structural-racism.

Merry, Michael S. 2013. *Equality, Citizenship, and Segregation: A Defense of Separation*. 1st ed. New York: Palgrave Macmillan.

Merry, Michael S. 2021. "Is Faith in School Integration Bad Faith?" *On Education. Journal for Research and Debate* 4, no. 11: 1–8.

Miller, David. 1997. "Equality and Justice." *Ratio* 10, no. 3: 222–237.

Mills, Charles W. 1998. *Blackness Visible: Essays on Philosophy and Race*. Ithaca, NY: Cornell University Press.

Mills, Charles W. 2017. *Black Rights / White Wrongs: The Critique of Racial Liberalism*. New York: Oxford University Press.

Monkkonen, Paavo. 2016. "Understanding and Challenging Opposition to Housing Construction in California's Urban Areas." *SSRN Electronic Journal*. http://dx.doi.org/10.2139/ssrn.3459823.

Mullainathan, Sendhil, and Eldar Shafir. 2013. *Scarcity: Why Having Too Little Means So Much*. New York: Henry Holt and Company.

Nagenborg, Michael, Taylor Stone, Margoth González Woge, and Pieter Vermaas, eds. 2021. *Technology and the City: Towards a Philosophy of Urban Technologies*. Cham, Switzerland: Springer.

Newman, Kathe, and Elvin K. Wyly. 2006. "The Right to Stay Put, Revisited: Gentrification and Resistance to Displacement in New York City." *Urban Studies* 43, no. 1: 23–57.

Nozick, Robert. 1974. *Anarchy, State, and Utopia*. New York: Basic Books.

Okin, Susan Moller. 1989. *Justice, Gender, and the Family*. New York: Basic Books.

Olasov, Ian. 2022. "Cities after COVID." *The Philosophers' Magazine*, October 2. https://www.philosophersmag.com/essays/302-cities-after-covid.

Orfield, Gary, and Susan E. Eaton. 1996. *Dismantling Desegregation: The Quiet Reversal of Brown v. Board of Education*. New York: New Press.

Österle, August. 2002. "Evaluating Equity in Social Policy: A Framework for Comparative Analysis." *Evaluation* 8, no. 1: 46–59.

Ostler, Jeffrey. 2019. *Surviving Genocide: Native Nations and the United States from the American Revolution to Bleeding Kansas*. New Haven, CT: Yale University Press.

Parfit, Derek. 1997. "Equality and Priority." *Ratio* 10, no. 3: 202–221.

Pastor, Manuel, Vanessa Carter, and Maya Abood. 2018. "Rent Matters: What Are the Impacts of Rent Stabilization Measures?" USC Dornsife Program for Environmental and Regional Equity.

Pateman, Carole. 1988. *The Sexual Contract*. Cambridge, UK: Polity.

Pateman, Carole, and Charles W. Mills. 2007. *Contract and Domination*. Malden, MA: Polity.

Patterson, Orlando. 1997. *The Ordeal of Integration: Progress and Resentment in America's "Racial" Crisis*. Washington, DC: Civitas/Counterpoint.

Patillo, Mary. 2013. "Housing: Commodity versus Right." *Annual Review of Sociology* 39: 509–531.

Pietila, Antero. 2010. *Not in My Neighborhood: How Bigotry Shaped a Great American City*. Chicago: Ivan R. Dee.

Perry, Andre M., and David Harshbarger. 2019. "America's Formerly Redlined Neighborhoods Have Changed, and So Must Solutions to Rectify Them." *Brookings*, October 14. https://www.brookings.edu/research/americas-formerly-redlines-areas-changed-so-must-solutions/.

Perry, Andre M. 2020. *Know Your Price: Valuing Black Lives and Property in America's Black Cities*. Washington, DC: Brookings Institution Press.

Plato. 1992. *Laches and Charmides*. Translated by Rosamond Kent Sprague. Indianapolis: Hackett.

Pogge, Thomas. 2007. *John Rawls: His Life and Theory of Justice*. Translated by Michelle Kosch. New York: Oxford University Press.

powell, john a. 2005. "A New Theory of Integrated Education: True Integration." *School Resegregation: Must the South Turn Back?* Edited by John Charles Boger and Gary Orfield, 281–304. Chapel Hill: University of North Carolina Press.

powell, john a. 2008. "Race, Place, and Opportunity." *The American Prospect*. http://prospect.org/article/race-place-and-opportunity.

powell, john a., and Marguerite L. Spencer. 2003. "Giving Them the Old 'One-Two': Gentrification and the K.O. of Impoverished Urban Dwellers of Color." *Howard Legal Journal* 46, no. 3: 433–490.

Putnam, Daniel. "Gentrification and Domination." *Journal of Political Philosophy* 29, no. 2 (June 2021): 167–87.

Rawls, John. 1993. *Political Liberalism*. New York: Columbia University Press.

Rawls, John. 1999a. *A Theory of Justice*. Rev. ed. Cambridge, MA: Belknap Press of Harvard University Press.

Rawls, John. 1999b. *The Law of Peoples*. Cambridge, MA: Harvard University Press.

Rawls, John. 1999c. *Collected Papers*. Cambridge, MA: Harvard University Press.

Rawls, John. 2001. *Justice as Fairness: A Restatement*. Edited by Erin Kelly. Cambridge, MA: Harvard University Press.

Reardon, Sean F., and Kendra Bischoff. 2011a. "Growth in the Residential Segregation of Families by Income, 1970–2009." US2010 Project. https://s4.ad.brown.edu/Projects/Diversity/Data/Report/report111111.pdf.

Reardon, Sean F., and Kendra Bischoff. 2011b. "Income Inequality and Income Segregation." *American Journal of Sociology* 116, no. 4: 1092–1153.

Reardon, Sean F., Lindsay Fox, and Joseph Townsend. 2015. "Neighborhood Income Composition by Household Race and Income, 1990–2009." *ANNALS of the American Academy of Political and Social Science* 660, no. 1: 78–97.

Rodrick, Dani. November 6. "Rescuing Economics from Neoliberalism." *Boston Review*, November 6. https://bostonreview.net/articles/dani-rodrik-rescuing-economics-neoliberalism/.

Rose, Damaris. 1984. "Rethinking Gentrification: Beyond the Uneven Development of Marxist Urban Theory." *Environment and Planning D: Society and Space* 2: 47–74.

Rose, Kalima, and Margaretta Lin. 2015. "A Roadmap toward Equity: Housing Solutions for Oakland, California." City of Oakland Department of Housing & Community Development's Strategic Initiatives Unit and PolicyLink. https://www.policylink.org/sites/default/files/pl-report-oak-housing-070715.pdf.

Rosenbaum, James, Stefanie DeLuca, and Tammy Tuck. 2005. "New Capabilities in New Places: Low-Income Black Families in Suburbia." In *The Geography of Opportunity: Race and Housing Choice in Metropolitan America*, edited by Xavier de Souza Briggs, 150–175. Washington, DC: Brookings Institution Press.

Rothstein, Richard. 2014. "The Making of Ferguson: Public Politics at the Root of Its Troubles." Washington, DC: Economic Policy Institute. http://www.epi.org/publication/making-ferguson/.

Rothstein, Richard. 2017. *The Color of Law: A Forgotten History of How Our Government Segregated America.* New York: Liveright.

Sampson, Robert. 2008. "Moving to Inequality: Neighborhood Effects and Experiments Meet Social Structure." *American Journal of Sociology* 114, no. 1: 189–231.

Sampson, Robert. 2011. *Great American City: Chicago and the Enduring Neighborhood Effect.* Chicago: The University of Chicago Press.

Sampson, Robert. 2015. "Individual and Community Mobility in the Great Recession Era: The Spatial Foundations of Persistent Inequality." In *Economic Mobility: Research and Ideas on Strengthening Families, Communities and the Economy*, edited by Alexandra Brown, David Buchholz, Daniel Davis, and Arturo Gonzalez, 260–287. St Louis, MO: Federal Reserve Bank of St. Louis. https://www.stlouisfed.org/community-development/publications/-/media/project/frbstl/stlouisfed/files/pdfs/community-development/econmobilitypapers/section3/econmobility_3-1sampson_508.pdf.

Scanlon, Thomas. 2018. *Why Does Inequality Matter?* New York: Oxford University Press.

Scheffler, Samuel. 2003. "What Is Egalitarianism?" *Philosophy and Public Affairs* 31, no. 1: 5–39.

Scheffler, Samuel. 2010. *Equality and Tradition: Questions of Moral Value in Moral and Political Theory.* Reprod. Oxford: Oxford University Press.

Scheffler, Samuel. 2015. "The Practice of Equality." In *Social Equality: On What It Means to Be Equals*, edited by Carina Fourie, Fabian Schuppert, and Ivo Wallimann-Helmer, 21–44. New York: Oxford University Press.

Schelling, Thomas. 1969. "Models of Segregation." *American Economic Review* 59, no. 2: 488–493.

Schelling, Thomas. 1971. "Dynamic Models of Segregation." *Journal of Mathematical Sociology* 1: 143–186.

Schemmel, Christian. 2015. "Social Equality—Or Just Justice?" In *Social Equality: On What It Means to Be Equals*, edited by Carina Fourie, Fabian Schuppert, and Ivo Wallimann-Helmer, 146–166. New York: Oxford University Press.

Scheutz, Jenny. 2022. *Fixer-Upper: How to Repair America's Broken Housing Systems*. Washington, DC: Brookings Institution Press.

Schlichtman, John Joe, Marc Lamont Hill, and Jason Patch. 2017. *Gentrifier*. Toronto: University of Toronto Press.

Self, Robert O. 2003. *American Babylon: Race and the Struggle for Postwar Oakland*. Princeton, NJ: Princeton University Press.

Shapiro, Thomas M. 2017. *Toxic Inequality: How America's Wealth Gap Destroys Mobility, Deepens the Racial Divide, and Threatens Our Future*. New York: Basic Books.

Sharkey, Patrick. 2013. *Stuck in Place: Urban Neighborhoods and the End of Progress toward Racial Equality*. Chicago: University of Chicago Press.

Shelby, Tommie. 2005. *We Who Are Dark: The Philosophical Foundations of Black Solidarity*. Cambridge, MA: Harvard University Press.

Shelby, Tommie. 2016. *Dark Ghettos: Injustice, Dissent, and Reform*. Cambridge, MA: Harvard University Press.

Shellenberger, Michael. 2021. *San Fransicko: Why Progressives Ruin Cities*. New York: Harper.

Steinberg, Stephen. 2010. "The Myth of Concentrated Poverty: How Do We Get There?" In *The Integration Debate: Competing Futures for American Cities*, edited by Chester W. Hartman and Gregory D. Squires, 213–227. New York: Routledge.

Smith, Janet L. 2010. "Integration: Solving the Wrong Problem." In *The Integration Debate: Competing Futures for American Cities*, edited by Chester W. Hartman and Gregory D. Squires, 229–245. New York: Routledge.

Smith, Neil. 1996. *The New Urban Frontier: Gentrification and the Revanchist City*. London: Routledge.

Soja, Edward W. 2010. *Seeking Spatial Justice*. Globalization and Community Series. Minneapolis: University of Minnesota Press.

Solnit, Rebecca. 2013. "Google Invades." *London Review of Books* 35, no. 3: 34–35.

Solnit, Rebecca, and Susan Schwartzenberg. 2000. *Hollow City: The Siege of San Francisco and the Crisis of American Urbanism*. New York: Verso.

Sowell, Thomas. 1987. *A Conflict of Visions*. New York: W. Morrow.

Spinner-Halev, Jeff. 2012. *Enduring Injustice*. New York: Cambridge University Press.

Squires, Gregory D., ed. 2018a. *The Fight for Fair Housing: Causes, Consequences and Future Implications of the 1968 Federal Fair Housing Act*. New York: Routledge.

Squires, Gregory D. 2018b. "Fair Housing Yesterday, Today, Tomorrow." In *The Fight for Fair Housing: Causes, Consequences, and Future Implications of the 1968 Federal Fair Housing Act*, edited by Gregory D. Squires, 1–13. New York: Routledge.

Stanley, Sharon. 2014. "Toward a Reconciliation of Integration and Racial Solidarity." *Contemporary Political Theory* 13, no. 1: 46–63.

Stanley, Sharon. 2015. "The Enduring Challenge of Racial Integration in the United States." *Du Bois Review* 12, no. 1: 5–24.

Stanley, Sharon. 2017. *An Impossible Dream? Racial Integration in the United States*. New York: Oxford University Press.

Sullivan, Daniel Monroe. 2007. "Reassessing Gentrification: Measuring Residents' Opinions Using Survey Data." *Urban Affairs Review* 42, no. 4: 583–592.

Sundstrom, Ronald R. 2003. "Race and Place: Social Space in the Production of Human Kinds." *Philosophy and Geography* 6, no. 1: 83–95.

Sundstrom, Ronald R. 2004. "Racial Politics in Residential Segregation Studies." *Philosophy and Geography* 7: 61–78.

Sundstrom, Ronald R. 2008. *The Browning of America and the Evasion of Social Justice*. Albany: SUNY.

Sundstrom, Ronald R. 2020. "Residential Segregation and Rethinking the Imperative of Integration." In *The Routledge Handbook of Philosophy of the City*, edited by Sharon M. Meagher, Samantha Noll, and Joseph S. Biehl, 216–228. New York: Routledge.

Sundstrom, Ronald R. 2022. "Integration and Reaction." *Dialogues* 62, no. 1: 77–83.

Sundstrom, Ronald R., and David Haekwon Kim. 2014. "Xenophobia and Racism." *Critical Philosophy of Race* 2, no. 1: 20–45.

Tach, Laura M. 2009. "More Than Bricks and Mortar: Neighborhood Frames, Social Processes, and the Mixed-Income Redevelopment of a Public Housing Project." *City and Community* 8, no. 3: 269–299.

Táíwò, Olúfẹmi O. 2022. *Elite Capture: How the Powerful Took Over Identity Politics (and Everything Else)*. Chicago: Haymarket Books.

Taylor, Charles. 1995. "Irreducibly Social Goods." In *Philosophical Arguments*, 127–145. Cambridge, MA: Harvard University Press.

Taylor, Charles, and Amy Gutmann. 1994. *Multiculturalism and the Politics of Recognition: An Essay*. Princeton, NJ: Princeton University Press.

Taylor, Paul C. 2013. "'Whose Integration? What Imperative': Commentary on Elizabeth Anderson's *Imperative of Integration*." *Symposia on Gender, Race and Philosophy* 9, no. 2: 1–5. https://web.mit.edu/sgrp/2013/no2/Taylor0913.pdf.

Tilly, Charles. 1998. *Durable Inequality*. Berkeley: University of California Press.

Tsai, Jack. 2020. "Is the Housing First Model Effective? Different Evidence for Different Outcomes." *American Journal of Public Health* 110, no. 9: 1376–1377.

Turner, Margery Austin, and Stephen L. Ross. 2005. "How Racial Discrimination Affects the Search for Housing." In *The Geography of Opportunity: Race and Housing Choice in Metropolitan America*, edited by Xavier de Souza Briggs, 81–100. Washington, DC: Brookings Institution Press.

Turner, Margery Austin, and Xavier de Souza Briggs. 2008. "Assisted Housing Mobility and the Success of Low-Income Minority Families: Lessons for Policy, Practice, and Future Research." Brief No. 5. Washington, DC: The Urban Institute. https://www.urban.org/sites/default/files/publication/31591/411638-Assisted-Housing-Mobility-and-the-Success-of-Low-Income-Minority-Families-Lessons-for-Policy-Practice-and-Future-Research.PDF.

van Leeuwen, Bart. 2018. "To the Edge of the Urban Landscape: Homelessness and the Politics of Care." *Political Theory* 46, no. 4: 586–610.

van Leeuwen, Bart, and Michael S. Merry. 2019. "Should the Homeless Be Forcibly Helped?" *Public Health Ethics* 12, no. 1: 30–43.

Valls, Andrew. 2007. "Reconsidering the Case for Black Reparations." In *Reparations: Interdisciplinary Inquiries*, edited by Jon Miller and Rahul Kumar, 114–129. New York: Oxford University Press.

Valls, Andrew. 2018. *Rethinking Racial Justice*. New York: Oxford University Press.

Van Vliet, Willem, ed. 1998. *The Encyclopedia of Housing*. Thousand Oaks, CA: Sage.

Vigdor, Jacob L. 2002. "Does Gentrification Harm the Poor?" *Brookings-Wharton Papers on Urban Affairs* 2002, no. 1: 133–182.

Vigdor, Jacob L. 2013. "Weighing and Measuring the Decline in Residential Segregation." *City and Community* 12, no. 2: 169–177.

Voegelin, Eric. (1968) 2012. *Science, Politics and Gnosticism: Two Essays*. New York: Regnery.

Wacquant, Loïc. 2008. *Urban Outcasts: A Comparative Sociology of Advanced Marginality*. Cambridge: Polity Press.

Wacquant, Loïc. 2016. "Revisiting Territories of Relegation: Class, Ethnicity, and State in the Making of Advanced Marginality." *Urban Studies* 53, no. 6: 1077–1088.

Waldron, Jeremy. 1993. "Homelessness and the Issue of Freedom." In *Liberal Rights: Collected Papers 1981–1991*, 308–338. Cambridge: Cambridge University Press.

Waldron, Jeremy. 2017. *One Another's Equals: The Basis of Human Equality*. Cambridge, MA: The Belknap Press of Harvard University Press.

Waldron, Jeremy, and Meir Dan-Cohen. 2012. *Dignity, Rank, and Rights*. New York: Oxford University Press.

Walks, R. Alan, and Richard Maaranen. 2008. "Gentrification, Social Mix, and Social Polarization: Testing the Linkages in Large Canadian Cities." *Urban Geography* 29, no. 4: 293–326.

Walzer, Michael. 1983. *Spheres of Justice: A Defense of Pluralism and Equality*. New York: Basic Books.

Wax, Amy, and Alexander Larry. 2017. "Paying the Price for Breakdown of the Country's Bourgeois Culture." *Philadelphia Inquirer*, August 9. https://www. inquirer.com/philly/opinion/commentary/paying-the-price-for-breakd own-of-the-countrys-bourgeois-culture-20170809.html.

Weber, Max. 1968. *Economy and Society*. Edited by Guenther Ross and Claus Wittich. Berkeley: University of California Press.

Weiner, Brian A. 2005. *Sins of the Parents: The Politics of National Apologies in the United States*. Philadelphia: Temple University Press.

Wilkins, David E., and Heidi Kiiwetinepinesiik Stark. 2018. *American Indian Politics and the American Political System*. Lanham, MD: Rowman & Littlefield.

Williams, Morgan, and Stacey Seichnaydre. 2018. "The Legacy and the Promise of Disparate Impact." In *The Fight for Fair Housing: Causes, Consequences, and Future Implications of the 1968 Federal Fair Housing Act*, edited by Gregory D. Squires, 169–188. New York: Routledge.

Williamson, Thad. 2010. *Sprawl, Justice, and Citizenship: The Civic Costs of the American Way of Life*. New York: Oxford University Press.

Wilson, August. 2007. *Radio Golf*. New York: Theatre Communications Group.

Wilson, William J. 1987. *The Truly Disadvantaged: The Inner City, the Underclass, and Public Policy*. Chicago: University of Chicago Press.

Wohl, Michael J. A., Nyla R. Branscombe, and Yechiel Klar. 2006. "Collective Guilt: Emotional Reactions When One's Group Has Done Wrong or Been Wronged." *European Review of Social Psychology* 17, no. 1: 1–37.

Wolcott, James. 2020. "Futilitarianism, or To the York Street Station." *Liberties* 1, no.1 (Fall): 202–220.

Young, Iris Marion. 1990. *Justice and the Politics of Difference*. Princeton, NJ: Princeton University Press.

Young, Iris Marion. 1999. "Residential Segregation and Differentiated Citizenship." *Citizenship Studies* 3, no. 2: 237–253.

Young, Iris Marion. 2000. *Inclusion and Democracy*. New York: Oxford University Press.

Young, H. Peyton. 1994. *Equity: In Theory and Practice*. Princeton, NJ: Princeton University Press.

Zasloff, Jonathan. 2017. "The Price of Equality: Fair Housing, Land Use, and Disparate Impact." *Columbia Human Rights Law Review* 48, no. 3: 99–153.

Zimmer, Tyler. 2017. "Gentrification as Injustice: A Relational Egalitarian Approach to Urban Housing." *Public Affairs Quarterly* 31, no. 1: 51–80.

Zuk, Miriam, and Karen Chapple. 2015. *Case Studies on Gentrification and Displacement in the San Francisco Bay Area*. Berkeley, CA: Center for Community Innovation.

Index

For the benefit of digital users, indexed terms that span two pages (e.g., 52–53) may, on occasion, appear on only one of those pages.

concentrated wealth and, 121–22
definition of, 117–18
in disadvantaged suburbs, 116
forced concentration and, 121, 124
voluntary means of, 117–18
Constitution of the United States,
   35–36, 50, 55–56
corrective justice. *See also*
      rectification
   context immobility and, 109–10
   intergenerational poverty
      and, 109–10
   liberal egalitarianism and, 29–30
   public apologies and, 53–54
   racism and, xvi, 53
   reparations and, 53–58
   spatial justice and, xix, 3
   tort law and, 53–54
COVID-19 pandemic, xiv–xvi
Crowder, Kyle, 118–19
cultural loss
   civil rights and, 96–98
   democratic equality and, 100
   demographic change and, 98–100
   displacement and, 76–77
   gentrification and, xx, 65, 81–82,
      83–84, 85, 94–100
   reciprocity and, 101–2
Cushing, Robert, 120

Dawkins, Casey J., 13, 16–17, 49–
   50, 178n.2
*The Death and Life of Great American
   Cities* (Jacobs), 160
*The Death and Life of the Urban
   Commonwealth* (Kohn), 85,
   196n.14
democratic equality
   distributive justice and, 10, 25–26
   gentrification and, 83–84, 100–5
   integration and, 133, 135–36,
      144, 149–50
   just city and, 13
   liberal egalitarianism and, 21, 58

nondomination and, 3
open communities and, 36–37
reciprocity and, 10–11, 13
reconstruction and, xvi–xviii
rectification and, 26–27, 59
relational equality and, 9–10
right to housing and, 48
spatial justice and, xviii–xix, 2–3,
   6, 9–10, 12–14, 21–22, 110,
   123–24, 170–71
substantive opportunity and,
   36–37, 49
Denton, Nancy, 114–15, 127
Department of Housing and Urban
   Development (HUD), 22–
   23, 38–39
desegregation
   Brown v. Board of Education
      and, 24–25
   Civil Rights Act of 1964 and, 15–16
   community change and, 98–100
   definition of, 126
   demographic evenness and, 132
   Fair Housing Act of 1968
      and, 24–25
   formal desegregation and, xx–xxi
   integration compared to, xx–xxi,
      126–27, 132, 136–38, 140–41,
      144, 148, 149
   moral duty and, xxi–xxii
   spatial justice and, 136–37
Desmond, Matthew, 1–4, 80–81
difference principle
   acceptable conditions for
      inequality under, 21–22
   fair equality of opportunity
      and, 19
   open communities and, 37
   primary goods distribution
      and, 17–18
   Rawls and, 19, 21–22, 34, 37,
      184n.25
   reinvestment and, 16–17
   segregation and, 21–22

social goods, 17–18
social-spatial arrangements. *See also*
    spatial justice
    geography of opportunity and, xix,
        6, 21, 49, 91
    housing shortages and, xiii–xiv
    injustice in, xiv, 15–16
    liberal egalitarianism and, 28
    neoliberalism and, xxii–xxiii
    relegation communicated
        through, 12–13
    social-spatial segregation, 112–21
        (*see also* segregation)
    societal values and, 6–7
    systemic-injustice framework
        and, 45–46
solidarism, 86–87
Solnit, Rebecca, 62–64, 94–95
Southern Christian Leadership
    Conference, 98–99
spatial injustice. *See also* spatial
    justice
    African Americans and, 21–22
    gentrification and, xx–xxi, 73–74
    housing crisis and, 2
    Native Americans and, 21–22
    NIMBYism and, 22
    racial injustice and, 53, 81–82
    wealth gap and, 22–23
spatial justice
    affordable housing and, 172–
        74, 175
    background justice and, 7
    basic equality and, 7–9, 46
    climate change and, xiii–
        xiv, 174–75
    corrective justice and, xix, 3
    democratic equality and, xviii–xix,
        2–3, 6, 9–10, 12–14, 21–22, 110,
        123–24, 170–71
    democratic governance
        and, 24–25
    desegregation and, 136–37

distributive justice and, 2–3, 4–5,
    6, 14, 15–17, 21–22, 110
educational segregation and, 9–10,
    11, 109
environmental sustainability
    and, 171
fair equality of opportunity
    and, 19
Fair Housing Act of 1968 and,
    xix, 42
geography of opportunity and, xix,
    6, 21, 49, 91
integration and, 134–35, 142–43,
    145–46, 156
just city and, 4–5
liberal egalitarianism and, xvi–
    xviii, 2, 16–17, 28–30, 58, 90–91
liberty and, xvi–xviii, 3, 15–16,
    21–22, 23–24, 45–46, 110
Marxism and, 16–17
moral equality and, xvi–xix,
    3, 15–16
policy recommendations
    regarding, 171–73
political equality and, 15–16
Rawls and, 16–17
reconstruction and, xxii–xxiii, 2,
    146–47, 152–53, 156–57
rectification and, 26–27
reinvestment and, 16–17
right to housing and, xix, 9, 46,
    48–49, 110, 170–73, 175
"right to the city" and, 5, 161
social equality and, 105–6
subsidized housing and, 173
urban planning and, 2–3
zoning and, 172–73
Stanley, Sharon
    on integration and conversion
        among white people, 159, 162–
        65, 166–67, 168–69
    on integration and group
        power, 162–63